Voices from Mutira

Voices from Mutira

Lives of
Rural Gikuyu Women

Jean Davison
with the women of Mutira

Lynne Rienner Publishers   Boulder & London

Published in the United States of America in 1989 by
Lynne Rienner Publishers, Inc.
1800 30th Street, Boulder, Colorado 80301

and in the United Kingdom by
Lynne Rienner Publishers, Inc.
3 Henrietta Street, Covent Garden, London WC2E 8LU

Library of Congress Cataloging-in-Publication Data
Davison, Jean, 1937-
    Voices from Mutira: lives of rural Gikuyu women/by Jean
    Davison.
    Bibliography: p.
    ISBN 1-55587-157-7 (alk. paper)
    ISBN 1-55587-158-5 (pbk.: alk. paper)
1. Women, Kikuyu (African people)—Kenya—Kirinyaga District—Interviews. 2.
Women, Kikuyu (African people)—Kenya—Kirinyaga District—Social conditions. 3.
Rural women—Kenya—Kirinyaga District—Interviews. 4. Rural women—Kenya—
Kirinyaga District—Social conditions. I. Title.
DT433.545.K55D38 1989   89-31703
305.48'8963954067626—dc20   CIP

British Cataloguing in Publication Data
A Cataloguing in Publication record for this book
is available from the British Library.

Printed and bound in the United States of America

The paper used in this publication meets the requirements of the American National
Standard for Permanence of Paper for Printed Library Materials Z39.48-1984
5 4 3

Contents

Acknowledgments

Many people on two continents contributed to my work on learning and change in the lives of rural Gikuyu women. First are two mentors, one American, the other Kenyan. Without the support of Shirley Brice Heath of the School of Education, Stanford University, to pursue the study of women's lives through retrospective accounts, it is doubtful the project would have begun. Without the determination and support of Stephen N. Mutunga of Kenyatta University in Nairobi, who took care of many technical details and later gave me the space to write, it is doubtful the work would have been completed. In addition, I would like to thank David Abernethy of the Political Science Department, Stanford University, for his helpful suggestions prior to my research and James L. Gibbs, Jr., of the Anthropology Department and Kennell Jackson of the History Department for their willingness to read the initial manuscript and for their valuable contributions as African scholars.

I would like to make special acknowledgment of the unfailing generosity of the seven women whose narratives are recorded here. They spent many hours sharing their lives and voices with me—*nĩ wega muno muno* (many, many thanks). Erastus Mwai, then chief of Mutira Location, greatly assisted my entrance into the location and subsequent work. Janet Mithamo, Teresia Giciku Karimi, and Flora Karoki contributed to my orientation to the community and became valuable friends. The Muriũki family, with whom I stayed, were my extended family in the field and graciously shared with me their daily lives, observations, and humor. Three women's group leaders, Joyce Wamithu of *Uritu wa Gatwe*, Pricilla Njagi of *Winyerekia*, and Margaret Wagithi of *Uthiri wa Kanitha*, welcomed me to their women's groups and provided valuable background on the activities of the groups. Finally, my research assistant, Joyce Karuana Kimenyi, spent many hours helping to transcribe the audio-taped life-history interviews. Without Karuana's assistance my research would have been a far greater task. I wish to thank the Stanford Center for International Studies and the Hewlett Foundation for making it financially possible for me to do the research in Kenya. In addition, to the Kenyan government, Kenya National Archives staff, Department of Adult Education, the Women's Bureau, and Maendeleo Ya Wanawake Organization for their hospitality and assistance—*asante sana.*

Jean Davison

The old Kikuyu women have had a hard life, and have themselves become flint-hard under it, like old mules which will bite you if they can come to it. They were more difficult for any disease to kill off than their men, as I learned in my practice as a doctor, and they were wilder than the men, and, even more thoroughly than they, devoid of the faculty of admiration. They had borne a number of children and had seen many of them die; they were afraid of nothing.

—Isak Dinesen, *Out of Africa*, 1937

Although far from negligible, the part played by women in the life of a savage tribe is very apt to be overlooked by a man. The reasons are obvious; the African woman is not obtrusive; she is perpetually busy, and one rarely comes in contact with her. Her inner thoughts and beliefs are a sealed book to the investigator. . . . The longer the experience, the more clearly one realizes that this lack of information about the woman is one of the weak points of any inquiry.

—C. W. Hobley, a colonial administrator, in
Bantu Beliefs and Magic, 1938

1

Change in Gikuyu Women's Lives

A Vignette from the Field

She came running down the track under the green canopy of banana trees, screaming at no one and everyone, her arms flailing, her eyes full of terror. I could only decipher part of what she was shouting, but the smell of fear needed no words. It entered my body like a quick, hot flash as I prepared to run from some unknown terror. I stood still, all senses alert, and tried to quiet the instinct to flee. I had been in the field for only three days and was wary of my reactions. Instead of fleeing, I found myself being carried along by a gathering crowd to a river—a river that moments earlier had swallowed the terror-stricken woman's husband.

A man—pewter gray in color—was stretched out on a grassy knoll above the riverbank, face up. He wore the mask of death. His four-year-old son stood over him looking bewildered. People gathered around them explained in agitated tones that, in the process of cleaning his wife's cooking pot after the midday meal, the man had slipped and fallen into the river and drowned. The woman—one of many I would come to know in Mutira—was now a widow.

In a few short minutes, her life had been transformed from one of relative security as a married woman to the insecurity of widowhood. The way she coped with this unforeseen event could alter her life course. Part of the change meant learning new skills to ensure the survival of her family. This change also meant modifying her behavior to fit a new social category. Both activities were to become part of this life transition.

Change and Learning

Change and learning, learning and change, over the course of lives, are the warp and woof of this book. We know something about the way people adapt to changes—both large and small—in the cultures of North America and Europe, but we know very little about the way learning and change are mediated in people's lives outside these regions.

Rapid advances in media technology force us to witness cata-
strophic changes, such as drought and mass migrations, affecting
entire populations in Africa, but the significance of such events in the
daily lives of individuals is elusive. We see a Somali woman passively
holding a dying child but do not learn about the survival strategies
she employed to save her other children. Nor do we learn how she
will change her life in the future to reflect her present experience. The
ways in which rural African women in one location mediate change
in their individual and collective lives is the major concern of this
book. The Gikuyu women who are the focus speak for themselves
through their life narratives.

The collection examines the lives of seven women ranging in age
from twenty-three to seventy-five years who live in Mutira Location,
Kirinyaga District, Kenya (see Map 1.1). From the time the oldest
woman was born on the eve of major European settlement to the time
the youngest woman entered school in the early 1970s was a period of
rapid social and economic transformation in this East African country.
Since independence in 1963, new opportunities for education, better
health care, new farming systems, and access to commodities previously unavailable have all made a major impact on the lives of rural
Kenyans. But these have affected individual Kenyan women (and
men) differently depending upon background and personality.

Change as a multifaceted phenomenon acts as both opportunity
and constraint depending upon the significance of meaning a person
attaches to a given situation. What constitutes a positive change for
one person—for example, the introduction of a new farming
method—may turn out to have a negative effect upon another.

Change in the lives of Gikuyu women results from historical and
sociocultural forces often working in tandem. These are forces over
which rural women have little or no control. At the same time,
idiosyncratic changes occurring within the lifespan of a particular
woman (a death in the family, relocation to a new place, the timing of
biological changes) contribute to shaping her life.

Although maturation, or biological growth, affects all individuals,
the rate of physical change and its significance varies for individuals.
For example, although the onset of menarche for Gikuyu girls occurs
on average at about 15.9 years of age, it can vary anywhere between
10.5 and 17 years (Worthman 1985:3). Moreover, for some Gikuyu
girls its occurrence must follow normative sociocultural practices
designed to mark the transition from childhood to adulthood, whereas for others menarche merely signifies a potential for reproduction.
The social significance of this biological event varies greatly.

Learning, strictly speaking, is the acquisition of new attitudes,
knowledge, and skills, which usually leads to a change in behavior.

Map 1.1 Kirinyaga District in Kenya

Learning occurs in many places, more often outside of schools than inside them. Over the course of a life, a person is apt to learn only 25 percent of what she or he knows in a classroom setting. The rest occurs in the home, community, workplace, or through travel. How and where do rural African women learn the knowledge and skills they need for survival? Has the indigenous learning process changed over time?

Learning and change are often linked in a mutually supportive way. Learning new ideas leads to change, and, in turn, change prompts an individual to learn new skills and behaviors. The two—change and learning—enjoy a symbiotic relationship that becomes apparent in the telling of a life story. Moreover, documenting ways women meet change in their personal lives may enable us to improve our abilities to understand how rural women learn best and how their needs might be served to enhance their social and economic development.

Women's Narratives and Global Development

A broad literature exists suggesting that rural women as a distinct gender category with specific needs ought to be included in development planning and policy at all levels (for example, Tinker and Bramsen 1976; Pala 1976; Giele and Smock 1977; Staudt 1982; Safilios-Rothchild 1982; Bay 1982; Barnes 1983; Spring 1985; Due 1985). Notwithstanding, the development process continues to be dominated by professionals—both men and women—who innovate change *for* rural women rather than *with* them. As an alternative, we might begin by listening to what rural women have to say about the kinds of changes *they* envision in their lives based upon past experience and present need.

In Africa, these women, who are often farmers, have been a singularly ignored category. Yet, they are responsible for 75 to 85 percent of the food production on this continent, which continues to face periodic food shortages, and they contribute substantially to the production of export crops, the linchpin of many African national economies (see Davison 1988). If for no other reason, they deserve to be heard.

One way of collecting women's perceptions of change is through interviews and observations that focus on the present. Another is to collect life histories and archival data that document change over time. The latter method enables us to better understand trends that can shape policies for women's development in the future. The two approaches are complementary. Both are used in this study of African women's lives.

The research upon which this collection is based began with a survey of 101 Gikuyu women, but the majority of time in the field (1983–1984, with a shorter visit in 1985) was spent collecting and validating the life histories through what has been described as "person-centered ethnography" (Langness and Frank 1981).

Person-Centered Ethnography

The process of ethnography requires spending an extended period of time (a minimum of one to two years) in a cultural community different from one's own, learning the language and nonverbal forms of communication, collecting ethnographic data through techniques of participant-observation and interviews with informants in the community. Often when reporting the results, however, the significance of everyday activities and the construction of their social meaning are lost in attempts to generalize about a particular group. Talking to an individual in the process of recording a life history reveals how events and activities are made meaningful, how change and learning are mediated through time. The actor becomes the focus.

From a conceptual point of view, sociologist Ken Plummer suggests that person-centered ethnography (and life-history research) best fit the approach of symbolic interactionism that concentrates on the communicative acts of individuals: "The cornerstones of interactionist thought embody a profound distaste for abstraction, reification, and absolutes; the humanly constructed, and hence ambiguous and emergent, meaning is their root concern" (1983:52–53).

Because symbolic interactionism focuses on the subjective, it is closely aligned with person-centered ethnography. Such an approach allows us to "know people personally and to see them as they are developing their own definitions of the world" (Bogdan and Taylor 1975:4). Attention to life changes as experienced subjectively may reveal how individuals create meaning out of change and contribute to their own learning process.

An ethnographic approach places the individual within a sociocultural context that depends upon oral rather than written communication. It is particularly applicable to life histories of nonliterate individuals where written records, such as journals and letters, do not exist. It allows us an opportunity to hear the voices of those who cannot write but who have opinions and ideas that we need to hear.

Person-centered ethnography requires lengthy interviews with a life-history informant, "tracking" his or her daily behavior, and cross-interviews with relatives and acquaintances to verify particular aspects of the narrator's account. In the past, however, scholars collecting life histories often failed to explain how their informants were chosen or how the data were collected (exceptions are Crapanzano's life history of a Morrocan outcast, 1981, and Shostak's portrait of a !Kung woman, 1981). In this introduction I explain how and why the narratives were collected and how they contribute to the literature.

Life-History Genre

Writing in 1945, Clyde Kluckhohn observes that life history as a genre is difficult to define: "The lumping of 'biographical' and 'autobiographical' documents is dictated by the circumstance that is often a highly arbitrary decision as to which category is the appropriate one" (81–82). Kluckhohn contends that often what results is more biography than life history in an autobiographical sense.

Rosaldo (1976) maintains that life history and the case study, like autobiography and biography, preselect their data into a meaningful whole and as such are separate literary genres. Although Crapanzano agrees with Rosaldo, he makes a distinction between the case history and biography, on the one hand, and life history and autobiography, on the other, suggesting that the first two bear the "impress of a narrator," who may analyze and evaluate the material, whereas the latter two present the informant from his or her own perspective (1980:8). In actuality, life history serves both purposes.

The life history that takes shape within an anthropological context is an oral account of a living person's life told by that person to someone from a different culture who records it. The process of collecting the life story becomes a collaborative effort negotiated by two actors— the elicitor and the narrator. Often, as in the life histories in this collection, the narrative is audio-taped, then translated and transcribed into a form that is rendered meaningful to a reading audience outside the culture of the narrator. As a result, life history as a literary genre straddles autobiography and biography. Whereas a life history is recorded by an ethnographer, and the transcribed text adheres to the informant's oral narrative, it approximates autobiography. However, once the ethnographer begins to rearrange or delete material found in the original transcription in order to clarify meaning for an external reading audience, the "impress" of a second person other than the original narrator is felt.

For purposes of analysis, a life history enables the social scientist to weigh to what degree an individual is like all other human beings, like some others, and like no others (Kluckhohn and Murray 1953:53). Human beings, regardless of where they live, share certain basic needs and common responses. At the same time, specific sociocultural communities (and groups within those communities) perceive themselves, and are perceived by others, as having a set of characteristics that differentiate them from all other groups and communities. Finally, within such groups, individual differences in personality and life circumstances contribute to the uniqueness of each person.

Life Histories of African Women

Although a number of life histories of Africans have appeared in the twentieth century (such as Gollock 1928; Perham 1936; Sachs 1937; Winter 1965; Barrett and Njama 1966; Barrett and Muchai 1973; Kuper 1978; Crapanzano 1980), only a handful have focused on women. *Baba of Karo*, originally published in 1954, is one of the earliest.

Written by Mary Smith, the wife of anthropologist Michael Smith, *Baba of Karo* is significant because it was the first full life history of an African woman. In an introduction to the life narrative, Michael Smith argues that his wife's account of Baba is valuable, not only as a cultural record of Hausa life in Nigeria, but as an illustration of the way society "governs and shapes an individual's life" (1954:14). Indeed, the narrative is a study in Hausa socialization as perceived through the lenses of one nonheroic woman. The account contributes to the reader's knowledge of Hausa life during the colonial period in Nigeria. Yet, we rarely get a glimpse of Baba's inner feelings or how she mediates the changes and transitions in her rich, event-filled life. For instance, Baba's mother's death by lightning is a traumatic event, but we lack a sense of Baba's retrospective feelings toward her mother's death, perhaps because she chose not to share this part of herself with an outsider. Nevertheless, in a period generally characterized by androcentric ethnographic accounts of African societies, *Baba of Karo* is a solitary light.

In the postcolonial period of the 1960s, more women's narratives began to emerge. Among them were Anne Laurentin's sketches of women in the Central African Republic (1963) and Iris Andreski's *Old Wives Tales* (1970), a small collection of Nigerian women's narratives illuminating the importance of storytelling in African women's lives. In East Africa, Charity Wacuima's small autobiography, *Daughter of Mumbi* (1969), was one of the first narratives written by an African woman. Brought up as a Christian, Wacuima provides the perspective of a "mission" Gikuyu (one educated in a mission) in describing her socialization into the Gikuyu way of life.

An increasing number of ethnographies have been published since the 1970s that focus on women in African societies (for example, Abbott 1974; Bledsoe 1980; Caplan 1975; Mullings 1976; Obbo 1980; Robertson 1976; Guyer 1984; Oboler 1985). But rarely have these included the individual histories of women. Sarah LeVine's study of six Gusii women in Kenya (1979), Marjorie Shostak's *Nisa* (1981), and Patricia Romero's *Life Histories of African Women* (1988) are exceptions. Each of these works takes a different approach.

LeVine's collection, although more psychological case studies than life histories, makes a valuable contribution to investigating the way rural Kenyan women in one location perceive themselves and change in their daily lives. All of the women presented in LeVine's book are married, economically poor, and in their thirties or forties. Although LeVine's selection of women is confined to those she knows and with whom she has rapport, she assures us that they are representative of other Gusii women of their age. She concentrates on their roles as wives, daughters-in-law, and mothers, eliciting each woman's perceptions of these roles in Gusii society. Given the variety of marital circumstances and personalities, no two women have quite the same perceptions. LeVine demonstrates that intracultural variability exists, but she does not attempt to situate the informants within a historical context of changes occurring in Kenya.

Marjorie Shostak's *Nisa: The Life and Words of a !Kung Woman* is the life narrative of one !Kung woman in her fifties, who, although she is a gifted storyteller, may not be representative of other !Kung women. Although there is no way of knowing whether Nisa is representative of women of her age group in !Kung society, the autobiography does provide an "insider's view" of the various age-stages through which Nisa passes as a !Kung woman and her feelings about the changes she has experienced. Individual personality and culture converge in this life history.

Patricia Romero's *Life Histories* draws on accounts of women from very diverse cultures in Africa, so it is difficult to draw conclusions about women in any one culture. In addition, similar to Shostak's life narrative and LeVine's collection, we are not told whether the women she selected are representative of their societies or not.

The collection of Gikuyu life histories in this volume contributes to the ongoing study of African women. First, it gives voice to seven women within one cultural group who vary by age, marital circumstances, work, and personality. Second, each woman has been selected from a larger sample of women in her age category so that the reader has some notion of how "representative" each woman is of her particular cohort. Third, the collection illuminates women's perceptions of historical events—for instance, the diverse experiences of women during the Mau Mau Rebellion (1950s) or their differing opinions on female circumcision in the 1980s. Collecting life narratives of African women, then, provides a unique opportunity to grasp the concrete dailiness of women's lives in the process of change—lives that are very different from our own.

The Setting: Mutira Location

This study of change in Gikuyu women's lives took place in Mutira Location (Kirinyaga District). The location was selected from a number of possibilities in Kenya for two reasons: First, the location's temperate climate made it an ideal working site, and second, my previous contact with two families in Mutira on earlier visits to the location in 1977 and 1980 facilitated reentry into the community in 1983.

Kirinyaga District is the smallest district (1,437 square kilometers, 555 square miles) in Central Province. Formerly, it was part of Embu District, but in 1963 the new Kenyan government redefined a number of former colonial districts to reflect a more equal distribution of population. Kirinyaga was created with its district headquarters at Kerugoya. Lying on the eastern edge of Central Province, Kirinyaga is bounded on the east and south by Embu District, on the west by Murang'a and Nyeri Districts, and to the north by the Mount Kenya Forest. It is located between 1° and .08° south of the equator. The southern part of the district contains the rice-growing lowlands of Mwea, whereas at the higher elevations coffee and tea are grown. Maize, beans, potatoes, and bananas are the staple crops of the majority of the people in the district.

Kirinyaga is divided into three administrative divisions —Gichugu, Ndia, and Mwea, with a total of ten locations that are further divided into seventy-six sublocations. Each location is administrated by a chief, with assistant chiefs appointed by the central government for each sublocation. The population of the district is about half a million, with the primary ethnic group being the Gikuyu. According to population figures for 1982, there are more females than males in all age groups in the rural areas (outside Kerugoya). It is probable that the war for liberation in the 1950s and the more recent urban migration of younger males have contributed to the discrepancy. In Ndia Division, where Mutira Location is located, there were 62,781 females to 57,603 males in 1982 (Kirinyaga District 1982:15). Furthermore, the population is unevenly distributed, with Ndia and Gichugu having higher population densities (including four locations with an average of 400 people per square kilometer), whereas Mwea Division in the southern, drier part of the district has only 139 people per square kilometer (Castro 1983:30).

The district is agriculturally productive because of its rich, volcanic soil, a sufficient water supply, and favorable climate. The volcanic soil is conducive to the growing of coffee and tea. There are normally two seasons for rain—*mbura ya njahi* (the "pigeon pea rains" or "Long Rains") that fall mainly at night between March and June and *mbura ya mwere* (the "millet rains" or "Short Rains") that fall between mid-October and early December. However, there is great variation in rainfall between years, and in 1984 there were no Long Rains. Consequently, some women living in the parched lowlands had to leave their families in search of wage labor among people living at higher elevations, who were less affected by the drought. Others had to wait in government food lines for maize meal.

Although Kirinyaga District generally has a favorable environment for agriculture, farming is limited to small-scale production. The *Agricultural Census of Large Farms, 1981–1982* (Kenya, Central Bureau of Statistics, 1984) shows no large farms (over 20 acres, 8.1 hectares) in Kirinyaga District in contrast to other districts in Central Province. However, in Ndia Division there are thirty tea-buying centers and one of Kenya's largest tea factories at Kangaita. Most producers in Mutira Location own between 1 and 15 acres of tea, which are harvested year round.

It takes a minimum of three years before a tea bush can be harvested, so the cultivation of tea is a long-term investment. Periodically, the tea bushes must be pruned back to encourage new growth. Pruning is done by section on a rotating basis so that only one section of a tea plot is unproductive at any time. The tea leaves are picked to select the best quality (two new leaves and a bud) and are transported in large baskets to local weighing stations where they are weighed and sorted according to three grades, with two leaves and a bud bringing the highest price. An experienced adult plucks up to 60 kilograms (132 lbs.) in a six-hour period. In 1983, a picker received 80 cents—less than a shilling—per kilo. The average amount earned in a day was 40 Kenya shillings ($3.00).

Mutira Location, in the northwestern corner of Kirinyaga District (Map 1.2), has four coffee cooperatives, each with its own factory. Similar to tea, coffee is a long-term investment from the time the saplings are planted to the harvesting of the first crop. The branches of the tree must be regularly trimmed so that lateral shoots and suckers are cut away allowing only the main branches to grow, thus assuring the best grade berries. Because the trees are planted farther apart than tea bushes, they tend to collect weeds more readily. Women spend a good deal of time weeding and hoeing around the base of the trees with a machete and hoe. The yield for coffee is higher per kilo than that for tea (1.50 Kenya shillings, in contrast to .80 for tea in 1983), but coffee requires more inputs in terms of fertilizer and copper fungicide to prevent coffee berry disease (*Collectoruhum coffeanum*).

In addition to tea and coffee production, there is some dairy farming. Most families keep at least one or two cows in addition to sheep

NORTH

MOUNT KENYA FOREST

Mutira Location

KIRINYAGA DISTRICT

Map 1.2 Mutira Location (shading indicates the four northern sublocations) and/or goats. Every sublocation has a cattle dip, and the Ministry of Agriculture encourages local farmers to bring their cows on a regular basis in order to prevent diseases such as East Coast Fever, which is carried by ticks. Some families, and several women's self-help groups, also raise pigs for slaughter. The Kagumo Town Council has a small slaughterhouse, but there is no industry in the location.

Because it was impossible to get around by foot to every one of the eight sublocations in Mutira Location, four in the north were chosen based upon representativeness of economic activity (in one, mainly coffee is grown; in another, mainly tea; and in two, a mix of coffee and tea) and accessibility. The sublocations included were Kirunda, Kagumo, Kaguyu, and Kabari, with elevations ranging from 5,400 feet to 6,500. Kaguyu and Kabari border the Mount Kenya Forest and were the site of heavy fighting during the liberation struggle in the 1950s. A broad trench still exists that local Gikuyu were forced to dig to prevent Mau Mau guerrilla fighters in the forest from entering the internment villages to obtain food and recruit followers. In addition, local people (including children) have accidently stumbled across active grenades left by the colonial army at the edge of the forest, sometimes with disasterous results. The legacy of the guerrilla war for liberation is still a part of the people's lives, as I learned from talking with older informants and from the women's narrative accounts. The majority who either fought on the side of the Land and Freedom Army (labeled "Mau Mau") or supported their efforts remain bitter toward the minority of Gikuyu who became Home Guards (those trained by the British to police the internment villages) or who remained loyal to the colonial government.

The research site that included the four sublocations forms a triangle cornered by three market centers—Gathuthuma and Gatwe in the north and Kamuiru in the south. In addition, the largest center in the location, at Kagumo, was part of the site. The southern end of the site (at the lowest elevation) consists of fairly flat land where coffee is the principle cash crop. Just north of Kagumo is a mixed area where both coffee and tea are grown. At the highest and coolest elevations, tea is the principle crop. The land north of Kagumo is composed of steep ridges, running north and south, separated by streams or rivers.

Historically, the ridges were occupied by different Gikuyu *mbari* (patrilineages). Since the early 1960s, the land has been subdivided by male *mbari* members who have legal title. The entire area was formerly part of the Gikuyu Reserve under British colonial administration. The southern end at Kamuiru was taken over by the British during the "Emergency" (1952–1960) for an internment village and is now subdivided into separate parcels, individually owned. Although the Gikuyu living on the ridges have historical roots in the location, many of those living at lower elevations around Kagumo were formerly squatters who were given small parcels of land previously held by the colonial government in the immediate postindependence period.

Kagumo (meaning "small fig tree"—every Gikuyu settlement historically had its own sacred fig tree at the center) is one of the oldest continually inhabited Gikuyu villages in the area. Today, it is more of a market center than a self-contained village. I spent about half of each week between September 1983 and March 1984 living in Kagumo. The other half of the week and from March onward I lived in the homestead of a Gikuyu family located in Kabari Sublocation, which gave me easy access to most of the life-history informants, the majority of whom lived at the northern end of the location.

The Sociocultural Context: The Northern Gikuyu

Before describing the Gikuyu, a word needs to be said about the spelling of the name of this major ethnic group in Kenya that accounts for 20 percent of Kenya's total population of nearly 25 million. The Gikuyu refer to themselves as *Agĩkũyũ* when referring to the plural form and *Mũgĩkũyũ* when referring to the singular. For this reason it is more accurate to refer to the group as "Gikuyu," following the lead of Gikuyu author Ngũgi wa Thiong'o (1967, 1977), than "Kikuyu," which was the way early Europeans spelled it (for example, Hobley 1910; Routledge 1910).

The Gikuyu are linguistically related to other Bantu-speaking groups in central Kenya (including the Kamba, Embu, Mbere, Tharaka, and Meru), who share common historical roots that date back to a prototype population known as the Thagicu. Migrating from the north, the Thagicu settled in the Mount Kenya region sometime between the twelfth and fourteenth centuries (Muriũki 1974). As splinter groups formed, it appears from archaeological evidence that one group migrated south and settled on the southwestern slopes of Kirinyaga (Mount Kenya). Artifacts found in a site at Gatung'ang'a suggest that the people who settled here hunted game, herded sheep and goats, and worked with iron to make simple tools and weapons (Muriũki 1974).

Subsequent Bantu migrations from the northeast, followed by periods of settlement, intermarriage, and further splintering, characterize the history of the Thagicu in the fifteenth and sixteenth centuries. It is from one of the splinter groups who settled at the convergence of the Thagana (Tana) and Thika rivers that Gikuyu trace their descent. From the settlement at Ithanga, subgroups migrated in several directions, some north to Nyeri, others northeast to Kirinyaga, and some south to Murang'a over the next two centuries. Those who migrated still further south toward Kiambu in the eighteenth century came into contact with a hunting people they called the Aathi, from whom they acquired land in exchange for goats and with whom they intermarried (Fisher n.d.; Kershaw 1975/76; Muriũki 1974; Leakey 1977).

Similar migrations followed, and the Gikuyu began to identify themselves as distinct groups that settled in particular areas. The result was the emergence of clans, each of which traced its descent back to a particular ancestress. The number of clans varies somewhat with informants (see Fisher n.d.; Middleton 1953), but the number usually given is nine.[1] Two clans may have originated through contact with neighboring Kamba: the Acera and Agaciku. The largest clan, the Anjiru, was formerly known for brave warriors and medicine men. Aithaga (also Eithaga) clan was composed of iron-smiths, and its members additionally had the power to control rain and to make strong curses. Others are the Ambui, Angari, Aithiegeni, Aithirandu, and Aithanga (the last four have alternative names depending upon geographic location). Although all Gikuyu trace their descent from one of the named clans, their oral tradition relates the existence of male and female progenitors—Gikuyu and Mumbi—from whom the nine clans arose. They are believed to be the "mother" and "father" of the nine clan ancestresses.

The northern Gikuyu settled on the steep slopes of Kirinyaga, whereas the southern Gikuyu who migrated south toward Kiambu settled around the Chania River (Leakey 1977; Muriũki 1974). The southern Gikuyu intermarried with the Aathi, from whom they acquired land in exchange for goats. Over time, regional dialects and local traditions developed that distinguish the two groups.

Gikuyu Economy

Originally hunter-gatherers, the Gikuyu gradually adopted horticultural practices, beginning with the cultivation of cocoyams, sweet potatoes, bananas, and millet. The cultivation of crops was segregated by gender: Men cultivated yams and bananas; women, sweet potatoes and millet. Women also gathered a variety of wild spinachlike greens, tubers such as arrowroot (taro), and berries. Sugarcane was grown and honey collected from men's hives in the forest for the production of beer (*njohi*). Maize was introduced early in the nineteenth century and has become a major staple crop (Hoorweg and Niemeyer 1980). When it serves as a food crop it is cultivated by women, but when it is sold as a commodity it tends to be grown by men. In addition, European potatoes, cassava, and rice have been added to the food repertoire. Legumes include dwarf beans, cowpeas, pigeon peas, kidney beans, lentils, and garden peas.

In addition to the foods named, Gikuyu today grow cabbage, tomatoes, onions, carrots, kale, and swiss chard. Seasoning is salt, chili peppers, or curry. There is a great variety of fruits known by the generic term *matunda*. In addition to bananas, these include passion fruit, mangos, papaya, loquats, plums, pineapple, oranges, and avocado pears. Women and children, especially, enjoy fruits, which they also sell in local markets.

The staple dish of most rural Gikuyu is *githeri*—maize kernels and kidney beans boiled together for several hours. Once cooked, the dish may be preserved in a cool place for up to three days without refrigeration. To give variety, pigeon peas, carrots, potatoes, onions, or kale are often added. Although the generic term for food is *irio*, the Gikuyu have a favorite dish—*irio cia Agĩkũyũ* (literally "Gikuyu food")—that they serve to visitors; it consists of maize kernels, potatoes, garden peas, and beans mashed together. In addition, older Gikuyu enjoy millet porridge, particularly when it is allowed to ferment.

Although Gikuyu were formerly hunters as well as gatherers, Kenyan game laws prohibit them from hunting today. Meat of wild game (such as antelope, impala, and bushbuck) and from herd animals (goats, sheep, and African cattle) was the prerogative of men. Pork and fish were prohibited; game birds and other fowl were eaten only occasionally; eggs were not a part of the diet. Women rarely ate meat and then only when it was handed to them by their husbands (Fisher n.d.; Karoki 1977).

Meat of goats and sheep was roasted, often at the end of a ceremony. The animals were used for sacrifical purposes to seal an agreement, as a means of restoring health to a community, or to honor someone on a special occasion. Usually the animal sacrificed was a ram that was kept indoors in a special place in a woman's house, was fed sweet potato vines, and was allowed to fatten for slaughtering. Strangulation was the ritual method of killing, after which the animal was slaughtered, its blood sprinkled on the earth (blood is symbolic of males, earth of females), and the meat and organs roasted for male elders. The contents of intestines served a special purpose. Referred to as *tatha*, it was removed and smeared on the head and body of an individual for protection or as a means of cleansing.

In addition, the animals were used as a medium of exchange to acquire property and as bridewealth(*rũracio*). Kershaw (1975/76) notes for the Southern Gikuyu (Kiambu) that in the nineteenth century Gikuyu from Murang'a acquired land from the Aathi (Ndorobo) through a series of payments of sheep or goats. Cattle—both African and imported European—were used similarly, but the Gikuyu did not keep large herds. Many Gikuyu now keep a few cattle mainly for milking. The milk is boiled with tea leaves as a favorite drink.

Today, meat is served only on special occasions to celebrate a ceremony such as *Irua* (circumcision) or to welcome a special visitor. Though women are allowed to eat meat, it is rarely a part of their diet. In sum, the Gikuyu remain largely vegetarian.

Cash-value crops such as tea and coffee were not grown by the Gikuyu until the 1940s, when the colonial government first allowed Africans to cultivate them (Leo 1984). Up until the 1940s, the only cash crop that Africans were allowed to grow in any quantity was maize, because it was needed to feed African laborers working on European plantations. In contrast, coffee and tea might compete with settler production of the same crops (Leys 1975). However, in Mutira Location, Gikuyu did not cultivate either cash crop until 1959 or 1960. First, during the 1950s, the large majority of Gikuyu in Mutira were either fighting with the Land and Freedom Army (the Mau Mau) in the nearby forest or they were interned in villages set up by the colonial government under its emergency powers to prevent collaboration with Mau Mau.[2] Second, the majority were largely unaware of colonial government policies allowing them to cultivate cash crops. While they were interned or fighting for liberation, in 1954, the colonial government instituted a land and agricultural reform package known as the Swynnerton Plan (named for then assistant director of agriculture R.J.M. Swynnerton) designed to encourage Africans who accepted land consolidation and entitlement to grow export crops. Most Gikuyu in Mutira were too preoccupied with the liberation struggle to notice that a "reform" was in the making. It was not until the end of the emergency that they began to plant tea and coffee, now their major cash crops.

In addition to growing tea and coffee for export, Gikuyu living in the Mwea Irrigation Settlement Scheme, set up in the 1950s, grow rice for sale in Kenya. Other northern Gikuyu cultivate pyrethrum, which is exported and processed abroad, then sent back to Kenya for local sale. Marketing boards, a colonial invention of the 1940s, now operate as parastatals of the state. They impinge on the daily lives of rural Gikuyu farmers by controlling the marketing and distribution of most cash crops.

Gikuyu Social Structure

Culturally, the northern and southern Gikuyu share the same social and political traditions, modified over time by interchange with the Rift Valley Maasai and later the Europeans. The concept of *mariika* is central to Gikuyu society. The term means "age-sets" (*riika* is the singular). *Mariika* provide a means of keeping track of generations related directly to the year in which a particular group (both male and female) was circumcised. The circumcision group (generation) is given a name that identifies it with a particular event or characteristic of the group. Lambert (1956) notes that in one location in Nyeri, those circumcised in 1893 were given the age-set name *Nuthi* (jigger fleas) because the abominable insects were unusually prevalent that year (1956:20). Another age-set might be called *Ngigi* (locusts). Later age sets in Nyeri (names varied according to location) came to be associated with the arrival of Europeans, notably *Chiringi* (with the introduction of the shilling in 1923) and *Ndege*—the Kiswahili word for bird that also means airplane (Lambert 1956:21).

Members of a particular *riika*, circumcised at the same time, were given a rank in the age groupings. The rank defined the behavior of individual members within a *riika* and their behavior toward members of other age-groups, both younger and older. The older a particular *riika* became, the more respect it was accorded. This is still true in rural Mutira. *Mariika* acts as an agent of gender-segregated social control.

Older informants, both male and female, relate that a strong bond forms between members of the same *riika* during *Irua* and continues as a form of mutual social aid throughout the lifespan. However, younger Gikuyu, usually circumcised in hospitals today, have little affinity for the concept of *mariika*. In place of *Irua*, today's young Gikuyu seek peer bonds through school classes. Moreover, as the life histories illustrate, the strict social segregation between the sexes seems to be breaking down as young people of both sexes come into contact with one another in primary classrooms, on the playground, and through church activities.

In the past, the transition from one life stage to another in Gikuyu society was marked by rites of passage, which play a central role in the life histories of the older women. Each stage was given a special name for both males and females. The terms used by southern and northern Gikuyu vary according to location, but the meaning is the same. Among the Gichugu and Ndia Gikuyu in Mutira Location the terms for female stages until recently were:

gakenge	newborn (applies to both sexes)
kaana	infant (applies to both sexes)
karigũ	a small girl
kirigũ	a big, uncircumcised girl
mũirĩtu	a grown, circumcised girl
mũhiki	a bride with young children
wamũng'ĩ	a woman with three or more children, one of whom is circumcised

mūtūmia	a woman with several children who have been circumcised
mūongia (also kiheti)	an old woman past menopause

Each of these stages was marked by a particular ceremony— the generic term is *mambura*. A *kaana* became a *karigū* once she had completed *mambura ma twana*—ceremony of the children—and had been removed from her mother's bed to a bed of her own or with other children. A *karigū* became a *kirigū* with ear-piercing; a *kirigū* became a *mūirītu* through the ritual of *Irua*. A *mūhiki* referred to a woman who had left her father's homestead to become a bride in her husband's father's homestead, if he remained in the paternal home, or in a separate homestead over which her husband had control. Marriage was not a single event, but a series of substages that brought together two clans and two extended families. Of utmost importance was *rūracio*, or bridewealth; the number of herd animals—usually goats and cattle—that the groom gave to the bride's family to compensate for the loss of her services to her natal family and to establish the parentage of future children (C. Clark 1971; Mathu 1971). Formal negotiations were held between adult males of the bride's clan and family and those of the groom to establish the amount. Usually, the payment was rendered through a series of installments over time. Today, *rūracio* often includes a payment of Kenya shillings, determined by the amount of formal education a family has invested in its daughter.

A ceremony called *nyumithio*, which was linked to the circumcision of a woman's first child, allowed a woman to be called *wamūng'ī*. During *nyumithio*, as we learn from the oldest informant, a woman received *kirira*, or "special secret knowledge" from the elders (older women). After several children had been circumcised, she became a *mūtumia* and was eligible for membership in the *kiama* —council of elders—which was composed of both men and women in Mutira Location. All old people were referred to by the general term *andū akūrū*, but a very old woman who had "lost most of her teeth" and was past menopause was known as *mūongia*. Accorded great respect, she was allowed to take an active role in sacrificial ceremonies. Hobley (1938) relates that old women were also feared because they had the power to bring evil or bad luck, especially if encountered in a group. Consequently, the respect may have been partly a result of fear. Old people (of both sexes) nearing death were treated with great deference and attention for fear they might inflict *kirume*—a curse put upon a living person or the property of the dying person (Hobley 1938).

Over time, the distinct age groups for females have merged into four groups: *kairītu*, which refers to any uncircumcised girl; *mūirītu*, referring to a circumcised, unmarried girl; *mūhiki*, a young bride with young children; and *mūtūmia*, which refers to any woman who has had several children. An almost parallel sequence of age stages exists for males: *kahii* (boy); *mwanake* (circumcised young man); and mūthuri (any married man with children regardless of age). Old people are still referred to as *andū akūrū*.

The Gikuyu family has been envisioned as circular rather than linear as in western cultures. Each new generation "replaces" their grandparents, who are then free to become ancestors. That such a belief still exists among older Gikuyu is indicated in the way many women in Mutira answered the question, "For whom were you named?" Quite often the answer was, "For my father's mother" or "My mother's mother." When asked why, the response was usually, "Because it was me who gave birth to my father (or mother)." The necessity of "replacing" four grandparents and trying until success is achieved explains why Gikuyu seek to have a minimum of four children and often have more to honor parents' siblings (see Herzog 1971).

The northern Gikuyu today live in homesteads (*micii*, singular *mūcii*) located adjacent to their fields. Spread widely over the steep ridges of Mount Kenya, from a distance the homesteads resemble clusters of brown mushrooms protruding from a green patchwork of maize, tea, and coffee. Each *mūcii* is enclosed by a hedge or log fence with a single entrance. Ideally, it contains the paternal head of family, his wives or wife, their unmarried children, often his married sons, and sometimes single male or female relatives. The Gikuyu are traditionally polygynous, but with the influence of Christianity and Western education, the trend has been toward monogamy. If a man chooses to marry more than one wife, theoretically he must provide *rūracio*, or bridewealth, and a separate house for each within the homestead. In practice, whether or not *rūracio* is actually transferred depends upon the integrity of the man marrying and the circumstances of the man's family, as we shall see in two of the life histories.

The Gikuyu living pattern is undergoing change. Until recently, the male head of the homestead lived separately in his own large *thingira*, or man's house, at the rear of the compound, with houses for each wife and her children extending in a semicircle on either side of the *thingira* toward the entrance. Behind each house were egg-shaped granaries woven from sticks and elevated slightly above ground. In front of the houses, which faced toward the center of the homestead, was an open, pounded earth yard called the *nja*, where many of the family activities—such as food processing, clothes washing, feeding of small herd animals—took place during the daytime. Unmarried, circumcised sons moved out of their father's *thingira*, where they

lived from about age six and built their own smaller bachelor houses—called *kithuni* —where they lived until they married. Upon the
birth of a first child, a married son built a house for his wife and her
future children. Until that time, she lived with his mother, learning
from her what duties she would be expected to perform in the new
homestead. With the increased cost of building materials, today more
husbands are building single-family houses that contain separate
sleeping rooms for the husband and wife or wives.

Homes are constructed of either mud and wattle with a thatch or
corregated iron sheet roof, or they are made of timber. Gikuyu
women, in particular, prefer iron sheet roofing because it means that
their responsibility for the yearly repair of thatching (a time-consum-
ing task) is avoided, and, in addition metal gutters can be attached to
iron sheets to catch rainwater and collect it in a metal drum, thus
reducing the never-ending task of hauling water from a river or
stream. Prosperous Gikuyu supplement timber walls with stone,
which provides permanency. In most cases, the cooking hut is a separate building divided into two rooms—a large room with a central
fireplace (*riiko*) in the packed earth floor formed out of three stones;
and a smaller adjacent storeroom where goats and sheep are kept at
night, called the *thegi*. Most homesteads in Mutira do not have piped
water or sanitary facilities. Water is brought from nearby streams or
rivers in metal or plastic containers on women's backs, bathing is
from a plastic tub, and the toilet is an outdoor latrine some distance
from the houses.

The Historical Context

At the time the oldest life-history informant, Wanjiku, was born
(around 1910) groups of British settlers, encouraged by land promises,
spread northward like so many greedy fingers from the small colonial
trading post of Nairobi in southern Keyna. The Gikuyu of Kiambu
and those further north in Fort Hall and Nyeri districts were directly
in the path of the land-hungry settlers. Many Gikuyu suddenly found
land they assumed to be theirs expropriated for "crown use" by a
colonial government they thought was only temporary. Some, forced
into landlessness, became squatters or laborers on settler plantations.
Others fled north and eastward into "reserves" set aside by the early
1930s for "native" use. Though well within the native reserve, Gikuyu
in Mutira Location began to experience crowding at the lower elevations as land became a scarce commodity. Increased population
within the prescribed confines of the reserve prevented the practice of
shifting cultivation and led to conflicts over land. At the lower elevations, intensive land use soon led to soil depletion and erosion of the

ridges. Nevertheless, women in Mutira prior to the 1950s were able to cultivate small plots in several ecological niches. As Wanjiku notes, "Before Mau Mau, we used to cultivate in different places— that way we could harvest at different times."

Production was limited to food crops for family members and visitors. Extra amounts might be exchanged for other items—such as goats—in local markets. Wanjiku describes learning to count as being important "so that one could count the equivalent thing for trading in the market." Although food was usually plentiful, Wanjiku was able to remember one year—historically recorded by British observers as 1918—when no rain fell. Her people had known droughts before and they would know them again. They labeled this one the Hunger of Kimotho, for a local chief appointed by the colonial government. Wanjiku was about eight years old at the time. Other droughts occurred in the 1930s and 1940s, when the informants in their fifties were children and Wanjiku was a mūtūmia who had given birth to two of her sons.

In particular, a drought in 1941 affected both settlers and Africans. To the Gikuyu, it was known as Ng'arugu ya Njuu (Hunger of The Storks) for the large Maribu storks who destroyed grain crops. Yet Wanjiku doesn't mention this drought, possibly because she was less affected than other Gikuyu living in the drier regions. At the time, she was living in her husband's home on the edge of the Mount Kenya Forest, at an elevation where mountain mists provide a certain amount of moisture during most months. Drought is cyclical in Africa and its effects are felt differentially, depending upon local ecology and climate. This was certainly the case with the drought that occurred in 1984 during my stay in the field. Those living in the lower, drier regions such as Mwea were far more affected than those living at higher elevations such as Mutira.

While a drought is a natural phenomenon, the arrival of increased numbers of European and U.S. missionaries in the early 1920s in Kenya had more profound consequences for the Gikuyu way of life, particularly for Irua. Wanjiku was probably circumcised around 1924 or 1925—at about the age of fourteen. Her description of Irua gives no indication that she was aware of any controversy brewing over female circumcision. Yet clitoridectomy became an issue that attracted the colonial government's attention the following year, largely through the concerted efforts of missionaries.

In 1926, the colonial government, under pressure from Church of Scotland and U.S. Inland Mission leaders, began a campaign to outlaw female circumcision (including clitoridectomy) among the Gikuyu in Central Province (see Sangren 1982). "Native councils, composed of Gikuyu male elders, were encouraged to pass resolutions reducing the severity of the operation (particularly the removal and suturing of the labia minora and half of the labia majora). Councils were directed to regulate the performance of clitoridectomy by female circumcisers to insure that sterile conditions were met. Female circumcisers, who were midwives, were to be issued permits by the councils stipulating under what conditions the operation might be performed. At the prospect of trying to police female circumcisers, council elders balked. In a resolution passed by the Fort Hall Local Native Council (1927), it was noted that male members attending a *baraza* (outdoor public meeting) in May of that year refused to commit local female operators to regulations imposed by the colonial government (Kenya, National Archives 1927a.)

A heated debate emerged within the councils, and factions developed between the few mission-educated Gikuyu who favored abandoning the practice or altering its severity and the many who advocated continuing the practice of clitoridectomy as an essential part of the Gikuyu way of life. The Nyeri Native Council, meeting on March 9, 1927, expressed the feelings of many Gikuyu that despite the chief native commissioner's dissatisfaction with the practice, "It is the custom of the Kikuyu people to circumcise girls, and the vast majority are in favour of the continuance of this rite" (Kenya, National Archives 1927b:49).

The controversy continued over the next several years, with most Gikuyu stubbornly refusing to succumb to the wishes of a foreign government. In addition, many Gikuyu left the European mission churches to start their own Gikuyu Christian churches so they could maintain those cultural practices they felt essential to the Gikuyu way of life—including clitoridectomy and the practice of marrying more than one wife.

By 1930, the controversy over clitoridectomy led a colonial district commissioner in Fort Hall (now Murang'a) to write to the provincial commissioner in Nyeri: "In the present state of native opinion, I think the less talked about the operation of clitoridectomy the better. Natives are sick to death of the subject, so is everyone else. Nothing but harm can result from constantly raising the question, and no matter how many resolutions are passed, they could never be enforced" (Kenya, National Archives 1930:23).

By 1934, in the minds of Kirinyaga Gikuyu and those of neighboring Embu (then lumped together in Embu District) the colonial directive to outlaw clitoridectomy had become identified with covert measures for controlling population and land. A request was made that year by the Embu district commissioner to the provincial commissioner for CID (Central Intelligence Division) assistance "to combat the disaffected native propaganda campaign in Embu District averring that Europeans are trying to depopulate the land by preventing the circumcision of women" (Kenya, National Archives 1934:28). Because female circumcision was a necessary prerequisite to marriage (see Kenyatta 1968), Gikuyu believed that the government was trying to control population growth in the reserve with the intent of claiming "unused" land.

Although the controversy raged among Gikuyu elders—both male and female—it does not seem to have reached young women like Wanjiku who were undergoing clitoridectomy during the 1920s. Clitoridectomy was the accepted practice—a girl did not question the wisdom of the elders. Nor did Wanjiku envision any alternative to achieving adult status.

Wanjiku believed, like most of her people, that one must "buy maturity with pain." Maturity, in a society that had no extended period of adolescence, meant an abrupt break with childhood and the assumption of an adult role with its accompanying responsibilities and privileges. One of the signs of a mature adult was her/his ability to endure pain with stoicism. By demonstrating her ability to withstand pain during *Irua*, a woman demonstrated to others that she was ready to accept the pain that accompanied childbirth. Moreover, Wanjiku points out that participating in *Irua*, in addition to providing socially acceptable *physical* maturity, equally provided the means for social transition to adulthood.

An explicit part of the ritual process was learning the social mores that governed adult behavior. "Now, a girl misses something by not going through *Irua*—she does not know when she is talking nonsense in front of a grown person," Wanjiku contends. "Part of *Irua* was learning how to behave around the elders and how to act with different age groups." Consequently, a transition to a new age status required learning a new set of behaviors identified with the particular social status. Although some mission Gikuyu began to give up the practice of female circumcision in the 1930s and 1940s, other Gikuyu held onto the practice as central to the Gikuyu way of life—a symbol of ethnic pride pitted against colonial domination.

In the 1940s, Kenya's neighbors to the north became embroiled in World War II, but for the older women in Mutira the war seemed remote. Although Gikuyu males, as British subjects, participated in the war, people in Mutira knew little about their experiences until men returned home with stories they told their agemates and sons. Wanjiku's husband was not involved. The only reference she made to World War II was when I ask her how she knew that her conversion to Christianity was in 1948 and she explained that it was three years after the end of the Italian war.

However, when war came to Mutira during the 1950s, Wanjiku, as a mother left with three growing sons by a husband working far away, found her life very much changed. The lessons of World War II had come home to roost, and Kenyans began demanding a role in government and control of their land. Young men without land took to the forests to form a Land and Freedom Army dedicated to liberation. The Mau Mau Rebellion erupted in 1952, taking the British by surprise. The following year, Gikuyu in Kirinyaga, including Wanjiku and her children, were forced into fortified villages, leaving their cultivated fields and homesteads open to pillage.

As new Christian converts, Wanjiku and her husband had enrolled their sons in a missionary school, but a state of emergency made school attendance dangerous. Wanjiku's sons attended sporadically. Long days of forced labor and nights of fear became a daily pattern for many Mutira women. "A lot of times we would hear the airplanes coming to kill the Mau Mau fighters in the nearby forest. Then we became frightened, " shudders Wanjiku.

In selecting the five older women, I was interested in finding out how these women had experienced the struggle for independence beginning with the Mau Mau Rebellion and ending with liberation in 1963. Personal accounts of men's roles in the struggle exist (such as Barrett and Njama 1966; Barrett and Muchai 1973), but at the time I began collecting the life histories little had been written about women's roles. What I discovered is that each woman experienced this period differently. At the same time, all of the woman suffered dislocation.

Two of the women in their fifties were married to husbands employed by British colonials in Nairobi during the 1950s. Both women were forced to leave Mutira at the beginning of the emergency to join their husbands in Nairobi. In one case, the woman traveled at great risk because the colonial government had put up roadblocks and she had to travel in secrecy to reach her destination.

The three women left behind in Mutira were interned in fortified villages during the height of the fighting in the location. Wangeci, the oldest, was never sure whether she was going to be beaten by Home Guards or Mau Mau, so she kept to herself and prayed for the end of war and liberation. Another woman's husband became a Home Guard for the British, much to the woman's consternation. She has bitter memories of his brutality during the digging of the trench. The third woman's husband was supportive of the Mau Mau freedom fighters, as were other members of her family who served with the Land and Freedom Army. She became committed to the nationalist struggle and served as a scout for the forest fighters.

It was not until shortly before independence, when the people were released from the villages, that Wanjiku's husband finally returned home. He found his hard-working wife having already cleared the ridges below the homestead for the cultivation of tea and coffee—a decision she made on her own, unaware that her economic future would be determined by an international market far beyond her control.

Wanjiku perceives Kenya's liberation from colonial rule as the beginning of her own freedom from the heavy responsibilities and hardships she endured during the 1940s and 1950s. Schooling became easier to obtain, and everyone rushed to enroll their children. The hope was that educated children would return the investment by becoming wage earners who would later support their parents in old age.

Although Wanjiku embraces the idea of schooling, the kind of education children now receive fissions the Gikuyu way of life, creating in her view, demands and new formations:

> But people today—those with a Form Four education—do not want to stay in rural areas like this. They want to work in a town. Also, we who are older, can have trouble from children who attend school because sometimes they can abuse somebody who is not schooled—even an older person like a parent! Long ago, when I was growing up, nobody dared to abuse somebody in an older *riika*. Today, you can see boys and girls of different age groups mixing and even joking with one another. The importance of *mariika* in Agĩkũyũ tradition has disappeared with schooling.

Wanjiku sees the life she knew as a child slipping away. Schooling is partially responsible, she believes. Once schooled, young people disappear from the rural areas. They no longer respect their elders, and social distance between *mariika* disintegrates. Wanijuku's life best reflects the changes that have occurred within Gikuyu society during the twentieth century because, of the seven life-history informants, she has lived the longest.

Changing Gender Roles

Formerly, both men and women shared the agricultural workload except when men were at war. Men usually cleared the land, helped to prepare it for cultivation, and cultivated yams and bananas; women cultivated most other crops; and both sexes helped with the harvest. Women produced, processed, and had control over the distribution of most food crops. From the parcels of land she was allocated by her husband at marriage—often as many as seven or eight in different areas—a wife was expected to raise enough food to feed her husband, children, and any visitors. Women in polygynous marriages in which the relationship between co-wives was favorable often shared cultivation, food processing, and preparation tasks. In homes in which the relationship was not good, each wife cultivated her own parcel with the help of her children and prepared her family's food. A similar pattern in polygynous households exists today. In addition, a custom known as *ngwatio* (whereby women formed groups to help one another collectively with agricultural tasks such as hoeing and weeding on a rotating basis) still persists.

In Kirinyaga District, where Mutira is located, an increasing number of men work in towns and in the capital city of Nairobi, leaving their wives and mothers with the major burden of cultivation and food processing (Davison 1985). In addition, women whose husbands are often absent, or who are widowed, must perform the bulk of tasks associated with cash-crop production, such as hoeing, weeding, and constant harvesting of leaves in the case of tea and weeding, fertilizing, and harvesting twice a year for coffee. Formerly, children contributed substantially to agricultural production, but with the introduction of formal schooling that source of labor has been drastically reduced. Further, schooling has meant an added financial burden, because it necessitates the earning of cash for school fees and uniforms. Cash crops provide the predominant source of income for school fees and commodities like sugar, kerosene, and clothing that cannot be made at home. In short, the self-sufficient Gikuyu are gradually becoming more and more dependent upon a money economy that, in turn, requires the growing of cash crops that are dependent upon the fluctuations of a world market economy.

Men currently control most political and ceremonial aspects of Gikuyu society, except those in which the orientation is strictly female, as in female circumcision ceremonies or, more recently, in women's self-help-group activities. Men, particularly in public, tend to dominate—though a woman's submissive position decreases with age. Male heads of homesteads, when present, have the final say in all matters concerning land use and the homestead. Nonetheless, the peripatetic habits of many adult males and an increased rate of absenteeism means that often women in a homestead are left with the responsibility of making decisions normatively recognized as belonging to men.

Although Gikuyu women in groups are assertive, their behavior as individuals depends upon their age and status. Husbands—at least in public—demand respect. Wifebeating as a means of controlling married women is still an accepted practice among some Gikuyu. Obedience and respect for elders, highly valued, extend to male-female relationships. There is often a five- to ten-year age difference between a husband and his first wife (and more with subsequent wives). Consequently, a wife's position is one of public deference to her husband, though in private she may have greater leeway. Age-rank applies as well to co-wives. First wives have primary authority over additonal wives, who are usually younger and less experienced in homestead tasks and family matters. Younger women defer to older women. Yet, within constraints of age and sex, individual women demonstrate that they have the ability to control certain aspects of their lives and to mediate change.

Related to the role and position of women is that of children. Children are highly regarded by the Gikuyu and are included in all aspects of life—whether it is a circumcision or a clan meeting. Child care is the responsibility of the entire extended family, not just the mother. Though the father is absent much of the time, when he is at home he shows great affection for small children in particular. Children are in close contact with their mothers' bodies for the first year and are held often by various members of the family. From then on, older siblings are responsible for much of the child care, and grandmothers are as important as mothers once a child is weaned.

Motherhood is not an end in itself. A woman's productive role does not terminate once her reproductive one commences but instead takes on new meaning. Sociologist Nancy Chodorow's historical observation of the typical U.S. woman that "A woman carried out her childcare responsibilities along with a wide range of other productive work" (1978:4) still applies to rural Gikuyu women. Nevertheless, children determine a woman's social status to a great extent, and a woman is usually called by the name of her firstborn child. For example, a woman whose first child is named Wawira is Nyina-wa-Wawira, or Mother-of-Wawira. The more children a woman has, the more prosperous she is considered. Mothers who have raised many children are highly regarded by both sexes.

It was my role as a mother of children that allowed me to gain an acceptable position in Mutira Location. I was known not by my family name but by the name of my firstborn child. In addition, it was my position as a mother that gave me access to certain information that I otherwise might have been denied.

Collecting the Life Histories

Selection of the Seven Informants

When I entered the field in 1983, I had a working knowledge of the Kikuyu language and had visited the location on three previous occasions (1977, 1978, and 1980). I spent the first three months interviewing 101 women between the ages of twenty-one and seventy-nine from every third homestead. From this sample, I select-

Figure 1.1 DIAGRAM OF LIFE-HISTORY INFORMANTS

Age in Years

Age	Wanjiku	Wamutira	Watoro	Wangeci	Wanoi	Nyambura	Wanja
80							
60	Anglican	Anglican	Catholic	Anglican	Adult ed.		
				Women's self-help group member			Teacher
					Catholic		Single
40	Widow	Married	Married (sep.)	Widow	Married	Married	Form 4
		1st wife	2nd wife			St. Five	Anglican
20					Midwife	Catholic	

ed the group of seven life-history informants.

They were chosen from three different age categories—old age, mid-life, and young adult. Intracohort selection was based upon a range of variability in marital status, educational background, religion, and economic status determined by the initial sample.[3]

Among women in their seventies, there were few differences. The oldest woman, selected from fifteen possible candidates, is typical of her peers. Wanjiku is a widow. She is unschooled and nonliterate. She lives with three grown sons, their wives, and fifteen grandchildren in a homestead on a ridge adjacent to where I lived. She is an Anglican convert to Christianity. She cultivates maize and beans and occasionally assists other family members in picking tea. At the time of my stay in Mutira, she was largely responsible for the child care of three small infants, the children of two daughters-in-law and a granddaughter.

Four women in their early fifties were chosen from twenty in this group in the initial sample. Here there was more variability. Two life-history informants—Wamutira and Watoro—were selected because they represented spouses in polygynous marriages. Wamutira is the first of three wives, Watoro the second of three wives. In Watoro's case, she had separated from her husband. Of the two women who represented those in monogamous marriages, the husband of one had died. Wangeci is a widow. The other woman, Wanoi, was chosen because of her profession: She is one of the few traditional midwives in Mutira Location. Three of the women had never attended school, and Wanoi, who attended for one day, ran away and never returned. Later, as an adult, however, she joined a literacy class so that she could write her name and keep birth records.

All four of these women are Christian converts—two are Anglican and the other two are Catholic. Three of the women had children who had died. One did not. All are full-time farmers and relatively poor. Watoro, the poorest, did not have sufficient income from coffee cultivation to buy a cow, whereas Wangeci, the widow, had enough income from selling tea leaves to purchase cement to construct floors in her house and to construct a well.

My original intent was to select only one woman in her twenties, but I discovered enough variation with regard to education and marital status among the sixteen women in their twenties in the original sample that I decided to include two women in this group to reflect the differences. One woman, Nyambura, represents the majority of her peers who have completed several years of primary schooling (the mean number of years of school attendance for this age group is 5.8). The other represents the minority of women in her age group who have attained a secondary-school education. Nyambura is married with two children. The other woman, Wanja, is a single mother with three children. One is Catholic, the other Protestant. In addition, Nyambura is a full-time farmer, whereas Wanja, who has a secondary-school diploma, is a part-time nursery school teacher.

A word needs to be said about occupation and economic status. Of the total number of women surveyed, only 4 out of 101 had wage occupations—3 as teachers and 1 as a social worker. The rest were full-time farmers who depended largely upon earnings from tea or coffee cultivation for income or, to a lesser degree, on husbands' incomes.

Economic status was not directly determined through the sample survey but was indirectly assessed through observations of housing and homesteads. Most women in the sample were at the low end of the economic scale; that is, they lived in mud and wattle houses with thatched or corregated iron sheet roofs, no electricity or running water, and no sanitary facilities other than a pit latrine. For most women, earning income for their children's school fees was a constant problem. In all cases, women raised and processed the majority of their family's food, but they used cash payments from tea or coffee production to pay school fees, buy school uniforms and books, and purchase commodities such as sugar, cooking fat, kerosene, and clothing.

The Interview Process

Once I had made the selection of life-history informants, I approached each one to elicit her cooperation, explaining that the oral narrative would be audio-taped with her permission and would eventually be translated into a written text. All of the women agreed to participate and were interviewed for one to two hours on a weekly basis over a period of nine months. The interviews were transcribed and translated at night by kerosene lantern. Notes on one week's interview with an informant became a springboard for the next week's session. As time progressed and a rapport was established, the women became more open in sharing the intimate details of their lives. For many of the interviews, my research assistant was present, but for others she was not allowed to participate because she was an "uncircumcised girl who has not yet given birth." This was particularly true for sessions with the older women having to do with *Irua* and childbirth.

At the end of the year, each woman was given a gift of her choice to compensate for her time. One woman chose a battery-operated radio, another a pedal-operated sewing machine. Most chose dresses. I was fortunate in beginning the interviews during the dry, postharvest season, (December–February) when women's agricultural tasks were at a minimum. Once the planting season began, women were more occupied. During this time, I compensated their time additionally by contributing my labor to their fields after each session.

Once the life narratives were recorded and transcribed, it was then necessary to go back and validate the material through cross-interviews with family members, friends, and community leaders who had known the women a long time and through archival research to validate with historical evidence the occurrence of certain events referred to in the life histories. The validation process took about four months.

The narratives of the women follow this chapter, beginning with that of the oldest, in her seventies, and ending with those of the two youngest, in their twenties. Although none of the women objected to having her real name used in the written text, I have chosen not to use the names by which the women are known in their communities. Instead, common Gikuyu names for women are used, and, where necessary, names of husbands and children have been changed to protect their anonymity. For the most part, the women's stories are presented as they were told to me, with minor changes in sentence structure when these would clarify meanings for a reader outside the Gikuyu culture. In addition, where stories and riddles became redundant across the narratives, I deleted some and retained others. Each narrative begins with a brief introduction describing the woman and my relationship with her. Further comments and analysis are left to the final chapter.

Notes

1. Gikuyu traditionally did not communicate amounts beyond "nine" to others because they believed it might bring death to people and animals if they were enumerated completely.
2. The 1954 *Handing over Report* for Embu District (which included Mutira Location at the time) indicates that, by the latter part of 1951, "Mau Mau activities" were giving the colonial government cause for concern. By 1953, "villagization" was well under way, with seventy-one internment villages constructed by the following year. In addition, detention camps had been set up at Kerugoya, Embu, and Ndoma and a total of 831 men had been detained by July 1954 (Kenya, National Archives, 1954:10).
3. See Appendix A for tables showing marital status, education, and participation in women's groups among the six different age groups in the original sample of 101 women in Mutira.

The research site—Gikuyu homes on top of a ridge planted in tea, Mutira Location.

2

The Life of
a Traditional Woman

Wanjiku, the oldest woman in the group of life-history informants, has the distinction of being born prior to the period of major British colonial penetration in Mutira Location. Born sometime in the year 1910, she has a vantage point from which to view the changes that are occurring in the Gikuyu way of life. She critically assesses those changes; some are "good" —for example, the coming of Christianity, which brought with it an alternative to "traditional" medical practices. Others are "bad" such as the breakdown of *mariika* (age groups).

Chosen for her representativeness, Wanjiku, like many of her peers in their seventies, is a widow. She lives in a homestead, formerly headed by her husband, with two grown sons and their families, who provide her major economic support. Because the homestead is only one ridge away from where I stayed, Wanjiku was easily accessible. In addition, she is related through marriage to the family with whom I stayed, which meant I saw her on many occasions. She is the oldest of four adult women living in her family compound; the other three women are her sons' wives. Fourteen grandchildren ranging in age from infants to young adults enliven the compound. Wanjiku has a special attachment to her youngest son's wife, who fetches her mother-in-law's water and firewood, shares the cooking, and picks what Wanjiku perceives to be "my tea." In return, the old woman takes care of the daughter-in-law's infant son when the young woman is cultivating or picking tea. Thus, a comfortable reciprocity exists between the two women, who share a cooking fire.

A heavy-set woman, Wanjiku has become somewhat lame and gets around with the aid of a carved walking stick. She also suffers from arthritis. The physical disabilities frustrate her efforts to participate in many farming activities—a frustration she openly acknowledges. She views her major usefulness in life as completed and accepts that death may come in the near future. She has no fear of death, accepting it as an inevitable part of life.

When we first began working together, Wanjiku could not separate her own life experiences from those of all Gikuyu—she is firmly rooted in her cultural community. However, gradually, as she came to know me and we shared the child care of her grandchildren, personal feelings began to enter her story. The fifth interview was a turning point. When we began to discuss *Irua* I observed her becoming uncomfortable as she sought anonymity in generalizations. I suspected that the presence of my research assistant—a young, uncircumcised girl—was making it difficult for her to talk freely. When I asked her if this was so, she seemed relieved and acknowledged that it was. She explained, "You are a grown woman with children—a *mūtumia*—so I can tell you these things, but I cannot share this *kirira* (secret knowledge) with a young girl." Her observation posed a problem in terms of the ultimate reading audience and I explained that young, uncircumcised women might eventually be reading her story. This did not seem to make much difference to her because, as she explained, "They are of a different culture, and what they read will be in a different language. I cannot share this *kirira* with a *mūirītu* from this place because she is too young to know such things." It was as if she understood that in going outside the immediate cultural community and in the process of translation to English, the power of the spoken word would lose some of its meaning. And so it does. The written, translated text can never capture the complete texture, nuance of meaning and physical expression that are implicit in the initial telling of the narrative in Kikuyu. What is told here is mediated by the writer in the process of translation and transcription—a process necessary to render the narrative comprehensible to an audience from a very different set of cultural communities. It is advisable to keep this in mind as you read the written texts.

For the remainder of the sessions related to the experiences of adult women—*Irua*, marriage, childbirth—I worked with Wanjiku alone. She was then far more relaxed and much more open with her recollections, but whenever a woman of a younger *riika* appeared, she'd shoo her away playfully, explaining that she was giving Nyina-wa-Stephen *kirira*.

As the months went by, Wanjiku and I established an intimacy born of shared experiences—childbirth, children's diseases, and death. We spent one morning a week together, caring for three babies in the compound whose mothers were away working in their *mashamba* (fields). The mornings gave me a chance both to observe Wanjiku in her role as a grandmother and to observe the behavior of the growing infants. Moreover, Wanjiku often contributed anecdotes about her life that did not enter the more formal sessions but that she allowed me later to include in the final account of her life.

Through many shared hours, Wanjiku came to trust me and "adopted" me as her special apprentice, sharing willingly the Gikuyu *kirira* she chose to tell me and those events of her life she could remember. At times, her voice was touched with a sense of urgency—as if she might not get the chance again to share the critical aspects of her culture. At other times, she displayed a sense of humor, musing over life's ironies. Wisdom and humor characterize *Cũcũ's* (a respectful term meaning "grandmother") narrative. This, then, is her story.

—J.D.

I am called Wanjiku. I am the second-to-last-born of my mother, Wangeci. I was named for the sister-to-my-father. I was born at Kiaritha. My father was called Gacoki. He was a big, black man. He did not have a temper, for he never beat my mother. He and my mother, who was his first wife, had eight children. Waminĩ and Mũthungu, his other two wives, each had three children that I can remember. Mũthungu, the third wife, was not Mugikuyu [a Gikuyu]. She was a Kamba [Bantu-speaking group to the south of Kirinyaga District].

There were many children growing up together in my father's compound. We would all eat together. The food—even a cob of green maize—was put together on one tray basket, and the child who did not want to eat from the same tray was forced to. We would sit together around the tray and share amongst ourselves. One year, when I was about Njoki's size [an eight-year-old granddaughter], we did not have much to eat because no rains fell. People called it *Ng'arugu ya Kimotho*, the Hunger of Kimotho. Kimotho was an important elder in Kirinyaga at the time (1918). We were very hungry. Even our cows died. But the next year the rains returned.

My older sisters—Waruguru, Muthoni, and Wainoi—took care of me when my mother was working in the *shamba* or cooking. As soon as I was walking, my sisters gave me a small gourd and I would go with them to the stream to fetch water. Later, I learned how to collect firewood with a *mũkwa* [tumpline] and how to fetch green vegetables and carry them home in a *kiondũ* [basket]. When I was young I was never beaten by my mother, because I was an obedient child. I was quiet, too—a child who did not disturb others.

My mother, who was a jolly woman, taught me how to use a digging stick for cultivating and later on I learned to use a *kibanga* [machete]. But even after I was married, I found that the *kibanga* can be dangerous if used without care. You see this scar on my leg? My husband's mother hurt me with a *kibanga* when we were cultivating close together, so it taught me not to go near anybody with a *kibanga* My mother used to tell me which ones I was related to when we went visiting. She would say, "If you see so-and-so, that is your *cũcũ*

Figure 2.1 WANJIKU'S FAMILY

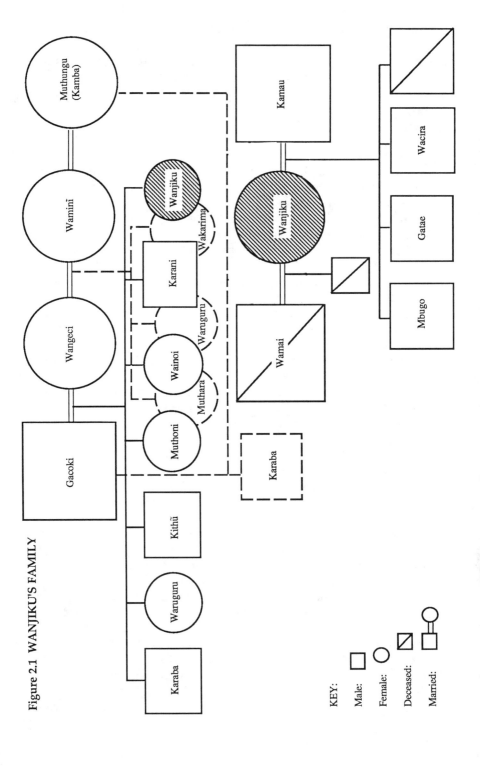

KEY:

Male: ☐

Female: ○

Deceased: ◩

Married: ♂

[grandmother] and that one you see there is your uncle. He is a relative and this one here is a clansmate." To know the members of our clan—Ũceera—was important then. That way one knew who could be called upon for a circumcision or wedding. We even helped each other at harvest time.

When I was growing up, there were terms given to girls for the stages they went through—from the time they were small until they matured to become women and then became old. The first was *karigũ*, which means a small girl. Then came *kirigũ*, which was for a big, uncircumcised girl like Njeri [her ten-year-old granddaughter]. After a girl was circumcised, she became a *mũirĩtu*. When she got married and had young children she was known as *mũhiki*. A woman with three or more children, one of whom had gone through circumcision, was called *wamũng'iĩ*. The woman who had three or more children circumcised was known as *mũtumia*. *Mũongia* refers to an old woman like me who has no teeth and can no longer give birth. These are the terms that were used when I was a child, but *karigũ* and *kirigũ* are not used now and even considered abusive. *Mũirĩtu* is used for any girl child before she gets married and has children. *Mũhiki* is still used to mean a bride and *mũtumia* refers to all married women with children. Sometimes *mũongia* is used for very old women, but not so often as it was used when I was a child growing up.

The first change that occurred in my life was when I was taken from my mother's bed—at about four or five years of age. There was a ceremony called *mambura ma twana* [children's ceremony] at that time. It came soon after I was weaned. How were we weaned? Our mother refused to let us suck anymore. A child would cry for a few days and then get used to it. When the mother wanted to get another child [resume sexual relations], a goat would be slaughtered by a *mũndũ mugo* [medicine man]. A strip of goat's skin called *rũkoro* was cut and put across the chest of the child. The slaughtering of the goat was to purify the child. At the same time, two women shaved the heads of the mother and child to make them clean. Then the mother and father, together with the *mũndũ mugo* and the two women ate the roasted meat of the goat. From this time, a child could not sleep in her mother's bed. She would have her own bed made of a soft skin or sleep with the older children

When I was a child growing up, we wore a goatskin. It used to be gathered and tied at one shoulder. When I realized that I was a girl is when I was given a *mwengu* [goatskin skirt with pointed flaps in front and back, usually decorated with beads].

As children we were taught how to count. We were told to collect sticks. Then we would count one to five and tie a bundle of five sticks together. We counted bundles of five sticks until we got to the number needed. Another way a young child was taught to count was by using the fingers. It was important to learn because of selling or buying goats. One needed to be able to count well so that one could count the equivalent thing for trading in the market.

We also learned to measure length using *ndigi* [string]. When building a house, a stick was placed in the ground where the fireplace was to be at the center of the house and strings of the same length were tied to the stick pointing out in all directions. Then other sticks were tied at the opposite end of each string and put in the ground to mark where the outside wall of the house would be. It was just like today's tape measure. So you see, even though we didn't have written numbers, we still could keep track of things and knew how to measure.

How did we exercise our brains as children? We were taught stories and riddles as we sat near the fireplace at night, waiting for the food to cook. The person with a riddle would say, "*Gwata ndai*" ["Catch a riddle"]. The person playing replied, "*Ndogwata* " ["I am ready"]. Are you ready? Here are some for you:

Ndarekia mũkoni haha watwarairu-
ruma Mbere.

I dropped a banana stem here, and its noise was heard at Embu [a distant place].

[Answer:] *Gĩkuo kia mũndũ mugo.*

The death of a medicine man.

Ciariranira.
[Answer:] *Thara mũrima ũria*
noyu ũngi.

They cry at each other.
Napier grass on both banks of a river.

Kanya gatune rware.
[Answer:] *Thathĩ wamũhiki.*

A red pot in the field.
Red soil smeared over a bride.

One used to "give cows" [metaphorically] to the person asking the riddle if he/she did not know the answer. It was not actually cows but just saying that cows would be given—that way one could get a lot of cows verbally if one knew the answers to new riddles that the other person didn't know. Often children were taught the answers to riddles by their parents in the same way children today are taught the answer to a math problem in school. A child was taught riddles so that when she went to tell them to other children, she would have a lot of cows and would win—just like when a child nowadays gets many good marks in school, she is given a number [rank] to show where she stands in the class. The one teaching riddles was happy with the child who had a good memory for the answers.

Some stories made us think, too. The boys were told stories by their fathers and grandfathers and the girls were told stories by their mothers and grandmother near the cooking fire. I remember one that was told by my grandmother about two big men created by *Ngai* [God].

Once there was a man called Mwaramwaka and another called Mũriakamiri. Mwaramwaka would sleep for the whole year. Mũriakamiri was a very strong man who was never defeated by any-body—he would even kill wild animals.

One day, Mũriakamiri thought of going to look for somebody who was as strong as he was. He ended up at Mwaramwaka's place. He met this one still asleep, for the year was not yet over. I tell you, Mwaramwaka had a lot of cows and when Mũriakamiri reached the place where they were kept, he started eating Mwaramwaka's cows. The servants went to call Mwaramwaka, but they had trouble waking him. Finally he woke, and went out to meet a man the size of a giant eating his cows. Mwaramwaka went to Mũriakamiri and told him to start eating the cows from one end and he would start from the other end. So they ate the cows and met in the middle and started to fight. They fought and fought and Mwaramwaka was defeated. Mũriakamiri took the very large bag that he never left behind when he went hunting and opened it. Inside were all the animals he had ever killed—an elephant, buffalo, lion, gazelle, and rabbit. Now he put Mwaramwaka on top of all these animals, closed it and went on his way.

Soon Mũriakamiri started feeling thirsty and when he reached a lake he went to take some water. Just then, a bird came and told him not to take water there for the place was dangerous. Mũriakamiri despised the bird for threatening him and bent down to take water from the lake. Suddenly, there emerged a water snake with nine heads, and it came toward him. Mũriakamiri started killing the snake by hitting it on the heads. But the ninth head jumped away and disappeared to tell the other snakes what was happening.

Now, Mũriakamiri picked up his bag, slung it on his back, and went on his way. But *Ngai*, the Creator, saw all that he had done with the strength *Ngai* had given him. *Ngai* regretted it and so he removed the strength from Mũriakamiri. All of a sudden, Mũriakamiri felt the bag grow very heavy. So he put it down. And when he did this, it opened up and all the animals he'd ever caught came out and ran away. Then *Ngai* told Mũriakamiri to go too. Now Mũriakamiri was weak. He realized that he had no strength to kill any longer.

This story taught us children to grow up fearing the power of

Ngai. It taught us to use our strength in useful ways and not to abuse others with it. If we went to fight somebody and overpowered him, we learned we might be killed too. Most of the stories we heard had a lesson in one way or another.

Whereas stories and riddles were usually told at night, a proverb could come anytime. These were wise sayings that were a way of counseling us. For example, we were told, "*Rũrigi rwenta gĩriria mũndũ mũkwa*" ["A string makes one wait for a rope"]. This means that first one uses a string to carry things before she buys a *mũkwa* [carrying rope]. We were also told, "*Gũkĩriria kũretagira mũndũ ainda*" ["Patience brings one rewards"]. As a girl got older, her mother might say, "*Wendo mũnene wĩ thina* " ["A lot of love has problems"], meaning that what you love so much today may destroy you tomorrow. We had songs that taught moral lessons, too. I remember one that came after the missionaries began to start churches and schools. It tells people to forget the old ways, like drinking *njohi* [native beer], and be baptized. Even nowadays, we begin songs for weddings and church ceremonies that give advice about wise behaviors.

* * *

When I was a child about the size of Njeri, my mother began teaching me about how I should behave around men. If I was sitting badly, with my legs spread apart, she would tell me that this is not the way a woman sits. I was told that moving about with boys is bad because when the time reaches for circumcision [actually clitoridectomy, though all women refer to it as "circumcision"], the blood during the cutting would go back into the stomach. Whenever I left cooking utensils scattered all around, she would come and tell me that a woman does not do this. If I talked rudely, I was told, "A woman does not talk this way."

When I got a little older, about fourteen, my ears were pierced—meaning that I had bought a new stage of maturity with the holes in my ears. First, I got the upper rim of the ears pierced—that is called *mbuci*. Then, after those healed, the lower lobes were cut and wooden sticks were put in. This is called *gũtara matũ*. Then, when I showed the first signs of growing breasts—before I had my first menstruation—preparations were made for *Irua* [circumcision].

It was the Agĩkũyũ tradition for one to undergo circumcision in order to be termed a grown person. At that time, one bought this stage with pain. The parents would see the girl was growing breasts. Other people might notice, too, and they would point it out to the parents and say, "You should not let your daughter stay a *kirigu* ."

By "buying maturity with pain," I mean that the pain of the old days and the pain of nowadays are different. First, I felt pain having *mbuci* done. Then later, I felt pain when *matū* were cut. But these were less than the pain of *Irua*. With *Irua*, I was cut deeply with a *kienji* [broad-bladed knife used for the operation]. It was like being slaughtered. The wounds were covered with castor oil, and *ithangu ria ithakwa* (a very soft, light green leaf with a texture like velvet) was used to cover the wound.

I began going to circumcision ceremonies even as a child so I had seen what happened. It was the old women and my mother, though, who told me that to go for *Irua* is a good thing. The old people wanted me to go before I began menstruating because if a girl had *mambura ma mūtumia* [menstruation] before being circumcised it was a bad omen, and the parents would lose the first goats of *rūracio* [bridewealth] when a girl was married. My mothers prepared me by telling me what would happen during *Irua,* and the parents informed the relatives and neighbors that on such-and-such a day, Wanjiku would be circumcised.

On the morning of *Irua*, those of us who were candidates were taken to the river by women of our clans. The women and the candidates would dip into the river and start washing each other. Then the women smeared mud all over me and after it was washed off, I was carried on the back of a woman of my clan who was married with only one child up to my mother's house. There, I was dressed for *Irua*. We were dressed with beads made of seeds and gourd tops which were strung across the chest. We wore a skirt made of reeds and seed beads called a *thira*. Those going to watch, though, wore ordinary clothes.

The women accompanying us to the field where we were to be circumcised blew on flutes made out of bamboo. They danced and sang special songs for the occasion. Once at the field, they sang and danced even more, waving clubs in the air.

Ĩi, ĩi, ĩi—ni mwana,	Yes, yes, yes—it is the child,
Nĩ mwana	It is the child
Watuma kuuma nyũmba	Who has made me come from
nyũke kĩbaro.	home to this field.

Then they sang:

Ĩi, ni mburi.	Yes, it is the goat.[1]
Ĩi, ni mburi ya Wanjiku.	Yes, it is Wanjiku's goat.
Ĩi, Wanjiku ndure itangi cunika.	Yes, Wanjiku, bleed so the goat can't be snatched away from you.

There were five of us circumcised together that time—Thegoiya,

Wakonyo, Wakũthii, Muthoni, and me. Many people came to the field to watch us. Everybody who was able to walk was there—even small children. They were surrounding us in a big circle. We went to the center and spread out our *mathangu* [leaves] on the ground where we would be circumcised. When I sat down, my supporter—my mother's mother who was chosen by my mother—stood behind me like this [she demonstrates how she was held so her legs were spread apart]. Another woman was holding my hands. The circumciser, who was an old experienced woman, was in front of me, cutting and hewing away meat from my body. I felt so much pain and I screamed very loud. After the cutting, the circumciser put castor oil on the wounds—oil that my mother had brought in a container especially for my circumcision. Then an *ithangu* [leaf] was tied over that place. So, you hear, that is buying maturity with pain. I give you this *kirira* because you are my friend and you will understand.

After I had been circumcised, I walked home very slowly because of the bleeding. If I felt faint, water was poured over my head. Many people of my clan were accompanying me, singing and dancing. When I got home, all I wanted to do was go to bed. I just went in and slept, but other people—the visitors—went on dancing and eating because the clan women had done a lot of cooking—things like *irio*, porridge, and beer. I was later given good food to eat, and my parents slaughtered a goat for me.

After *Irua*, there was a whole month of being washed and having oil put on the wounds and *ithangu* changed until the wounds healed. So now, if you were to see me there, where the meat was stripped off, you would find it very hard [scar tissue].

Anybody who has not felt the pain of *Irua* cannot abuse me. If an uncircumcised girl abused me, we would fight. The girls nowadays do not know such pain. The ones who went through *Irua* together, we have felt pain together—that shows body maturity. We are of the same *riika*. We cannot abuse each other. We are known by our *riika* name—that, and the pain we shared, kept us together from that day.

From *Irua* I learned what it meant to be grown-up, with more brains. This is because after circumcision, I began to listen to my mother's advice that moving about with men could easily make me become pregnant once I begin menstruating. Also from *Irua*, I learned what it means to be pure Mũgĩkũyũ—to have earned the stage of maturity when, being a circumcised person, one no longer moves about with those not yet circumcised.

These things I am telling you, Nyina-wa-Stephen, make my lips fearful to think of the way things have changed. Now, a girl misses something by not going through *Irua*—she does not know when she is talking nonsense in front of a grown person. Part of *Irua* was learning how to behave around the elders and how to act with different age groups. Nowadays, because there is no transition to adulthood, people go talking to anybody. And when a girl goes to school, she is warned by the teachers not to say to any girl, "You are not circumcised" [as a taunt]. In school, they do not want to know which girls are circumcised and which are not.

If a girl gives birth today, she starts moving with those who have not done so yet. In the old times, that would not happen. A woman who had had a child would not talk with one who hadn't, telling her the secrets of childbirth. But today, *hiya*, a woman who has had a child talks and talks about it. That is when her friend knows she has gone through another stage and is no longer of her age group.

There are no *mariika* nowadays as in our time. Then, we who were of the same *riika* could do anything. We would share our secrets. We would agree to sit down with our legs apart so that we could see who in our *riika* was loose in sleeping with men. There was an old woman, like me, who would take all the girls together and inspect them to see who was having sex.

*Riika*mates used to help each other and straightened each other's behaviors if they saw one of the group doing things that were wrong. How did we help each other? If a girl was caught by a man who tried to have sexual relations by force with her, she would scream for help and the other girls of her *riika* would run and pull the man off, beating him. That happened once to me with a man who wanted to marry me. When he tried to carry me off, I screamed and my agemates rescued me. Also, we would help each other with work in the *shamba*, rotating to each girl's place, and at the end of our work the girl whose *shamba* we cultivated fed the rest of us. We called this *ngwatio*. Even after we got married we helped each other. If one gave birth, the rest would go to see her, carrying millet porridge, bananas, and even firewood. Today, we still have *itega* [custom of bringing gifts to new mother] after a woman gives birth.

In those days, you would not find any girl who was a *mūkoma ndi* [one who was impregnated and gave birth before she was married]. At that time, a girl feared to become pregnant while still living at her father's home as she knew she would never marry as a first wife. The difference now is that if a girl gets pregnant, she will be married as a first wife or she can go back home to live. If she wants to continue her schooling, she can leave the child at home with her mother and go back to school. Now a girl may get married even though she is not circumcised, but back then, if a girl refused, it was considered a bad omen and she never could marry. It was the missionaries who found that circumcision was meaningless. The girls who went to church refused to go for *Irua* and so others began to follow. But it was brought up again during Mau Mau—then the tradition was followed to show one's loyalty to Gikuyu traditions. When we got *Uhuru* [Independence], things changed even more—after that it was not practiced so much here anymore. Now, the government has banned it for girls. A girl no longer has to buy maturity the way we did.

* * *

After Irua, I was counseled to wait for my first menstruation and to notify my mother immediately when it came. When I first saw blood, I went to my mother and she cautioned me to stay in the house until the days were over. Then my mother gave me water, and I washed and she started telling me to be careful around men when going to dances because I could easily become pregnant. By this she meant that when I went to dance ceremonies with men or visited a man's place, I should not let him touch my clothes. If a man tried to touch my clothes—to undo them—I told him it was bad, and he would not go any further because young men had also been counseled by older men on their behavior. If a man raped a girl and she became pregnant, he had to marry her and no one else. The relatives of the girl made sure it happened. When we went to dance ceremonies was usually at night. We'd hear somebody playing a flute, and we knew there was a dance. We'd dance *mūgoiyo* [a dance held on a night when there was no moon and the *njahi*, or beans, had been planted]. A circle of fires was made, and the dancers encircled them. Men stood with their backs to the fires, each holding his partner who stood with her feet on his. The two bounced up and down slowly in time to the music. [The same dance among Gikuyu is described in Hobley 1910.] We'd also dance *mweretho* [a young people's dance in which each man would toss his female partner in the air while she shook her body. It was erotic and considered distasteful to British colonial senses.] *Mweretho* was later forbidden by the missionaries. Then *ndumo* came at the end of the year after the harvest. *Ndumo* was danced by the girls naked—I have danced it many times. We would gather in the field and dance all night. We wore beads around the neck and a little reed skirt, but the rest of the body was naked.

It was at one of the dance ceremonies that I met Wamai, who became my first husband. We were of the same village—Wamai and me—but from different clans. We both came from *Itūra ria mbari ya Nguna* [village of the Nguna people]. His clan was Unjiru, mine Ūceera. Wamai was a man whom we called *kiumbi*. It means one who is attractive to girls. He is also a good dancer, can talk well, and laughs a lot. Girls would go and visit him for the night at his *kithuni* [unmarried man's house]. We liked a young man with such characteristics.

When Wamai first started showing an interest in me, he came near the granary at our home and blew his nose. I went out to see who it was. We talked. He said we ought to cultivate together. Yes, men and women often cultivated together. Men liked to cultivate yams and bananas, but they would help with the millet and sorghum. They did not like cultivating sweet potatoes—that is a woman's crop.

Wamai visited several times this way, blowing his nose, and then one time he told me he wanted tobacco—you know, the kind you pinch in the nose [snuff]. I went to my father and asked for tobacco and told him who I was giving it to. I would not have asked if I had not liked Wamai—a girl had her own mind. So my father gave me tobacco and I took it to Wamai. Love started from there.[2]

Wamai took the tobacco to his father and told him it was from the daughter of Gacoki called Wanjiku. When a young man informs his father who the tobacco comes from, the father begins to check to discover if there has ever been a relationship in the past that would prevent the marriage. For example, where the mother comes from—if there has been any bad feelings with these people, that would prevent the marriage. Or if the man is a clanmate who has not been seen in the area for so long that one's parents don't know you are of the same clan, then you will be told not to marry. Another thing, if it is the Ūmboi Clan and Ūnjiru Clan—they are clans that do not marry with each other because of past relationships that were not good between them. It is the same with the Ūithekabuno and Ūnjiru, because long ago the Ūithekabuno would carry oaths against other clans and no girl would marry into such a clan. But in our case, it was found that there were no bad relationships between my clan and his.

Wamai's father told him to tell his mother to brew beer—the local beer made from sugarcane that we call *njohi*—and to take it to our place to give my father in exchange for the tobacco. The giving of beer is called *gūthokia*. A man carries the beer in a very large gourd to the father of the woman to be married. With *gūthokia*, Wamai's parents and mine became *athoni*, meaning that as their children were marrying they will be joined as parents.

When Wamai and his brother brought the beer, I took it to my father and he asked, "Wanjiku, have you given us this beer?" I said, "Yes, Father—it comes from the father of Wamai." Then I began to make sour porridge for Wamai and his friends to show the community that we had become friends.

After some time, the arrangements began for *rūracio*. Now the elders of both our families met to decide how many goats and cows Wamai should give to my father. Women were there, too. They had brought the beer and prepared the food for the occasion. After a lot of talk on both sides, the men settled on the amount. Wamai began to bring the cows and goats that had been agreed upon, but not all at the same time—just a few at a time as he got them. Then my father told him it was time to *gūthinjiro*. This meant that Wamai brought another goat to my father's place that was slaughtered as a sacrifice and eaten by all who were there so that people would know that now I belonged to Wamai—I would only marry him.

My mother and my other mothers counseled me about being a good wife. They told me, "Now that you are going to Wamai's home, do not go there with *ng'aa*—empty feelings. There are some women who marry and do not give the people in her husband's home food and do not listen to their advice—those ones talk *ng'aa*. It means that such a woman will not show respect for the man's family. I was told to give respect to any woman or man I met at Wamai's by talking nicely to them. I should be hardworking and hospitable. If I cooked food, I was told to give it to all the children I saw and to the husband's parents. My mother warned me that if people discovered I had *ng'aa* and did not care for other people there, the *rūracio* might be taken back because it showed that I was one who could not be ruled [controlled]. My mother said to me, "Now that you are going to your husband's place, you are no longer in my hands, but under your husband's care and rule. Respect him and do as he wants—whether it is washing his clothes or heating water over the cooking fire for his bath. Go and be a good woman."

Then one day, Wamai came and removed me from my father's place and took me to his home. He came alone, because there was no need for anybody else to help him take me as I loved him and had agreed to go. It is only those women who refused to go after the *rūr a-cio* had been paid that were taken by force to the man's place. But even though I wanted to go, I felt sad about leaving my home that day because I realized that I was separating from my family.

Once I went to live at Wamai's, I became a member of his clan and from that time I have remained Ūnjiru. When I first came here, I stayed in Wamai's mother's house until my husband built a house for me and I was officially put into it. During the time when I was staying with the mother, I was observing how she was cooking food and taking care of her house. She also gave me *kirira*. She would tell me how a married woman should behave toward her husband and the moral codes of our people that only elders know.

Finally, the day reached for me to *kumanda*—to get some raw vegetables from the *shamba* and cook them in the new house, which meant that now I would live with my husband. A goat was slaughtered by my husband's father and a piece of its skin was tied around my ankle. Before I went to *kumanda,* I removed the dress I had on and put on a woman's dress made out of a skin. I tied a *mūkwa* around my waist as a sign that now a woman will be installed in her own house. Then my husband's mother took me by the hand and led me to the *shamba.* She got some yams and put them in a basket, collected bunches of bananas and sugarcane, then took me back to the new house. Now Wamai and I could live together in the house. Up to that time he had been continuing to live in his *kithuni.*

I found that marrying was a big change—learning about sex and my husband's habits once I moved to the new house. I had been advised to be obedient to my husband and his parents—now I was experiencing what it meant. I was cooking for Wamai and heating water for his bath. And after staying together that way for awhile, I found I was pregnant.

I knew I was pregnant when I missed two periods and then began to feel changes. I did not feel well and could see my body changing. After about nine months, I was ready to give birth. I was in my house and my husband's mother and my own mother were there. They told me to sit on a stool and then to hold my breath and push hard. Then the child just came out. It was my husband's mother who caught the baby and washed her over a broken piece of cooking pot. Then she cut the umbilical cord. My mother pushed on my sides and stomach to make the afterbirth come out. Then they washed me.

After the umbilical cord was cut, those two women cried, *"Ariririti, ariririti, ariririti, ariririti*—whom have you called the child?" And I answered, "Wambui," which is the name of my husband's mother. The first girl is always named for the husband's mother, the first boy for the husband's father. If the child had been a boy, the women would have called *"ariririti"* five times instead of four to tell people in the compound that it was a boy.

I stayed for about one month without working, just taking care of the baby. All that time, my husband's mother was cooking for me, fetching water, and washing me. She taught me how to wash the child in a broken cooking pot and how to care for her. My own mother brought food to me from home. My husband slaughtered a goat so I could take the soup to get strong again.

After I had my first child, I felt different because I was no longer a girl. One cannot be a girl after she has felt the pain of childbirth. That is why Agĩkũyũ girls are told that they do not know the pain one feels when the ear of the child cuts a woman's body as the child pushes its way out. A woman who has given birth is different from somebody like Karuana [my research assistant], because now that woman knows two things—how to get pregnant and how to give birth. She has a new kind of knowledge. But long ago we would never share this knowledge with a woman who had not had a child. It was considered *thiri* [secret]. That is why I cannot share these things with Karuana.

* * *

The baby was not even one year [old] when my husband died. When one loses somebody like one's husband through death, she experiences a lot of changes and differences. Like me, I was married to Wamai who later died and left me with only one child. Then after a short while, the child died too. The husband's parents refused to let me go back home to my parents' place.

Yes, I saw Wamai die. What happened is that one day he went to the marketplace and he was given a piece of cooked meat that might have been poisoned. When he came home, Wamai was seriously sick. His father told him to sleep at his mother's house because I had a child. He slept that day, but with a lot of stomach pains. The following day, it was recommended that *kubibo* should be done. *Kubibo* means that if one got sick, there were people who used to be called to come and make cuts using a *kienji* on the sick person's body and then that one would suck out the sick one's blood and spit it out. No, the person who did the cuts and sucking was not a *mūndū mugo*. It was just an ordinary person who knew how to practice *kubibo* on other people. Though *kubibo* was practiced on Wamai, he never recovered. He died the following day, and I was there to see him.

I felt a lot of pain and cried to see him dead, thinking that now he was leaving me all alone. My friend, I was really shocked. For a time, I was feeling lonely and found myself with no energy to do anything. And then, soon after, the child died, too. Now my thoughts were always sad and my heart missed happiness. First the husband and then my first child—I thought life was grim for me. I wanted to return to my father's home, but my husband's parents would not allow it. They continued to treat me well. They were not eager to see me gone. At times, I felt like going, and when I went home, then my husband's parents would come and take me back. So I finally decided to stay here as I had been given some land at their *shamba* where I could cultivate. They told me that I should never marry elsewhere because they liked me so much.

I stayed there for about three years without marrying. At the time, Wamai had a younger brother close to my age. He was an uncircumcised boy when his brother died, though he was big. His name was Kamau. He had been very happy when Wamai married me and I came to stay at their place. He even helped his brother bring the beer to my parents before we married. And when I arrived here, he was always helping me to dig in my *shamba*. That boy loved me, but he kept his love for me in his heart. Other boys used to tease him after Wamai died and tell him that if they were him, they would have gotten circumcised so as to marry me. The father also liked me, and so to make sure that no other man talked to me we would go to cultivate together with Kamau in the same *shamba*.

Kamau was not younger than me. Girls used to grow and mature faster than boys. You see, my age and his were the same, but I got circumcised earlier so as not to begin menstruating before *Irua*. Finally, when Kamau got circumcised, then we were able to marry. But I knew he liked me even before that because once when I returned home after Wamai died, Kamau came for me at my parents' home and told me that I had to go back, and if I didn't, he would never marry another. With Wamai, we got married in the Agĩkũyũ tradition. But with Kamau, we married traditionally when I moved into a house with him, then later we went to church and he put this ring you can see on my finger. When we married, Kamau did not have to take *rũracio* to my parents because his brother had taken most of it by then. He was only asked to take the few goats that had not been taken. It was common in those times for a man to marry his brother's widow. And you can read in the Bible where it says that one can take his brother's wife if the brother happens to die.

Wamai and Kamau were similar in character. Wamai never mistreated me nor beat me and neither did Kamau. Even up to the time Kamau died last May, he had never beaten me. He loved me so much. With Kamau, I had three sons. We would have four, but one, born after Wacira, died when he was not yet one year. So there were two of my children who died—the first born and the last born.

* * *

It was at the beginning of the Italian war [World War II] when Kamau and I became Christians, but it was in 1948 that I became saved. You know, in the church there are Christians, and then there are those Christians who have been saved. The saved ones do not take tobacco [snuff] nor drink. And they don't abuse anybody. Christians just go to church, but they may spend the rest of Sunday abusing people at home. Some drink beer, others gossip or take tobacco. But the one who is saved can't do any of these things. When I became saved—that was the most important change in my life.

How did I come to be saved? It was when the *mũndũ mugo* was unable to heal the swelling that was here below my ear where you see this scar—that is when I decided to go to God for His healing. What happened is that my face started to swell so that I could only look to the side and not straight ahead. After my face and neck swelled, it turned into a large, puss-filled wound that hurt a lot.

The *mũndũ mugo* came to cleanse me of the bad omen that had befallen me to cause the sore. He dug a hole in the ground and put a folded banana leaf—curved like a container—into the hole. Then he poured water into the banana leaf. He put *muthaiga*—a chalklike powder that was his medicine—into the water. Now he dipped a bunch of leaves into the water mixture and sprinkled it over me saying, "*Rũmuka. Rũmuka, wariga. cio wanariga mũndũ mugo, una mwoni wa mbũgu.*" ["Get well. Get well, you who is not known. The one who is medicine man, the one who sees *mbũgu* (objects such as stones and bones used by the medicine man in divination) has washed away all the bad omen."] When the *mũndũ mugo* did all he could, and the wound did not heal, and it had cost a lot of cows to have his ceremony, I decided that *ũgo* [a medicine man's healing ceremony] was not important. All during the years when I was having my three sons, I had stayed suffering with that wound. But in 1948, I began praying to God for his healing, and the wound healed—that's when I got saved.

At the time, I joined the Mother's Union [Anglican women's support group]. It was a group that vowed never again to carry out old Agĩkũyũ customs and to end those things that would not please God—like taking beer and abusing one another. If one of the women in our group got sick, we would help her by going to her *shamba* and cultivating it, fetching firewood and water and anything else that people in her homestead were missing. It was a group of women that helped each other.

I felt happier in my heart when I became saved, knowing that now I was not on bad terms with anybody and that even if I died now, I would gain afterlife. I know that even now when I am old and unable to walk well, God is waiting for me to come. Anytime He comes for me, I am ready to go and rest with Him. I know that one day I will die, for nobody remains on this earth forever.

* * *

It was about four years before Mau Mau [the rebellion against the British in 1952] that I was saved. When Mau Mau came, it changed things very much for our people here. When I first heard about Mau Mau, I was staying together with my children in a house at Kabare. Mbugo, the firstborn, was about John's age [a grandson, aged fourteen], Gatae was a little younger, and Wacira was the size of Karimi [grandson, aged five]. The one who followed Wacira had died by then. My husband was away working in the railway station at Voi then. He was the one who swept the station and kept it clean. So I was alone with the children. During emergency time [1952–1960], one was not allowed to move from place to place. We had to stay in one of the villages that the government had assigned us to. Nobody wanted to go—we were forced to stay in a village. When going to the toilet or to the river for water, we were taken by Home Guards carrying their guns [Home Guards were Africans appointed by the colonial government as local police]. A lot of times we would hear the airplanes coming to kill the Mau Mau fighters in the nearby forest. Then we became frightened.

While living in the villages, we had to dig a big trench up here [at the edge of Mount Kenya Forest] to keep Mau Mau fighters out of the villages. We would wake very early in the morning, before the cock crowed and the trumpet sounded. It was still dark. The British soldiers came round telling people to open up their houses and come out. If you were met asleep, you could be killed. Then we would start walking all the way from Kiaritha up to the place where the trench was being dug and arrive after sunrise. We were each given a portion of the trench to work on. Then we would dig with our *jembe* [hoes] all day, removing the soil until the hole became deep. If we started to drag behind working, we were beaten. Later, the trench was filled with bamboo sticks, sharpened at each end, to keep the Mau Mau fighters from crossing, but some came across anyway. Nobody knew where or how they used to cross to get to the villages for food. It's like if a human being is closed in a house, he/she will find all means possible to get out.

After we were released from digging the trench at the end of the day, we would go to the *shamba* and cultivate just a little portion—that was supposed to be enough for our food. There was a curfew and beginning at three o'clock we were forced into our houses and the doors were shut. Later, we were taken to the toilet and river for water, then back to our houses. We were like prisoners.

I never took the Mau Mau Oath because on the night when the freedom fighters removed people from their houses for the Oath, they happened to skip my house and I kept quiet. The good thing about Mau Mau was that they never killed anybody who didn't reveal them [to the British]. If you had seen Mau Mau but didn't reveal them, they'd leave you alone. They did not use my house because I had not taken the Oath—those who had not taken it were called "lice" or "bedbug" and were avoided.

So me, I only prayed to God that He would protect me and my children as my husband was away. At times, we would be met by white soldiers carrying very long guns. They would come and ask us in Kiswahili, "*Wapi Mau Mau?*" [Where are the Mau Mau?] We would say, "We don't know," and they would just pass on and not ask again for awhile.

During Mau Mau, if I was seen with you [a white person], I would be beaten and killed and my house would be burned down by Mau Mau supporters. And you, being white, would be killed, too. Those times were bad. People were living in between fear of Mau Mau and fear of the Home Guards. Both were our enemies. The Home Guards supported the British and the Mau Mau were on the side of the Agĩkũyũ. If you made a mistake with the Home Guards, you would die. If you made a mistake with the Mau Mau you would die, too.

During that time, my children were going to a school run by Anglican missionaries at Karaini. But the attendance was poor because people were sad and afraid. The students were always afraid of Mau Mau coming and burning down the school and beating or killing people there. They never burnt Karaini, but they went there once. So going to school was hard then.

The day that we got our independence [December 12, 1963], we started shouting "*Uhuru na Umoja*" ["Freedom and Unity"], and the news traveled fast from one person to the next. There was an agreement amongst us that nobody would go to sleep, and we spent the whole night before dancing and singing, "Munyao, raise the flag on Mount Kenya" [Munyao was a Kamba who climbed the mountain to plant the first Kenyan national flag on the summit]. We were so happy because we would never be ruled by foreigners again. It also meant the end of the beatings we were experiencing during the emergency.

After *Uhuru*, when all the roads were cleared [of British roadblocks], my husband came home from Voi. He found us here, having cleared the forest. Before Mau Mau we used to cultivate in different places—that way we could harvest at different times. We might plant maize and beans down near Karaini first, then up here later—that way we had food for eating and food for storage. During Mau Mau, some of the *mashamba* were taken by the British, and so we had to come back here and clear more of the forest. We began to plant tea and coffee on the hillsides. Some people at Embu had begun planting coffee before Mau Mau, but here we did not start until after *Uhuru*. The tea and coffee factories gave us seedlings to plant, and government officials came and showed us how to cultivate them. Later, we paid back the factories for the seedlings out of the first harvest.

I decided to try both tea and coffee, but tea grows better up here. Once I learned how to pick coffee and tea from the officials, I taught my sons how to do it. Now it is my sons and their wives who are responsible for the cultivation. Coffee only has to be harvested twice—in late May and November—but with tea you have to pick it all year round.   We get more shillings for coffee but tea is easier to grow. Why? Because it does not need spraying with pesticides the way coffee does. There is a disease that can destroy coffee if one is not careful.

* * *

After *Uhuru*, my sons went back to their schooling. The oldest one—the one who stays at Kagumo Teacher's College—he has gone up through Form Six and has even gone abroad. The other two finished Form Four [secondary level]. One works in the coffee factory as an inspector and the other was just appointed an assistant chief.

How is schooling different nowadays from when my sons went to school? The level of schooling my sons acquired was the highest one could go then. But today, people are not satisfied with four years of secondary school—that has become the lowest level of schooling that people want to achieve, because a good job requires more schooling now. But people today—those with a Form Four education—do not want to stay in rural areas like this. They want to work in a town. Also, we who are older can have trouble from children who attend school because sometimes they can abuse somebody who is not schooled—even an older person like a parent! Long ago, when I was growing up, nobody dared to abuse somebody in an older *riika*. Today, you can see boys and girls of different age groups mixing and even joking with one another. The importance of *mariika* in Agĩkũyũ tradition has disappeared with schooling.

There is no use taking a boy to school nowadays and leaving a girl behind, because girls who have been to school are more helpful to the family than boys who've been to school. Why? Girls help their brothers and sisters acquire the things they need—even school fees—with the money they earn from a good job after completing school, but a boy may move to the city and forget about his family.

When Kamau was working at Voi and I used to receive letters from him, I wished then I had gone to school so I could read the letters without anybody reading them for me. But just because we couldn't read, didn't mean we didn't think. Before there were schools, we thought a lot, but in different ways. When a person was sick, the *mũndũ mugo* had to think out the cause of the disease and make a cure. When one saw she was pregnant, she used to tie knots on a string from the day she had sexual relations to the day she gave birth to keep track of time. When counting cows or goats, men used sticks to represent their property so they could keep track of the number of animals. Young children had the responsibility of keeping track of all the cows and goats when they went herding, and sometimes the father would test them to make sure they knew which were his from those of the neighbors. We exercised our minds with riddles and songs. The one solving a riddle had to have knowledge of Agĩkũyũ customs and the surroundings [environment]. Unless you know our traditions and the way we live, you cannot solve the riddles. So we had a different way of thinking that did not use books. Sometimes, I experiment by thinking—I see what and how others do something like building a new house and I remember how they did it, then come back here and try to do the same from what I can remember. That way I am able to learn new things.

* * *

A long time ago, if the first child of a woman was mature and ready to go for *Irua*, the father and mother would be shaved [hair from their heads] while all the elders were sitting in a circle. Then the two parents would be given *kirira* by older people, and a goat would be slaughtered and eaten for the occasion. It was the *mambura* [ceremony] called *nyumithio*. It means the oldest child is removed from the house of the parents—*kumithio*—and must build his own house if he is a boy. Or if it is a girl, it means that soon she will leave her father's home to be married somewhere else. After *nyumithio*, the mother's head was shaved completely to show that she is now at a new stage of life—an elder with a grown child—*wamũng'ĩĩ*. She put *mikwa* [large ear plugs] in her earlobes. The man put metal rings in his. At *nyumithio*, no woman whose first child was not circumcised was allowed to attend. They wouldn't come because they knew that they wouldn't be given anything to eat at the ceremony. It was a ceremony only for older women.

When Mbugo went for *Irua*, he was taken to a hospital for the operation. When he came back, I stayed with him at home, cooking *ugali* [hardened maize meal porridge] until he healed. By that time, I was a Christian, so I didn't have my head shaved or go through *nyumithio* as other women did. I was already a member of the *kiama* [elders' council], too. Usually men and women whose first child had been circumcised could join the *kiama*. Yes, the *kiama* was for both men and women here. There never was a council for just men or just women alone. But all the members of a *kiama* had to be of the same clan. Nobody outside the clan was ever given *kirira*. The role of the *kiama* was to initiate new elders and to decide on punishment for wrongdoers. If somebody stole a goat, he would be tied up with rope and put in a beehive [located in a large hollow log] and rolled down a hill with burning banana leaves stuffed into the beehive to make the bees angry. The decision would be made by [members of the clan who were] the *kiama*.

Usually, men and women whose first child had undergone circumcision could join the *kiama*. If a woman went to seek *kirira* from the elders, she would be given it. She would go to an older woman who belonged to the council for *kirira*. She would do as the older woman advised, a goat would be slaughtered, and then the elder woman would initiate her while all the other elder women were seated around them. The woman being initiated had not reached menopause, but had had her first child circumcised. But the one initiating her had to be past menopause.

I was a member of the *kiama* of my husband's clan, but I joined earlier than most women. The reason is that I was initiated by my husband's mother after I was married there. She gave me *kirira*, then later initiated me. She never tested my knowledge as is done nowadays in secondary school or university. I was given all the Agĩkũyũ knowledge required and we just learned it. If we became a member of the council, it was assumed we knew it. So I became a member of the *kiama* from that time.

I went through menopause a long time ago—before Mbugo was married. I never felt any headaches or anything you are telling me of [headaches, sweats, hot flashes, depression were described]. It's only that I noticed menstruation had stopped. It was not a big change for me. Long ago, I was happy because I was young and healthy and had the energy to do my own work. Now, I am feeling tired and my leg aches, so it is hard to walk long distances. All I can do is wait for God to do His will.

As an old woman, I try and counsel my sons now. Gatae—now that he is a man of the people [assistant chief]—I remind him that he cannot come home late at night with a family here waiting for him; he must learn to carry the country [sublocation] with *rũrigi* [strings] rather than a *mukwa* [carrying rope]. We have a saying—"*Thina ndiguaguo na mukwa, ukuaguo na rurigi*" [Why carry it with a rope when you can use a string]. When I hear that any of my sons have quarreled with their wives, I call that son and tell him it is not good to quarrel because it will teach the children bad behavior.

Yes, I have had many roles in my lifetime. The most important roles are, first, to take care of the husband and at the same time, care for my children—cooking and washing for them. But equal with these is my role as a farmer—taking the cows to river to drink and feeding them, taking a *kibanga* to the *shamba* to cultivate and from the *shamba* carrying home firewood for the cooking fire. All these three—wife, mother, and farmer—are equally important. They are all one—they cannot be separated. Being my parents' daughter and a daughter to my husbands' parents have been less important. I could not take care of my husband's parents the way I took care of my own because now I had my own house and children to care for. When we met at the women's group, we were advised how to live peacefully in one's home without quarreling, and this helped me to keep my home happy. So that role as a member of the Mother's Union was more important than being a daughter. Being a member of the *kiama* was less important than being a member of the women's group because after the missionaries came, the *kiama* did not have as much meaning.

What has been my greatest accomplishment? All the work I have done on this earth. And I am proud of being a Christian and being saved. When I was a young girl, I used to have dreams about the young man I would marry, but now that I am old I do not have dreams anymore. My strongest character is staying at home without wandering from place to place or abusing anybody. I am also patient and follow Jesus. I used to have bad desires, like desiring somebody else besides my husband or wanting somebody else's bananas, but I called upon the Lord and was saved from those desires.

Being a woman means being one who is married and has joined her home together. It also means being able to hear things and keep them sealed inside. I think of myself as Mūgīkūyū before I am a Kenyan. Being Agīkuyu means having followed the steps of *mbuci*, *matu*, and *Irua* as I told you.

It is only because you are my friend that I have given you this *kirira*, Nyina-wa-Stephen. Now you are the one to benefit from it in your writing. I have talked all the things I have seen without refusing or hiding anything. You are learning and I am learning from you too. One can never finish learning. Learning only ends when one dies, isn't that so?

Notes

1. The goat refers to the present a father gives his daughter when she returns home after being circumcised, to celebrate her bravery.
2. Among Gikuyu, the term *mūrata* (friend) is often used to signify a love relationship between members of the opposite sex. However, in this case, Wanjiku used the term *wendo*, meaning "love."

3

Wamutira:
The First Wife

Wamutira, the first of the women in their fifties, was chosen from among several women in polygynous marriages because, in addition to being a first wife, she never joined a women's group, nor has she attended adult education classes. Of the four women, she is least affected by educational change—either formal or nonformal. A late convert to Christianity, Wamutira is an Anglican who attends church but is otherwise uninvolved in church activities.

When I met Wamutira in the process of conducting the initial survey, she left me with few impressions—negative or positive. When I returned to request her participation as a life-history informant and explained why she had been chosen, she listened with bowed head, thought it over for a moment, and then gave one of her indefatigable smiles and agreed to work with us. The first two sessions were somewhat hesitant—she was very shy about answering questions and kept her eyes on the ground much of the time. At the end of the second session, I asked Wamutira how she was feeling about the interviews and whether she wanted to continue. She replied, looking directly at me for the first time, "I feel good about them because they are making me think about my life." She wanted to continue.

There was a marked change in Wamutira's behavior with the third session. Her earlier shyness began to evaporate as she grasped her importance as a teacher. Further, she became more confident in volunteering information about herself. By the fourth session, a few key questions were prompting detailed retrospective responses with regard to her experience with *Irua*. Wamutira's ability to remember detail as we moved forward in her life and her candid self-perceptions enhance her autobiographical account. In fact, from her buoyant behavior I sensed she rather enjoyed the opportunity to reminisce.

Another positive aspect of our sessions was Wamutira's relationship with her co-wives. Both women seemed pleased that we had chosen Wamutira and welcomed any chance to cooperate. At the same time, they respected our need for privacy during the sessions and after providing us with tea always withdrew to work in their *mashamba*. They would reappear at the end of the hour, learn what the topic had been, and contribute their own observations and knowledge. For instance, when the topic was basket-weaving, the three wives collaborated in preparing samples of basketry, using different materials and at various stages of completion, to illustrate the task involved in learning as children. All three women taught me how to *gwokotha*—the process of binding together plant fibers to make a string for weaving. And all wanted an opportunity to express their views on *Irua*. In a sense, the three wives jointly accepted the responsibility of my education. They also expressed concern for my well-being, remarking that as I spent more time in the community I seemed "healthier."

Wamutira and the second wife, Karuana, are agemates and have a particularly close relationship. The third wife, Muthoni, is about ten years younger but over the years has made a place for herself in the homestead. Unlike the older wives, she has had a few years of schooling, which seems to give her an advantage she lacks in age. Nevertheless, she always defers to the two older women in decisions concerning the homestead. Of the three women, the second wife, Karuana, is the most self-assured, and often, when the session with Wamutira was over, she would appear and want to visit with us. It was Karuana who volunteered that none of the three wives had *cuka*—wraparound material used as a sort of apron-skirt. She asked if I could bring them each one from Nairobi the next time I visited there. Wamutira is the most reserved of the three women, often deferring to Karuana in our casual conversations. On the other hand, when we were alone in sessions, she blossomed. In short, Wamutira's story must be viewed within the context of her relationship with her co-wives, thus their perceptions of certain events, such as *Irua* and marriage, are included.

—*J.D.*

I am the second child of my father, Kŭruga, and my mother, Kabuci, who was my father's eighth wife. My father was a headman and very important. He had, altogether, twenty wives, but I can only remember the names of twelve of them. First, there was Nini, our oldest mother. Then came Kamira, Wairima, and Keru. Keru had two children who were my agemates. Then there were Wagatwe, Wamuruana, Wanguku—and Kabuci, my mother. She was followed by Waguu, Ngŭngi, Kagure, and Wamumu. I can't remember the names of the rest. Our compound was like a village—with so many of us growing up together. Each wife had her own house where she and her children lived. My father stayed in his own *thingira [man's house]*.

My father was a good man who liked everybody and never had a

Figure 3.1 WAMUTIRA'S FAMILY

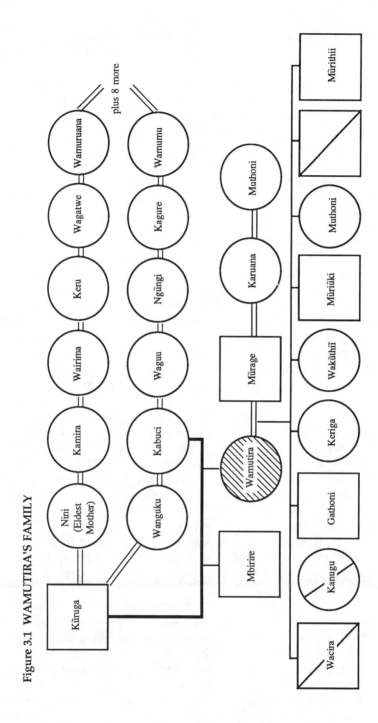

bad temper. My mother was similar. I had only one older brother called Mbircire, who was jolly and would never fight. The reason I came to be called Wamutira is because I was named for my father's mother who came from a place called Mutira. It was important to name the first daughter after the father's mother, the second daughter after the mother's mother. The same was [true] for sons. This way, the grandparents would always have a place in the clan. Our clan is Waithirandu, but I married later into the Ũgaciiku Clan.

Every morning, my brother and I would wake up and go to the house where porridge was being cooked. After being given calabash of sour porridge by our mother, we went to the *shamba*. During the day, while we were working there, food was brought to us. After working some more, we would go back home and start playing in the compound. What did we work with in the *shamba*? My mother gave me a sharp, pointed stick to dig with and I never lost it.

By going with my mothers and other girls of my compound, I learned how to fetch water. I would take a small gourd and a basket, just as I used to see the women do, and follow them to the river. I would fill the gourd and put in a maize cob to stop the water from spilling out, then put the gourd in the basket and carry it back from the river. Even collecting firewood, I took some string and went to the forest with other girls and women. When I had collected enough pieces of wood, I was shown how to tie them together with the string and carry them on my back. But I lost most of the pieces on the way home.

I never started cooking until I was a big girl because my mother would not allow me to cook with her pots from fear I would break them. [Traditionally, pots were made of fired clay.] But later, when I was bigger, I watched the way she cooked—how she peeled potatoes with a knife and the amount of beans and maize she put into the cooking pot for *githeri* [a beans and maize mixture that is the staple of the Gikuyu diet in rural areas]. When I was finally allowed to cook, I copied what I had seen my mother doing.

It was my mother who taught me how to make baskets, too. I would watch her when she was making the strings for weaving. She would place a sisal thread on her lap and roll it over and then place another with it and roll them together in the same direction to make a string. This is called *gwokotha*. Here, I will show you. [She demonstrates.] You take these two threads and roll them each in the same direction with a little saliva against your leg. Now roll them together in the same direction, with a little saliva on your hands to make them stick together. I first learned to make threads using banana fibers and grass. I would make some threads and go and show them to my mother and ask her if that's the way she does it. Then she would say,

"No, you have made the strings like a boy"—that's when the two rolled threads failed to join together in a tight string.

I used the tall grass to make threads at first. After picking it, I would bring it home and cut it lengthwise into long, thin strings and then I would *gwokotha* the strings and use them for weaving. After using grass and banana fibers and acquiring enough skills, then we [girls in the compound] made threads out of *migio*—a wild plant that grows around here. First, we'd strip off the leaves and then peel back the outer bark from the main stem. The inner bark was stripped back in long threads, and when it dried its fibers were good for weaving. We did the same thing with *ngutwii*—stinging nettle fibers. Later, we began to use sisal fibers when we were grown and more experienced. The baskets you see nowadays, those are made with sisal fibers and then decorated with woolen threads to form a pattern.

While the girls in our compound were learning to cultivate and weave baskets, the boys would make *mbara* [long thin branch of a tree joined at both ends with bark to form a hoop]. They would roll the *mbara* with a stick across the ground. They also made pointed sticks to throw and play with. Boys did some herding of goats and cattle, though usually this was done by old people. If a family had no sons, then a girl would herd. But me, I never herded because my father had a lot of sons. I didn't learn to herd until I got married. But nowadays, one sees more girls herding.

My brother and I were treated the same by my mother. He had his own gourd and calabash and I had my own gourd and calabash of the same size. The gourd was for porridge and the calabash for *irio* [general term used for food]. Nobody ate each other's food, but if my brother came with friends and he had drunk all his porridge and I had not taken mine, I would give it to his friends. When my brother grew big and started coming with lots of friends, then he was given more food, as I was still a child and was not able to finish as much. But when I grew up and started coming with my girlfriends, then my mother started giving me more, too. Sometimes, when I went and visited my brother in his *kithuni* I wished I could be a boy. I used to hear of a big rock whereby if you sat on it, you would change to a boy. I wondered about it, but never went to sit on it.

As small girls, we never wore very much—only a piece of blanket on the upper body and sometimes another piece for the skirt. But grown women like my mother wore a dress made out of three pieces of antelope skin, called a *njuri*. One piece was used as the front part, and the other two pieces went behind. When sitting down, my mother would wrap each of those pieces around her thighs and then tuck in the front piece.

What was I like as a child? I can't remember well, but I was told that I used to just stay at one place and mother would bring my food there. Maybe I was quiet.

We played games after we returned home from working in the *shamba*, like wrestling with each other and a game where we used to collect smooth stones from the river and gather in a group on the ground. Then one of us would throw the stones up in the air and try and catch all of them on the back of the hands. The game is called *ciũthi*.

Because there were many children in our compound, sometimes we would fight. But then any grown person nearby would come and threaten us with a beating if he or she ever saw us fighting again. That usually stopped us. It was only our mothers who were involved though, or some older son of my father. My father, being a chief, was never at home to know what happened to us children. He was always away on some business.

Mariika were important because, as one was growing up, she learned how to treat people in different age groups. People of different *mariika* would not abuse each other or even greet each other. But you, if you were of my same age group, when we met we would greet one another and laugh and tell jokes or do anything we wanted together. We would never talk with those of other age groups, especially those younger than us.

My mother used to tell me never to appear near a place where older people were gathered talking. We never stayed in the same house with my father, and when he came to visit my mother we children were told to leave so that we would not hear what their talk was about. When we got to be a little older, we went to our oldest mother, the one called Nini, and she taught us things—like not to play with boys as their games are never good and would end up in bad things, such that they would lie on top of us. Nini told us how we should behave at dances once we were circumcised. And sometimes she would tell us stories at night around the cooking fire. There is one I remember well:

Long, long ago, during the time of Ndemi and Mathathi, there was one man who used to go to the forest to make knives, spears, and shields. He was a blacksmith. When he went there one day, he left his wife pregnant at home, and as the time reached for her to deliver she was assisted by a giant.

The giant never used to give the woman any food. Each morning it would spread castor-oil seeds out to dry and weaver birds would come to eat the seeds. The woman tried to talk to the birds in order to send them to her husband in the forest with the news that she delivered. But the birds did not know how to talk, and so the woman chased them away.

The following morning, there came a dove, and the woman asked it whether it would go where the woman might send it. The dove said, "Yes, I will go," so the woman told it, "Go to the forest and find my husband and tell him I have delivered and I have never eaten anything." The dove went to where the men were making things in the forest and started to sing.

Mũturi, ũgutura ĩl.	Blacksmith, you who makes things.
Cangarara ica.	Turn your head a bit.
Ndutrage naĩhenyaĩi.	Make your things quickly.
Cangarara ica.	Turn your head a bit.
Mũkagwuo ara ciarire.	Your wife gave birth.
Cangarara ica.	Turn your head a bid.
Agĩciarĩthio nĩ irimu, ĩ.	A giant assisted her, yes.
Cangarara ica.	Turn your head a bit.
Nduke tutui ũrie, ĩl.	Get this little to eat.
Cangarara ica.	Turn your head a bit.
Warega merukie ĩũ.	You refuse that I swallow it.
Cangarara ica.	Turn your head a bit.

All the men started asking themselves if there were any of them who had left a wife pregnant at home. The blacksmith said he had left his wife pregnant, and so he started sharpening his swords and spears and then went home.

On reaching home, the man found that the giant had gone to fetch firewood to come and cook. The man's wife told him the story and how she almost died of starvation. The blacksmith cooked for his wife, and she ate until she was satisfied. Then he did himself in the *thegi* so nobody would see him and waited for the giant to return. When the giant came and dropped the bundle of firewood outside the door, it started singing a song it always sang.

Wagiciiri, wagiciiri	You who have given birth
Wĩ nyumba ino?	Are you in this house?
Wogwa na mururumu	May you fall together with the
wa ngu icio.	sound of firewood

And the woman replied:

Onawe wogwa nacio.	Even you may fall with the sound of them.

The giant asked her whether the one who was in the forest making things had come back and that was why she was so brave in shouting back at him. The woman kept quiet. So the giant entered the house, but before it could do anything it was pierced with spears and arrows until it died.

That's all I can remember of the story, but I tell you, the giants used to scare us a lot as children. We thought they came from the forest, so we were afraid to go there alone.

While our oldest mother was telling us stories, two of my older brothers, one of whom was her son, were going to school. They were Mbicire, the one who died recently, and the other Mbicire at Kianjagi. Yes, they had the same name because they were both named after my father's father, just as my brother was. Our father did not have a good opinion of school, so he did not encourage us to go, especially the girls. But my brothers went anyway. My father did not see school as important and used to stop us from going by saying that once a girl goes there, she will become a prostitute. Yes, I had a desire to go to school, but I never got encouragement from the other girls in our compound either. None of them went to school, so I didn't want to go and be left behind [behave differently].

When Mbicire grew up and got married to his first wife, Wangeci, with a modern wedding and then built a new big house, he called all of us to come there one day. He told us that by using a *tawa* [kerosene lamp] in the house, we could start learning at night. Us, we just laughed.

* * *

What were the major events in my life? First, there was the piercing of the ears—the upper part of the ear first, called *mbuci*; then the lower part, called *matū*. After showing signs of growing breasts, I was circumcised. I stayed for quite a long time until I got married, then had my first child. I was bigger than my daughter there [she refers to her twelve-year-old daughter] when I got my ears pierced. Piercing your ears was a sign that a girl was getting mature and soon would be ready for *Irua*. My mother told me I could not get circumcised if my ears were not pierced, and as I had seen a friend getting hers pierced, I told my mother I wanted mine done. There were two of us who went together to have them pierced, and many people watched.

A man called Kibui was the one who pierced our ears. People gathered very early in the morning to see him do it. First, the upper hole was cut. That was for putting in decorative beads called *cioma*. Later, a hole in the lower lobe was cut for putting in shiny pieces of wood called *ndebe*. That is called *matū*. Kibui took a sharp razor blade and went round the lobe in a circle, cutting out a piece of meat. I had seen him do this before with other girls. After the meat was removed, a round piece of wood that had been heated over the fire, then oiled, was put in the hole. In a few days, the stick was changed, and one would have to turn it around in the hole until it came out. Then another stick of a larger size was put into the hole.

After my ears were pierced and I went home, my mother spread some banana leaves on the ground for me to lie on to try and get used to the pain. Yes it was very painful. When my ear lobes got pus, I could not do anything as they were swollen and heavy on my head. I only removed the sticks, washed the holes, and put in bigger sticks. I continued this way until the lobes were healed.

After *matū* and *mbuci*, my head was shaved with a razor blade along the front edges and then smeared with oil [rendered fat]. A sheet was bought for me to dress in. I was shown by my mother how to tie it using maize seeds to make a knot at one shoulder after folding the sheet twice to cover my body [like a toga]. Getting a sheet and our ears pierced made us feel more mature. Just recently, though, when we started wearing dresses, I paid money to have my pierced ears stitched up. Mine [holes in ears] were so big and drooping that I wanted them stitched so they wouldn't tear.

After I had my ears pierced, I didn't stay long before I went for *Irua*. I had not seen *mambura ma mūtumia* [menstruation] yet and even stayed for a long time after *Irua* before getting it. Those times were not like today, when young girls are having their first menses at a very early age. I stayed for seven years before menstruating.

I heard about *Irua* from my mother. She told me, "You see so-and-so? She is circumcised now. You are also going to get circumcised." She told me that first we would make beer for her brothers who are my uncles and ask them for permission. The reason that it was my mother's brothers is that my father's brothers were not as important, as my mother's brothers had to be paid back the number of goats and the amount of beer that were given for my mother's circumcision. The daughter had to give exactly what her mother had given to the uncles.

I saw many people come to my father's compound, and they drank the beer we brewed and then a day was set for me to be circumcised. On the day of circumcision, I was told to go to my oldest uncles's [mother's brother] place and dance for my uncles so that they would give me money and a goat. I went and danced, holding a wooden club and showing my uncles my body. Then they gave me three shillings and a goat, and I went home with the permission to go for *Irua*.

I was never told exactly why I was going for *Irua*, but I heard from people that a certain man—who was the first to refuse having his girls circumcised—had daughters who would never marry. So we used to get circumcised so we would be able to marry, because no man wanted an uncircumcised woman.

I was circumcised at Giagato, where there is a coffee factory now. First, in the morning we went to the river where women would smear themselves with mud, and then in the river we would be washed by the newly married women with one child. The same women then carried us on their backs back to the field. We were washed to make us clean [pure] for the ceremony, and the reason they carried us was they did not want us to touch the ground—we were well taken care of.

There used to be so many people at the field, young and old, who made a circle surrounding the girls being circumcised. The women would be on the inner part of the circle singing, "*li, ii, ii, nĩ kiama*" [Yes, yes, yes, it is the truth]. My circumcision mother [also called "supporter"] was Nini, our oldest mother. She helped me spread the *mathangu* [leaves] on the ground where I would sit so that no blood would touch the soil. It was she who held me from behind, with her legs over mine so that my legs would stay spread while I was circumcised. Another mother held my hands away.

How were we dressed? The girls being circumcised had put on beads across the upper part of the body and a short skirt made of reeds and beads called a *thira* over our thighs. The bead necklace had gourd tops and was worn from one shoulder across the chest to the armpit of the other shoulder. Some girls were given containers called *ithitu* from the *mũndũ mugo*. These containers had *muthaiga* in them—a white powder like ground ashes or chalk. *Muthaiga* comes from herbs. It is what we call *miti dawa* [literally "tree medicine"] that has been burnt and ground to a fine powder. Having a *githitu* [singular of *ithitu*] protected one from becoming bewitched. The *muthaiga* in it was good medicine. But us, we were protected from any harm in our compound because *muthaiga* was put all around the houses—that way, there was no need of a *githitu*. So me, I did not need one around my neck when I was circumcised because I was already protected.

Kamira and another woman called Watene from Gichugu were the circumcisers. Kamira was slender and black. She did not dress in any special way. She just had a blanket wrapped around her and tied at the shoulder. Before circumcising us, she got a small gourd and emptied some *muthaiga* into her palm and touched herself with it on the face to cleanse herself for the ceremony.

The circumcisers used a *kienji*, a metal knife that was very sharp with a wide blade like an axe and a handle that was thin. But nowadays, they use razor blades because there is not so much cutting done. Each time a girl was circumcised, the *kienji* was washed in water and wiped with a *mathangu* [leaf] of the *muigoya* plant.

Our father, Kũruga, had given those of his girls being circumcised some shillings. He told us that those who never cried during *Irua* and were brave could keep theirs but those who cried would have their's taken away. Me? I lost my shilling. I was crying because I was afraid, and I knew it would hurt even before they started cutting.

During the ceremony, women of the clan sang special songs called *ndaiho*, but I can't remember how they go at the moment. Three deep cuts were made [removing the clitoris], and it was very painful. They used to cut deep until a *mathakwa* leaf fit in. But nowadays, those who want to be circumcised, only the tip of the clitoris is removed. After the cutting was done, the wounds were spread with castor oil because there was no medicine then. The oil was brought to the field by my mother in a bamboo container, and I used the oil to put on the wound until it healed. Then a *mathakwa* leaf—which is very soft—was stripped of its stem and tied over the wound, using thread, in between the legs to keep the leaf still and in place. [At this point in the interview, Wamutira stops to demonstrate how the *mathakwa* leaf is prepared for use as a bandage.]

How did I walk home with all that pain between my legs? I was being supported by those near me—by supporters who were my circumcision mothers. They were one on each side and another woman was ahead with a small gourd of water so that when I fainted she would pour water on me.

When I reached my mother's house, I went right inside. As I was not able to climb onto the bed, banana leaves were spread on the floor for me. I had to sleep on my back because if I slept in any other way, the leaf covering the wound might come off and then I would have to have another put in, which was a painful operation. So you see, it was no joke. I was told never to sleep on my sides, as the wound might close up the hole and then I would never give birth. But I only stayed that way at night. During the day, one could sit down on a banana leaf comfortably. Each evening, I would remove the leaf and smear castor oil on the wound and then put another leaf in.

All the people who had come to escort me home—who came from all places— were feasting at my home. There was so much food and beer, but it was not enough for all those people. My father had given me a goat when I went inside the house, which I never saw again.

I felt weak and light for a long time before I got back my normal health. Girls used to lose a lot of blood, especially if the uncles demanded that there were some goats that had not been paid them. The girl would bleed until the goats were given to the uncles. Then the bleeding stopped.

In those times, one never refused to get circumcised. Even those who were poor and could not afford the things asked for by the uncles, other members of the community would make sure they got them so the girl could be circumcised.

Nini told me after I was circumcised that now I would be waiting for *mambura ma mũtumia* and I should take care and not wander about. And she told me that the calabash one eats from when circumcised—that one is never used again by another person, for it would mean contaminating the person who used it.

After I had gone through *Irua*, I felt different. I felt like I was a grown-up girl now, ready for dances. And everybody saw us as adults. People treated us differently and we were expected to act differently. Nowadays, you wouldn't know who is mature and who isn't because few girls go for circumcision, and even when a girl gets menstruation, you don't notice because girls do not have to stay in the house as we did.

Nobody ever told me about what menstruation was, and when I first saw it I got frightened because I learned that now I had to take extra care with men so as not to get a child before I was married. That was a very bad thing to happen to a girl then. I also wished that I had stayed long without it so that I would have enough time to go to more dances. [Here Wamutira contradicts an earlier statement relating that she waited a long time—7 years—before menarche. It makes for a contradictory, bumpy chronology, but older Gikuyu women did not seem to be concerned about gaps in time or the rationality of a perfect chronology.]

But now I would not want *Irua* to come back. Even the one who forbid it [Kenyan President Daniel arap Moi] did right.

*   *   *

[As we finished the session on *Irua*, Karuana and Muthoni, Wamutira's co-wives learned what we'd been discussing and wanted to express their opinions. What follows is a discussion between the three wives.]

Muthoni: If it's now and I'm told to go and get circumcised, I would run away and leave all that food and beer there.

Wamutira: Yes, there is one girl who ran away and left the circumciser and beer in the gourd and even the cooked food.

Karuana: It [circumcision] was a stupidity that was liked very much by Agĩkũyũ a long time ago.

Wamutira: With Wandia, she was bleeding badly, so we took her to the hospital. When the nurse came, she wanted to beat us when she saw Wandia and told us we were very foolish to be doing that kind of thing nowadays. She told us to take the girl home and heal her. I said we were sorry and would never repeat it again. And I pleaded with her to just give Wandia an injection. But the following morning, the girl was still bleeding. What I saw that time, that was the end of it for me.

Muthoni: I feel good because the banning of circumcision means that none of mine [daughters] will be destroyed that way.

Karuana: The things nowadays are not the way they were long ago.

Muthoni: Yes, that is so. A long time ago, if a girl matured and had her menstrual period, she would never go out. She told her mother and was shown where to stay and would stay there in the house until the days given her by God were over.

Karuana: You would not go anywhere, nor cook or go to dances.

Muthoni: So your clothes would all soak with menstrual blood, one after another, until the days were over.

Wamutira: But nowadays, things are better because nobody calls another *karigũ* [silly uncircumcised girl] or *kahii* [same applied to a boy], and so there are no fights between the circumcised and uncircumcised.

Muthoni: The only fights you get nowadays are between drunkards. You can't hear a girl fighting with another girl because of *Irua*.

Karuana: If you met an uncircumcised young man and a circumcised one you would not distinguish between them. It is only when he goes to school and is beaten by others [for not being circumcised] that he comes home and does it.

Muthoni: Now, you can't tell the difference between one who is circumcised and one who is not. Long ago, if you were of my age group and we met and my ears were pierced, you would never joke with me or abuse me until yours were pierced, too. There was a difference between those who had been circumcised and those who had not. Now, there is no difference. The old traditions are gone.

[Wamutira nods her head in agreement.]

*   *   *

[Wamutira resumes her narrative in the next session with an account of what, for most women, seems to be the happiest period of their lives—between *Irua* and *ũhiki*, or marriage.]

I stayed for quite a long time without thinking about marriage because of the happiness I got from dancing. Once we were circumcised, then we could go for dances. There was *mweretho*, where each man would dance with a girl and would throw her up in the air and the girl would shake her whole body. There was *gicukia*, which was attended by those not circumcised and another by only those who were circumcised. We used to go to dance very far from home when there was moonlight.

I remember one dance organized by boys for their girls in the area. We would spend the whole night there dancing and then go home the following morning. Those who were a bit brave would walk home during the night. When I was a *mūirītu*, I used to laugh a lot and sleep out in the cold night without even a blanket after dancing. As I had nothing to think or worry about, it was the happiest time I can remember. After dancing, I would go home and meet food already cooked and would just start eating. But now the mind is occupied with where to get food, what needs to be done next—like cultivating the tea or coffee, getting food for the cows.

In those times, the man who was very attractive—who was *kiumbi*—had his own unmarried man's house, which was just one room. Girls, during dances, used to go there every night. We washed ourselves, beautified ourselves, and went to this man's house and spent the night and would not return home until morning. Our oldest mother taught us how to dress ourselves when going there to prevent anything from going wrong. This was by tying ourselves with ropes so that the skirt was tight around the body. This is how we did it—I will show you. [She demonstrates.] Take one edge of the skirt in front, gather it into a knot and tie the rope around it. Then put that knot in between the legs toward the back. Now take the end of the rope and wrap it around each thigh so that when we are fondled by the man he cannot do anything [have sexual intercourse].

A man who is *kiumbi* is the best dancer, one who is handsome and able to lead in songs. The voice, itself, was enough to make one leave a pot cooking over the fire and go and dance! We would spend the night there in his big bed being turned over and over by him all night. So in the morning we would go tell others of our agemates who had not come with us and then they would go that evening to be turned over. With agemates, you can joke about things like that—where you spent the night and who was there. But with those of other *mariika*, you had nothing to talk about.

We used to go dance just near our home, and one day afterwards Mūrage (husband) made beer for us at his home. He never invited me but invited my friend, Kanyiba, and she took me with her. When we went there, Mūrage started talking to me on the subject of love and I told him that I was not interested in him. He realized it, too.

So, it happened that we had to pay back the beer we were given by having visitors to our place. When Mūrage came, I refused to listen to him, and he thought I was refusing him because of the beer we were taking. One night he came to the granary outside my mother's house and started blowing his nose. When I heard, I started asking, "Who is that?" I vowed not to marry him if it was the same person. I went out and told him to go home because we were going somewhere. He left, but the following night he came again. I went and told him to never come to our house again. But he started coming near the granary from day to day without stopping. He finished a month doing that.

My parents asked me who this man was who always came to the granary. I told them it was Mūrage and that I could not marry him, because I heard that at his place they beat their wives. Still he never stopped coming. So, I decided—because of his insistence—I would give him tobacco for his father. I went for tobacco from my father and gave it to Mūrage—that's the way our friendship started.

Mūrage took the tobacco to his father, and he was told to go to the sugarcane *shamba* and get some sugarcane to make beer. When it was made, it was brought to our place in large gourds by two women from Mūrage's place. Then I made sour porridge to pay back the beer, and Mūrage and his many friends came to take it. During *gūthokia* [the "gourd-having-period"], a girl would sit with a gourd of sour porridge on her lap, and an agemate, a girl who was a friend, would sit next to her passing the calabashes of porridge as she served them. So when Mūrage came with his friends, I would shake the porridge, then pour it into a calabash, and my friend would pass it to Mūrage and his friends. If a girl happened to put the gourd of porridge down on the ground, the man and his friends would not take it, because it showed that the girl was not interested in the man as she didn't respect him enough to keep the gourd off the ground.

After this period, Mūrage made more beer, and I made more porridge. When my father got enough beer, he asked for *rūracio*. It was the men of the two clans who were the ones who carried out the negotiations as to how many goats and cows would be brought to my father. The women cooked food to take to the place where negotiations were going on, and they brewed beer for the occasion. During that time, I was very far away, cultivating in the *shamba*, and was not allowed to come near. When all the goats and cows that had been agreed upon were brought by Mūrage and his helpers, a ram that was part of *rūracio* was sacrificed at our place and its blood poured into the yard. The mixing of the blood from the groom's ram with the soil of the bride's home means that peace is made between the two sets of parents and clans. *Uthoni* [in-laws] is how they refer to one another from then on. The process of mixing the blood of the ram with the soil is called *gūthinjiro*. Now I was promised to Mūrage.

I had been told by the older women in our compound that when you get married, you are carried shoulder high from your place to where you are marrying—to your husband's home. They also told me that I would go first to the man's mother's house and never come out and would always wear a veil covering the head as a bride to show respect for the mother.

So when Mūrage came to get me, I told him I wouldn't go. The following day, Mūrage and four others from his place came and insisted in knowing the reason. They threatened to carry me by force to his home. I got scared. I went into the house then and packed a few clothes, and we started walking. It was during the night, for they did not want to be seen. Sometimes, when people saw their daughters were being removed, they would refuse and would try and beat the man and his relatives because they did not want to lose the girl. I went slowly with Mūrage, sometimes sitting down because I did not want to go. Sometimes I wondered whether I could escape and go back home, but then I was threatened with a beating and I would start walking again.

When we reached the gate of Mūrage's homestead, I refused completely. I became afraid wondering what we were going to say to each other at his house—just the two of us. Then his father heard us and asked why we were refusing to go in. I had not even told my mother I was going. I knew that they would discover in the morning when they missed me. So the following day, food was brought to me from my father's place, for they knew I had been taken to Mūrage's.

I got food from my home until that time when I was welcomed to Mūrage's family by his parents with a goat. What happened is that when one married and went to her husband's home, she could not eat cooked food prepared there until she was welcomed officially. Up to that time, she was being given *kirira* [secret knowledge] by the husband's mother on what to do in that compound and how to behave. For instance, I was told by Mūrage's father's older wife not to wander about or go outside my husband [commit adultery]. She said, "You are newly married so you should not be seen outside until the time you will be allowed to." If I did go outside the house, she told me to cover my face and legs with a veil—a big sheet—so as not be bewitched. Also, it was hard for the husband's father to see the bride that way, and [it] showed respect for his wives.

Above all, I could not eat meat during this time until a goat was slaughtered for me. I can remember it was slaughtered when I got my first child almost two years later. That was our custom. The bride would not eat any meat. Even if the husband came with meat, she would just cook it for him and not eat it.

I did not go to Mŭrage's mother's house as I had been told because he had already built a house for me. After we stayed together for awhile, I learned what he wanted and how things should be done. So we stayed from that time without fighting.

I did not meet Mŭrage's mother when I went to live there because she had died. Only his father's other two wives were there. Their behaviors were very bad—they refused to give me a gourd, a calabash, and a tray basket for winnowing. I had to ask for these from my father's place. And those two did not get along with each other and used to fight sometimes, calling each other names. It made me feel sad to see them.

I stayed for one year before I got pregnant. What happened is that I was called home by my father, who was worried that I had not gotten a child yet. He called me so I would be washed in the river by the *mŭndŭ mugo*, just as happened to my mother when she did not get pregnant. The *mŭndŭ mugo* fetched some water from the river, using a calabash, and in a hidden place between some arrowroot plants, he washed me saying, "I have washed you of the bad omen that refused to let you have a child. May you have a child. I have washed you completely. I have cleansed you completely." His words worked, for I never finished that year without becoming pregnant.

Soon after the *mŭndŭ mugo* cleansed me I missed my monthly flow. I went to a short woman in my husband's father's compound called Waduru. She told me that I was pregnant and I would know when the baby inside was three months old. After three months, I started feeling sleepy during the day and vomiting. When I started feeling the child playing in the womb, I knew then that Waduru had told the truth.

Once I knew I was pregnant, I could not sleep with my husband anymore. He called me to come to stay with him in Nairobi, where he was working then, but when I told him I was pregnant, he said there was no need for me to come. We were told by our mothers that if a woman had sexual relations when she was pregnant, she would make the midwife vomit because the child would be very dirty.

As time neared for me to deliver, I was always feeling sleepy. When I went to the *shamba* to cultivate, I would sleep there until it was late—toward sunset—then go back home. I was not able to cultivate well. So my husband called me to come to Nairobi. His father was not happy. He told me that I should not go to Nairobi, for even here at home there was now a hospital. But I made up my mind to go because my husband wanted me to be near him so that he could take care of me as there was nobody at home to care for me—my husband's mother being dead and the other wives not friendly. When I left for Nairobi, the *Mzee* [Kiswahili word meaning "old one," a respectful term] was annoyed and started complaining and muttering.

After staying in Nairobi a short time, one day I started feeling some stomach ache and feeling like going to the latrine. A woman neighbor came, and I told her how I was feeling. She told her husband that I should be taken to the hospital because my husband was at work. It was not my wish to give birth in a hospital, but in Nairobi there was nowhere else I could have gone. People in Nairobi go to the hospital for delivery.

When I went into the hospital, there were doctors there and a woman midwife. I was put on a bed. After some more pains the baby came out, and the midwife took scissors and cut the umbilical cord and tied it using thread. Then she started pressing my sides to make the afterbirth come out. I felt pain when the afterbirth fell out. But one of the doctors game me some medicine. A nurse attendant came and went with the child—even before I had seen him! I was taken back to my bed. I slept for a awhile, and then the baby was brought to me to suckle. But the child refused. I knew it was because I had made the *Mzee* angry. You know, in those days, if an old man was made angry and grumbled, the one who was the cause could be inflicted with some kind of unusual thing—like a curse. So that is why the child refused to suckle—because *Mzee* was angry that I had gone to Nairobi to deliver.

So my husband decided to go home and get *Mzee*. Let me tell you, when the old man arrived, everybody was astonished to see that the child began to suckle—suckling fast and a lot. What the *Mzee* did is he brought milk from home for the child and then he blessed the child by spitting on his own chest [a traditional Gikuyu blessing], and that ended the curse.

Because I had been stitched after I was cut to make room for the baby to come out, I stayed in the hospital about three days. We gave the baby the name Wacira, as Mūrage's father, for whom he was named, had always wanted to act as a judge and wanted people to solve their problems by consulting a judge—Wacira means "judge."

I felt nothing but happiness when I had my first child because I had always been asking myself, "When shall I have my own child?" And now, because I had a child, I felt myself a woman. My breasts dropped because now I was suckling the child. And I found that when I came home to Mūrage's place, people treated me differently. When I came here with the child, a goat was slaughtered because now I had named the child after the father's father. The women here started cooking food for me, and I could begin eating meat.

How had I been prepared to be a mother? As small girls, we were always playing at taking care of babies. We would take roasted bananas and chew them to make them soft, then feed them to toy babies. We would wash them and clothe them the way we saw our mothers do. When we got a little bigger, we chewed the bananas and fed them to the smaller children in the compound with a finger straight away without keeping the chewed bananas in a calabash the way our mothers did. We also learned how to carry babies on our backs, tying them securely with a cloth so they didn't fall.

Being a mother means having happiness and sadness too. Six of my children are alive, but many of them died before they were big—three of them. Wacira, the first born, died before he was two years old. But there was a girl called Kanugu who followed Wacira who died when she was nine years old. I say that the child who dies when he/she is very small is less heartache than the one who dies when she has fetched water and firewood for you and has cooked for you. That one is hard to forget.

What happened is that Kanugu started swelling in her stomach. We took her to Tumutumu Hospital, and she was admitted. They removed the water that made her stomach swell, and then she was discharged. We went for her and paid the hospital bill and brought her home here.

When she came home, she started telling us that she could feel her stomach swollen again, so we took her back to Tumutumu and she died there. I thought maybe she was given poisoned food, as she had come from school and got sick that afternoon. I first took her to Kerugoya, but when it turned out to be more serious I decided to take her to Tumutumu. Before we took her to the hospital, though, we had taken her to the mũndũ mugo, because the grandmothers were so much for him and thought he would help. We went to my father and he told us to go and buy a cow and a goat and slaughter them. He cooked beer for her to get well. But she never did.

When we went to the hospital the next morning after she was readmitted, we were told that she had died. So we went to the mortuary to see her and then started making arrangements for the burial. My husband made the arrangements for the coffin and grave, and then he came and told me she was buried.

Even after Kanugu died, I stayed for a long time thinking that it must have been somebody who gave her poisoned food so that she would have a disease that would not kill her right away but she would suffer before dying.

The one who has never lost a child has not seen any problems in her husband's house. That one might ask how one looks when one is dead because they have never seen a dead body. But me, I have been to see, so I can't go asking.

When the girl died, I went home, and my father asked me

whether Kanugu felt better. I was unable to tell him because I was crying, and my heart was heavy with tears. I could not find the courage to tell him. So others told him.

I changed very much after that child's death. I started fearing that I might never be given others. The ones I had later after Kanugu's death, I took much care of so that they might not die—like making sure they were clean, had good food, and went for clinic. At times, I keep quiet and think, "I had very strong children who died compared to ones I have now"—like when the two-year-old boy died, I had just given birth to Mūrithii, my last born, and I prayed, asking, "Why has God taken the bigger one and left this tiny one?" But you see, Mūrithii is the one fetching water for me now. There are none of my children that I take for granted. Kanugu's death taught me that lesson.

*   *   *

After that time when I had Wacira, my first born, I returned here to Mūrage's place, but I was not happy. As I have told you, Mūrage's mother, Wagathare, who was the father's first wife, had died, leaving the other two wives here. I found these two women would not give each other food, nor did they share food with me. They never wanted to talk to me, and they hated each other. But it was their husband, Mūrage's father, who was at fault. He liked one more than the other and bought her better things, like clothes. The other one stayed feeling bad. Another thing, if the two wives made beer, *Mzee* would not give the second wife the beer but would share some with the younger wife. Those two women were very uncooperative, and I began wishing I had somebody I could talk with. I remembered how I'd seen my father's wives having good talks when sitting eating their evening meal together after the day's work. Then one day Mūrage came home from Nairobi to visit. He had been working for some Europeans as a houseboy. He told me that he could see the child and I were not very happy, so he was going to marry another wife so we could be working together. I agreed with him. "Yes," I told him, "that is a good idea, because now I will have somebody to talk to and work with." So we started looking for a bride.

Mūrage heard about Karuana from another woman who was her neighbor. We were told that she was a very good girl—hard working and not naughty. She knew how to control her mouth. So I told my husband to marry Karuana, because if he married a woman who was *ng'aa*—a woman who didn't care and wouldn't listen to me—then the home would collapse.

When I saw Karuana, I liked her and wanted to have her as my co-wife. I knew she would help with the work and was one I could communicate with. From then on, I felt a lot of happiness. Like today, when I'm visiting you, she is the one home cooking for the children, and when I return home I will meet things well taken care of. That's why I like Karuana so much.

I am able to remember well the day I went for Karuana, even though it was a long time ago. It is only that I don't remember the year, but I know it was during the start of Mau Mau [1952]. I can remember Mũrage and me taking beer to her father's home near the Kariko Coffee Factory, where there was a homestead of some Britons. And it was me who went for her on the day that was arranged for her to marry, because the husband was in Nairobi.

The first night after I brought Karuana home she spent the night here with me in my bed. Then, the next morning, I escorted her to the bus stop to go to Nairobi. It is me who married her. After becoming pregnant, Karuana came back here. When she came, my son got sick, so she told me to go to Nairobi so the child could be taken to the hospital. I went and left Karuana here. But I was only in Nairobi for a short time. Then I came back here and stayed with Karuana until the husband wrote a letter telling me to go back to Nairobi. Karuana and I, we each had our houses here, but she would always cook with me—even now.

At the time that Karuana came to live here, there was no coffee planted, only cultivating of food crops like maize and beans. We had our own *shamba* in different places, but we cultivated together. I never felt any jealousy toward Karuana. I was happy because the husband was finding children her, which I also wanted. And he would also come and give me mine. And after one of us got pregnant and was unable to work, it was the duty of the other to cook for her, cultivate her *shamba*, and feed and wash that one's children. Jealousy? That would be a waste of time. Mũrage would spend the night with Karuana and then come in the morning and ask me to warm his bathwater, and I would gladly do it. And the same with Karuana if he spent the night with me. The thought of where he slept and what he did was never in us. When two or three wives are good friends, that home is always warm and lively. But if they hate one another, there is no home.

* * *

[In order to find out Karuana's perceptions of her marriage to Mũrage and her relationship with Wamutira, I interviewed her on a day when Wamutira had gone to the clinic in Kerugoya. This is Karuana's account.]

First Mūrage came to our home, and we talked with him about the marriage. So when he came for tobacco, I gave it to him and he went and took it to his father. Then he brought beer, after which came gūthokia. Finally, the negotiations for rūracio were completed. My people had talked with Wamutira and she told them she had asked Mūrage to marry a girl who would keep her company. So he had that pressure from Wamutira because she wanted a co-wife.

After rūracio had been brought, I stayed at home until the day Mūrage said he would come for me. As I was told when the day was, I washed all my clothes and got ready. It was Wamutira who came, about three in the afternoon, carrying the child who was her first born on her back. We stayed at my home until dark because I would not agree to go in daylight. We met Mūrage at Karia coming to get us, as it was dark. The following morning, Wamutira escorted Mūrage and me to the bus stop in Kerugoya.

When Wamutira escorted us to the bus stop she was pregnant with that girl, Kanugu, who later died. When I went to Nairobi, I never changed in my feelings about Wamutira—I liked her. While we stayed there, a letter came telling us that she had given birth. At this time, there were difficulties in traveling because of the state of emergency during the Mau Mau times—the British put up roadblocks. Mūrage feared to go home, as he was a Mau Mau supporter. I felt very badly that he was not sending anybody to take money or soup to Wamutira. I reached a point of quarreling with Mūrage until he sent somebody home.

I had gone to Nairobi in May, and the following May I returned home to Mūrage's place and was three months pregnant. When I came here, I met Wamutira and we stayed together in the same house. You could even see me carrying her child when I needed to go somewhere. And if I went for a visit to my parents' home and was given something to eat, I would not eat it but instead carry it back here to share with Wamutira. We stayed together until we were taken to the villages run by the British during Mau Mau.

During that time, Wamutira was called to Nairobi with the komerera [type of bus that secretly transported Africans], and she left me here. When we were forced into the villages, it was me who carried all our things. Then I went back to my parents' home and there gave birth to my firstborn girl. When Wamutira returned home, we lived in a house with two rooms, but the doors were very close together. We are still good friends. Even if the husband would not wish it, we would still be close, and he would not be able to separate us, for Wamutira and I are of the same clan. But Muthoni is from another clan.

* * *

[Probably the other major change in Wamutira's adult life in addition to the births and deaths of her children was her relocation to Nairobi during the emergency. She describes her trip.]

It was the beginning of Mau Mau when I went with other women to Nairobi. We were taken by a bus called a *komerera*. It was a vehicle that had canvas covers for hiding people underneath. I walked with other women wanting to see their husband up to Baricho and got into the *komerera* to Nairobi. I had left Karuana here that time. When we reached outside Nairobi, those who went further into town were taken prisoners by the British and taken to Lang'ata Police Station. But us, we got off very far from town at a place that was all forest. We walked awhile and then were met by an old *mzee* who told us there was no roadblock near the railway station. So we passed through there. At the station, we met a man who was Mūgīkūyū, who took us to his house. The man cooked for us, and we washed and slept there overnight. We were very tired. In the morning, the man sent messages to each woman's husband, telling him where his wife was waiting. So each husband came to that house without being noticed by the police.

While in Nairobi, Mūrage and I stayed in two rooms of the "railway houses," which were many rooms in a row built for Africans by the British. The rooms had concrete floors and were built of stone. Mūrage was a supporter of the Mau Mau freedom fighters, even though he was working for a *muzungu* [European] at the time. The supporters of Mau Mau had made groups, one at Karatina, another at Sargana, another just before reaching here. The last one was at Nairobi. These groups would communicate with one another and tell each other when the roads were clear of roadblocks. That way, Mau Mau people would move from Nairobi to here and back without meeting government soldiers. Mūrage was part of the Nairobi group.

Before I went to Nairobi to join Mūrage, I had already taken the Mau Mau Oath, but Mūrage took it while in Nairobi. The Oath was being given by force to everybody here. Even when going to take it, one did not know that was what one was going to do. Somebody would come and tell you to accompany him to go and eat rice and broken maize. When you got to the place, it was a bitter experience. If one had plaited her hair, it was cut off using a blunt *panga*. If one made an attempt to refuse, one would be slapped hard. Also, we were made to take off all our clothes, and if one tried to cover her private parts with her hands she was beaten. The meat eaten in the ceremony was rotten, and one had to swallow it and could not spit it out. One would not even utter a word in that hut. It was bad. You only hear about the Oath. You do not know how it really was. Me, I know.

I went to Nairobi when the trench was being dug, so I never had to dig it. But I was involved because my husband was. The Mau Mau supporters brought money to me, and I would go and buy soup to give to the freedom fighters.

We returned home from Nairobi while the fighting was still going on but was not as great as it was at the beginning. Mũrage lost a lot of money when he left Nairobi and his job there. When we got here, we discovered that the goats and cows that he had left here were gũtaho [commandeered]. They had been taken by British government soldiers to Mwea and Ndomba to feed government soldiers. It was that time when people were just being released from the villages [1958-1959]. We began to build the houses here and they were not yet completed by the time Uhuru came.

I was feeling very happy the day of Uhuru because now we would not be beaten again. I could not eat anything, because I was excited that we were no longer slaves. There was a lot of dancing and singing that night and all the next day. People were ululating and telling Munyao to raise the flag on Mt. Kenya. We were not sad to see the British leave.

*   *   *

After Mũrage came to settle here, he became a tailor. He worked at a tailor shop on the other side of the market. Muthoni was sewing there, too. So it happened that every night he would visit her in her room next to the tailor's shop on the pretext that he was staying there to keep watch over the machines—that's what he told us. We did not know about it until Muthoni, who was only a girl, got pregnant, and then Mũrage came to tell us that he was going to marry another wife. Karuana and I, we told him that he couldn't marry again because we wanted to stay just the two of us. He told us he could not leave Muthoni, because she was already pregnant and she was a good girl—even had been to school.

We told Mũrage to go and hear what his father had to say. When he went, the father told him that he would not allow him to marry another wife. But Mũrage went and made beer and bribed his father with four gourds of it. And so the father gave his consent to go ahead and marry Muthoni.

Before, when Mũrage came home from Nairobi, he often wanted to beat Karuana and me because of our friendship. He would ask me, "Is it me who married Karuana or you?" This was when he found Karuana always staying at my house. Karuana told him it was me who married her because I went for her at her father's homestead. The husband would try and separate us, but he was unable to. It is our hearts that like each other—Karuana and me.

When Muthoni came we just kept quiet. But later, we reasoned that even if we three lived together feeling bad because of one another, there were none of us who had the power to take another back to her father's home. Karuana and I stayed for almost one year feeling bad about Muthoni, but we found that even if we fought with her or tried to abuse her, we were doing nothing because she was there to stay. Karuana knew Muthoni because she comes from the same place, but I did not know her. Finally, we agreed between ourselves to get united together as wives, the three of us. Like now, if a visitor comes and I'm not around, the others will welcome her and entertain her for me. The husband has never told us to be friendly, but it is our wish and what our hearts want—to like one another and be friends.

*   *   *

[Karuana, when interviewed, had a different perspective on Muthoni's arrival as a wife, as she relates here.]

When Muthoni came she found me with only one child. When the husband told me that he was going to marry Muthoni, I never felt bad. During that time, Wamutira and I never used two pots to cook—we always cooked together. The houses were two, but if you were told that one had an owner you would not agree. I only went to my house to sleep. Sometimes Mũrage would come and ask me, "Karuana, are you unable to get firewood for making your own fire?" Then I told him, "Wamutira is my mother, and she is the one who came for me from my mother's house. If you want me never to go to Wamutira's house, then take me back to my mother's. You knew very well we would stay together when you came for me. Leave us alone to do our work."

When Muthoni came, we welcomed her. At times, you cannot differentiate which children belong to whom here. Those children who are away, when they come home they always go to Wamutira's house. So sometimes you might say, "Wamutira has a lot of children." In my house, there is never a child. If there is food to eat from my house, the children will carry it to Wamutira's and eat it there. There is no difference between the way we treat the children—they are all the same.

*   *   *

[Having heard Karuana and Wamutira's perceptions of Mũrage's marriage to Muthoni, I approached Muthoni to hear her version.]

When I first came to live here at Mũrage's, I met Wamutira and Karuana. I was eating and drinking without seeing anything bad about the home, and I decided to stay. When I first met Mũrage, he was a tailor. I stayed with him next to the tailor's shop, and then I got pregnant. After seeing me, he would go to his other wives at home. They would cook food and send it to me at the shop. When time reached for me to have my baby, I came here and gave birth as I never went to the hospital. My co-wives were the ones who caught the baby—my first baby girl. They cooked for me for a long time and treated me well until my body got back its strength. So I started helping them in their work, and we stayed together, eating together and laughing a lot.

When I first knew Mũrage, he did not tell me he was married, because he wanted us to be friends [lovers]. But when I stayed with him and got pregnant, I pressed him for more news of his home, for I knew my fate was to marry him. He told me that he had two wives and I was going to be the third. I felt very bad inside and even wanted to leave him then. I went to my parents' home and stayed for two months. But Mũrage came and told my parents that I was free to go and marry elsewhere but I should not take his child along. When I thought about it, I decided to marry him. And when I came here, I never found him changed. If he brought anything home, he would give to each of us the same.

When I came here in 1962, I was a young mũirĩtu [newly circumcised] and a child to the other two wives. I was not even cooking. I started cooking when I had my second child. There have never been three houses for cooking. In this house, each wife has her own sleeping room and one for the children, and the other separate room—that one with a lock—that is the husband's. So there is no discrimination.

We help each other with the work here, but each wife has her own shamba and knows its extent. But when it is plowed, we plant together, and during weeding, when the plants are young, we do it together with the children. But when it comes to harvesting, one knows where her shamba reaches and harvests that one only.

Before we had the cart with the bullocks, we used to carry the coffee harvested in sacks on our backs to the coffee factory—all three of us. Now that Mũrage has the cart, our work is easier. When there is pay from the coffee harvest, if Mũrage gives one wife 100 shillings, he will give the other two the same. If he thinks of buying meat, he buys it and divides it equally, giving each her share.

*   *   *

[Karuana, in a separate interview, agrees that Mũrage treats all wives equally.]

When Muthoni came here nothing changed, because the husband

never started to differentiate. If he had something to give, he gave it to all of us. The same with the children. If one of the girls' dresses gets torn, he will buy a new one for that child. But if he is buying new clothes, he buys for all of them when he has the money. If the children are sent home from school for lack of school fees or uniforms, he will not differentiate amongst them but will help them as they need it. He treats us all the same. You are not the only one who is surprised, Nyina-wa-Stephen. Many people ask what makes us stay such good friends—all three of us.

* * *

[Wamutira, in a separate interview a week later, agrees.]

Each of us wives has her own portion of land to cultivate, but Karuana and I work our lands communally with the children. We start with one of our portions then go to the other one. The food that we cook, all three of us, the food cooked first is given to the children and husband. Then the food that is cooked later will be saved for cooking again the next day.

If disagreements occur, the husband calls me and shows me the mistake. But if we three wives have quarreled amongst ourselves, Mũrage calls us all, starting with me, and hears each one's account. Then, later, we talk and solve the problem with him. He never likes seeing us quarrel. He asks what we are missing here that makes us quarrel.

Mũrage treats us all the same. If it is school fees, he pays for all the children. He takes all the children to get new school uniforms, and also he loves all the children more than he loves us three. No, it would not have been so peaceful at home if he had favored any one of us over another, but he is equal in the way he treats us.

* * *

[One day when I was visiting the homestead, Karuana made the following analogy of our occupations.]

Nyina-wa-Stephen, you see how you use a pen and paper and that machine [she referred to the tape recorder] as your tools for work? Well, Agĩkũyũ women use the *mũkwa, kibanga,* and *oma* as their pens and pencils in the *shamba,* and they use the *nyungo* [pottery cooking pot] and *mũiko* [long stick that is rounded and flattened at one end—used for mashing food] in the house.

[The *mũkwa* is the woven rope carried by all women to haul containers of water, bunches of bananas, sacks of potatoes, and firewood home on their backs. The *kibanga* is the machete used for weeding, planting, cultivating, and digging out tubers. It also serves as a cutting tool around the homestead. The *oma* is a short-handled pitchfork, with the fork set at a right angle to the handle, used in cultivation. Finally, the *kiondu* is the term used for any woven basket used to carry produce home from the *shamba* or market. Karuana's analogy is perceptive, because the tools she refers to provide a rural Kenyan woman with the ability to support herself economically, just as my pens, pencil, and tape recorder provide me a means of support. Mutira women are full-time farmers who cultivate not only subsistence crops but have major responsibility for the two cash crops grown in the area—coffee and tea. Wamutira describes how she learned to grow them.]

We first began planting coffee after Mau Mau. We were shown by government agricultural officers how to plant the coffee, take care of the bushes—pruning them when needed—and how to pick the ripe seeds [coffee berries]. They showed us that we should pick the seeds when they are red. Before, we were fearing to pick coffee because we were afraid that it might not sell. But now, we do not fear it, and through practice we have learned to pick better and faster. Coffee is picked twice a year, in late May and again in November. Everybody helps then. We put the seeds in large sacks and carry them to the coffee factory for processing. The coffee factory is a cooperative. When the skins have been removed, we collect them and use them as fertilizer around the bushes.

With tea, it has to be picked year-round. The government took us to a training course at Kagosi to learn how to cultivate and pick it. We learned from extension workers that we should pick two leaves and a bud. At first we used to pick using one hand, as though picking vegetables, but now we are able to pick using both hands at the same time, putting the tea leaves into *gikabu* [large baskets] on our backs. Because we have learned how to pick better through practice, now we get a bigger yield. So, more kilograms of tea and coffee are sold now than when we first started. We take tea to the weighing stations and are paid at the end of the month according to the number of kilos picked. One of the things I am proudest of is that it was me who planted all these coffee bushes you see here. From what we earn, we can pay for the children's school fees.

Yes, it is true that school has taken our children from the *shamba*. When I was a child, we were expected to help our mothers once we learned how to handle a digging stick and a hoe. Nowadays, children have to go to school, so they can help us only on Saturdays and holidays. But I think it's important for children to go to school so that they can get educated and get the good things I see—like more knowledge and the ability to read road signs so one doesn't get lost.

Those who go to school are able to get employed and support themselves, unlike us who were foolish enough not to go to school. School might have helped me, because I would know some things I do not know now—like how to write letters to people whom I want to write. Like now, if I had gone to school, I would be writing to you, Nyina-wa-Stephen, and even talking to you in English.

Nowadays it is just as important for girls to go to school as for boys. Even a girl can do a lot of good things to develop her home. It is not like the old days, when people used to say that they would not take their daughters to school because they thought they would become prostitutes. Our fathers were foolish then.

My daughters did not get enough schooling. When we tried to force them to go like other people, they preferred to get married. But they do not have the best marriages. I know they regret, now, that they never finished school. Even my sons did not get much schooling.

What do I think is important to teach my children at home? To teach a child obedience—that is important. That means waking your girl very early in the morning so she can wash herself and go to school. It means when I send her for something, she should obey me. If it is after school, I tell her to go and fetch water for me and cook. I tell the younger ones to respect the older ones because they are just like their mothers. I would also like my daughter to be hard working and somebody who is able to rely on herself later on. After educating herself, she should be respectful to me and her father, knowing that she was able to go to school because of our hard work. It is the same with a boy, but, above all, a boy should be clever and study hard to be a teacher or an officer in a big company somewhere.

I taught the girls how to cultivate with a *kibanga,* how to pick coffee, cook, and wash their clothes. But I remember I never showed them how to dig with a hoe. They used to follow me in the *shamba* with a hoe and do as they saw me doing. That way they learned how to use a hoe. But for picking coffee, I had to show them how to do it. They learned how to pick just the red berries, putting them into their baskets without spilling them on the ground. Sometimes one of the children would find a chameleon on one of the branches and become frightened. Then I would take that child away—for a chameleon is a bad omen.

The main difference between being a grandmother and a mother is that my sons' children are told to go to *Cũcũ's* [Grandmother's], but the children of my co-wives are told to go to their eldest mother's house. But there is no difference when I'm taking care of all of them. If it is giving food, I share it equally amongst them—they are all my children. The most important thing is to take care of *all* children, regardless of whether they are yours or not. When giving tea or food, one should not discriminate—that way the home will stay in good harmony. To be a good mother is more important than being a good wife.

Which do I think is my most important role? The one of cultivating, picking coffee, fetching firewood and water, and cooking. Also that includes feeding the cattle. It is a difficult thing to think about the rest, but I told you being a mother is more important than being a wife because my children depend upon me very much. I only need to obey my husband as a wife. But now I am not very interested in him sexually. The next most important role is being a co-wife, which is more important than being a daughter, as that was long ago.

When did I become a Christian? It was after Mau Mau. Everybody had joined, and I was left behind like a fool. I found that so because when somebody died, she was buried by the church she belonged to. And me, I did not have any church, and so I would not be buried properly. So I joined the Anglican Church at Mutira.

Before I started going to church, when somebody began quarreling with me I would fight back. But now I don't do such things, even if somebody abuses me. The things I used to do—like nagging or feeling bad when my husband came asking me whether the cow had been given food and water, and I'd tell him to go and take the cow to the river himself—I don't do anymore. Now, I never talk back rudely to him, because I know he is the wheel and pedals of the bicycle and if he can't take the wheel and push the pedals, then we wives can't move.

* * *

[I asked Wamutira if when her first child was circumcised she had gone through *nyumithio* in order to achieve elder status.]

My oldest son went through *Irua* not so long ago, but there was no ceremony for me like in the old days when a woman's head was shaved and she got new ear plugs. And the tradition of the *kiama* for elders I never met—it had passed, too. Not long ago, I went through menopause, but I never got any headaches. I got some hot feelings and chills and sometimes I felt low. But I never felt sad when menstruation ended. I felt only happiness because I had layed down a burden that I did not want anymore.

What am I proudest of having achieved? I'm proud because I planted all the coffee trees you see here. I do not have any future dreams because I am satisfied with my life the way it is. My strongest character is being hardworking. I work in the *shamba* all day and feed the cows. I generally like working. My weakest is that I have a very bad temper when somebody does me wrong—but everybody loses her temper at times. The thing in my life that changed me the most was when my children died. I started worrying and wondering whether I would ever get others to keep. I was not able to eat or drink anything, and even working was a problem. I started taking extra care to see that my children were well fed, clean, and when they got sick, I took them to the clinic.

What does being a woman mean to me? A woman is one who plants herself firmly at her own homestead without wandering. Being Agĩkũyũ means that I took the Mau Mau Oath—for if you did not take it, one was not considered a true Mũgĩkũyũ.

I liked the way we talked, Nyina-wa-Stephen. The things you have asked me about my life make me think. I will keep them in my heart and never forget.

A mother shows her daughter how to place a gopher trap in the midst of the woman's sweet potato field.

4

Watoro's Story:
Poverty Is Like Dust

Watoro, the second woman in her fifties, represents another aspect of polygynous marriage—one in which the relationships are not copacetic. Watoro's case is atypical because she decided to leave marriage, a drastic step in a society that does not look kindly upon marital separations. I hypothesized that such a change might prompt unique experiences in Watoro's life—a hypothesis that turned out to be wrong. In addition to being separated from her husband, Watoro had had minimal experience with an adult education class and belongs to no women's groups. She is the poorest of the women in their fifties.

My relationship with Watoro proved to be difficult in two ways. First, as we began to know one another, Watoro's extreme poverty caused her to make material demands of me that I found hard to meet, leaving me with a certain sense of guilt and resentment. Second, her acute bitterness toward her estranged husband prevented her from discussing her marriage or him in any detail. The bitterness is woven into the fabric of her narrative, and she refused to tell me the man's name, referring to him only as "the husband."

Watoro is the only woman in her age group who has no land of her own to till, and to be without land, say the Gikuyu, is to be nothing. A woman's access to land once she marries is through her husband. Watoro lost that access when she left her husband. Instead, she cultivates her absentee brother's land and earns enough from the harvest of coffee to buy books and uniforms so her two youngest sons can go to school. Watoro is the major economic provider for her four sons, aged ten to twenty-four, and beyond what she earns from coffee, there is little financial security. As a result, Watoro is constantly under stress. Her two oldest sons are married and living with her in the overcrowded compound, rather than with their father as is customary. Both have young children, adding new mouths to feed.

Because the survival of Watoro's family depends upon her labor, we usually met during her midday "rest hour" in the middle of the coffee fields under a shade tree. After the session I'd spend an hour or

Figure 4.1 WATORO'S FAMILY

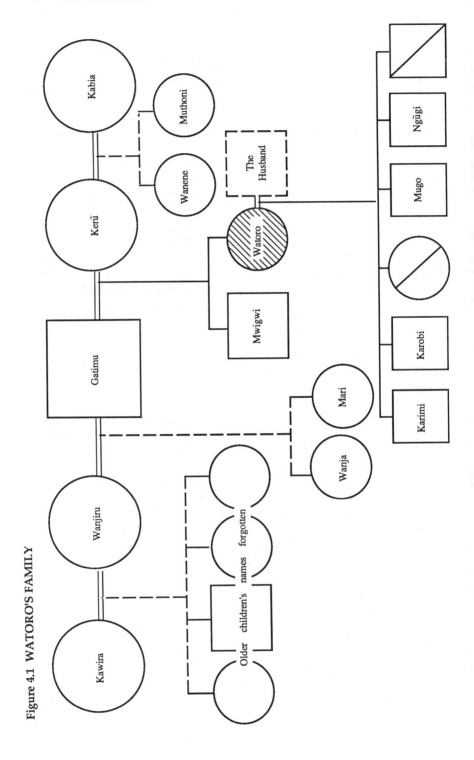

so working with her in the *shamba*. The two times I met her at home,
she willingly shared the little that was available with her visitors.
Such a gesture is characteristic of the hospitality one finds among
rural Kenyan women.

One day, as we were sitting in the coffee field talking about what
led to Watoro's drastic decision to leave her husband, I remarked that
often a crisis can turn into a learning experience. She gazed off tiredly,
fatigue and disconsolation showing in her dusty face, and then retort-
ed, "If you are cultivating here in this field and a big wind blows over
you covering you with dust, would you say that is a learning experience?"

—J.D.

I was named Watoro for the mother to my father. My clan is
Ũnjiru. My father, Gatimu, was a black man who was not very tall
and not fat either. He was of medium size and jolly. He had married
two wives before my mother came to live with him. They were
Kawira and Wanjiru. The first wife, Kawira, had three girls and a boy,
but I don't remember their names because they were big by the time I
was born and had already moved away. The second wife had two
girls. My mother, called Keru, was the third wife. She was a good
woman—hardworking, always cooking, and she did not talk badly to
people. After some time, my father married his fourth wife, Kabia,
who had two daughters who were my agemates—Wanene and
Muthoni. I have only one elder brother called Mwigwi. These are the
children I grew up with in the compound. I can remember that all my
father's wives were similar in character, because when you went into
any of their houses you were given food to eat—they never bothered
to ask if you were hungry.

Our homestead was at Gatitu. Also living there was my father's
mother whom we called Cũcũ. She was a short woman, neither so
black, nor so brown. She was a patient woman who did not show a
bad temper. She would never scold us if we bothered her with questions like "Where does the mongoose hide his house?" I can
remember she would cook millet porridge and drink it while she was
singing.

We children would ask Cũcũ lots of questions like "What is the
best food to cook?" She would answer, "Porridge and *irio*." Cũcũ's
food was always good and sweet, so we used to go to her house and
eat when we were small. We also used to ask her how one looks for
firewood and ties it together with a *mũkwa* [tumpline], and she would

show us how to wrap the rope around each end of the firewood, leaving a long loose piece in the middle to put at the forehead. She was the one who showed us what kind of work a girl does and which is for boys.

Long ago, when boys got to be about eight years old, they would only go herding and after that they would come and sit near the fireplace outside—the one set for old men—warming themselves and waiting for food to be brought to them. But us girls, we used to go to the river to fetch water, go with our mother to cultivate, and when we were older, help with the cooking.

I was shown how to fetch water using a very small gourd. When we went to the river, the mothers would fill the gourds for us to carry home. Later on, we learned how to tie a larger gourd on our back with a *mūkwa* until now we carry big barrels of water. After we were through our work, the girls would go inside and sit near their mothers and the grandmother at the cooking fire when the sun disappeared and it began to feel cold. This is how we learned to prepare food—by watching how the mothers chopped the greens and added them to the big pot of *githeri* [maize and bean mixture] cooking on the fire. Sometimes they would add some chopped onions or carrots to make it taste good. We still do that now and some people even add tomatoes.

It was my grandmother who taught me good character from bad—like when I go along the road, I should not abuse anybody. We learned through songs and stories and sometimes through wise saying. I remember she told us, " *tamahe nī mūigīre*" ["The one who has not given already, hers is stored"]. It means that if you have not given anybody something you may be required to give, you are still keeping it.

I can remember a story my grandmother told us about being a good mother:

Long ago, there was a man who was a *mūturi* [carpenter]—a man who makes and molds things. He had two wives and each wife had a son. The two boys loved each other very much and they were both called Mwira after their father's father.

One day, the first wife died, leaving her son behind. After a short time, the husband went back to his place of work leaving the two boys with the second wife. It happened that the second wife did not like the other boy and so she planned a way to eliminate him. She dug a hold in the *thegi*. Then she sent her own son to his grandmother's place and put the other boy in the hole and kept quiet. When her son returned, he asked where his brother was and his mother told him that she had sent him also to the grandmother's but he had not returned.

The boy took the goats and cows to graze. When evening fell he asked his mother again, "Where is my brother?" But his mother scolded him and told him to go and sleep.

The following morning, when his mother had gone to the fields to cultivate, the boy began singing:

Mwĩra uĩ Mwĩra,	Mwĩra, oh Mwĩra,
Kaninindume na nja	Small one come out.
Ũĩ, Mwĩra	Oh, Mwĩra
Baba mara guka	Our father has come
Ũĩ, Mwĩra	Oh, Mwĩra,
Na tuthanyu twĩrĩ	With out herding sticks
Ũĩ, Mwĩra	Oh, Mwĩra
Gakwa na ka Mwĩra	Mine and that of Mwĩra
Ũĩ, Mwĩra.	Oh, Mwĩra.

His brother, in the hole, heard him and sang in reply:

Mwĩra, uĩ Mwĩra	Mwĩra, oh Mwĩra
Kanini ndurarĩmuuru,	Small one you are not bad,
Ũĩ, Mwĩra	Oh, Mwĩra
Nĩ nyukwe urarimuuru,	It is your mother who is bad,
Ũĩ, Mwĩra	Oh, Mwĩra
Kwenja irima thegi	Digging a hole in the thegi
Ũĩ, Mwĩra	Oh, Mwĩra
Ria gugĩkia Mwĩra	For throwing Mwĩra in
Na tunyungu twao	With all the pots
Ũĩ, Mwĩra	Oh, Mwĩra
Na tuuga twa nyina	And mother's calabashes
Ũĩ, Mwĩra.	Oh, Mwĩra.

So the boy came to know where his brother was and he stayed near the hole singing that song and not eating anything. So he lost weight and grew sick.

At his place of work, the father of the boys started getting feelings that something was terribly wrong at home. He decided to go home for a visit. He reached there in the morning before the boy had taken the goats outside but found that his wife had already left. When the father did not see his other son, he asked Mwĩra where the other Mwĩra had gone. The boy told his father to follow him into the thegi, and he would show him. Mwĩra sang the song again, and the other son answered from the hole. The father removed the soil from the hole until he found his son. He pulled him out and went and slaughtered a goat and gave the boy tatha [contents of intestines], and the boy vomited all the soil and dirt he had eaten in the hole. Then the father roasted some of the meat for his two sons and hid the boy who had been in the hole in his own house and waited for his wife to return.

When the wife returned, she welcomed her husband and he gave her some meat to cook and went to his house. The wife told him that the other Mwĩra had gone for a visit to the grandmother. The wife's own son refused to stay at his mother's house and followed his father to his *thingira*. When the meat had cooked, the wife brought it to them. The man ate with his two sons and then smeared both with animal fat.

The next morning, the father told the wife to go and get his other son from the grandmother's. If she should not find the boy there, then she should come back with all the family members of both their clans.

So the two clans met and the elders told the wife to give them the child because they knew he had not gone to the grandmother's as the wife had told everybody. The boy who had been hidden was brought into the presence of the clan members, and the story of how he had been put into the hole was told. The family members told the wife that because of what she had done she could not stay there anymore, and she was to go back to her own people. But her own people refused her when they heard the story and killed her. The father went to his place of work, taking his two sons with him.

That is the end of the story. You see, a hospitable woman is the one who, when she marries away and meets young children, she takes care of them as her own. Our grandmother told us that if one marries she should not go abusing the children she meets, and when she cooks, she should give food to all children she meets. We were told, *"Gũtanaha na kũigwanira tha mũndũ ndagaga mwoi"* ["To be hospitable and merciful to others, one will not miss somebody to collect her"—help her in times of need].

As a child I was very playful, but I wouldn't provoke other children as some do. I remember we sang and danced a lot. We had one type of play where we would pass a ball around a circle of us, singing, *"Marombo na Mwarau"* three times, then *"Mwendi gũceca nĩa cece rĩngĩ"* [The one who wants to play can play again], then *"Marombo na Mwarau"* again as we passed the ball around.

When I grew up to be about four or five—still a child—a *mũndũ mugo* slaughtered a goat, and the skin was spread out for a bed for me, and *rũkoro* [a strip of goat's skin] was put around me. It was taken off the next day, after it had hardened. The elders gathered for the ceremony, then ate the goat's meat to celebrate. We called this *mambura ma twana* [ceremony of the children]. It usually occurred when the mother wanted to remove the youngest child from her bed so she could have sexual relations with her husband again and get another child. Up to that time, a child would sleep with the mother until it was weaned—no matter how big. All this time, the father was staying in his *thingira*. I don't remember too much about *mambura ma twana* because I was still small, but I was told about it.

The first major change that I remember were *mbuci* and *matū*; then, after these healed and I grew up some more and showed signs of growing breasts, I was circumcised. Then I was a grown person and could go to dances during the night. After many dances, when I was more mature and had begun to menstruate, I got married. Later, I separated from my husband and went back to my father's home—these were the big changes in my life that I remember clearly.

When I was about fifteen, that is when I went to my mother and told her I wanted *mbuci*. The reason I wanted my ears pierced was for beauty and putting on beads and decorative metals. Also, one would not be very happy to see her agemates with decorations in her ears while she had none. The ones who did not have their ears pierced were like fools, because they were trying to cut themselves off from the community. We would not joke with them, nor could they joke about with us.

As soon as I told my mother I wanted *mbuci* she went to my uncle to get permission. He was the brother to my mother who was born together with her [her twin]. It was the tradition that every girl had to get permission from her mother's oldest brother. My upper lobes were pierced with small holes, using thorns of a tree called *mūthūthi* [a type of acacia]. Then sticks were put in. When mine were pierced they began to swell, and so the sticks were removed and the holes joined together and disappeared as you can see. Like me, you would not say that I had *mbuci*, because the flesh grew back.

When we were to have our ears pierced, it was an old woman with experience who did it. She did not have any fear. But I felt pain when she poked the holes in my ears. After my upper lobes had healed, my mother again went to the same uncle and told him that I was ready for *matū*—that is the large hole made in the bottom lobe. A goat was slaughtered, called *ndonya matū*, and was eaten by my uncles. When I got the bottom ones pierced, hot pieces of wood were put into them to make them bigger—like these holes you see now. It was painful, but we wanted to have it done. Later, after a woman's first son got circumcised, she used to put beads in the upper holes, called *ngoni*, and *mwikwo*—large plugs—in the lower lobes. After I got *matū* I felt more mature, for I had already started getting breasts. It meant that now I could go for *Irua*, so I was excited.

I went for *Irua* before I had gotten my first menstruation. We were told by our mothers and grandmother that *Irua* was a way of buying maturity. It was me, together with my agemates, who decided when we were ready. When a girl feels ready she tells her parents to go and tell her uncles and ask for their permission. In return for the favor, the uncles are given a goat or beer. That was the custom. Then preparations would begin—one month before the actual ceremony. Dances were conducted at the homestead of the girl being circumcised and people would hear the sounds of the drum, rattles, and singing from far away and come to join the dancing. It was a festive time. Beer and porridge were prepared by women and taken freely until the day reached for the ceremony.

From the time of *mbuci*, our eldest mother had been counseling me that I should take care of myself and not be a wanderer. She told me that now that I was to become a grown girl I should be careful when moving about with boys and not do anything else apart from dancing when I attended the dances. She told me, "Soon you will go for *Irua* and will be discovered that day." By this she meant that people at the ceremony would discover whether or not the root I came from was good by the way I behaved that day—"A good club grows from a good root" is our saying.

Irua occurred after the harvest, when the main work was done and there was plenty of millet and sorghum to make sour porridge for the celebration. The first day of *Irua* was the "Day-of-*Mugumo*." Boys and girls were circumcised on the same day—boys in the morning and girls when the sun had begun to go down. On that morning, we went to the *mugumo* tree [sacred fig tree—enormous in size—that was similar to a shrine where prayers on behalf of the community were made by the elders], which had been singled out for that occasion. The candidates for *Irua* would go there and throw pointed sticks with dyed cloth tied to one end through the branches of the tree. Then branches were cut by newly married women for the candidates to take home. If the candidate was a boy, five or nine branches were cut, and if a girl, four or eight. [The number five of something is associated with the male sex, whereas four is associated with females.] The branches were carried to my home as good medicine and to sooth me after I had been circumcised.

It was on this day that one put on *mathangũ* [leaves] tied around the waist so they rustled when dancing. We also had a skirt made of beads, called a *thira*. The one whose circumcision was well prepared had people to borrow beads and other decorations from to make her appearance beautiful. Then the dancing would begin.

During the circumcision dances anybody was free to do anything—abuse another person, chase a woman, or any other social evil until the next morning of *Irua*. If a man had a desire for a certain woman, he could try and take her by force, so women would prepare themselves and come armed with sticks and clubs and move only in groups. We used to hide a club behind our sheets [tunics], putting them down the back so when somebody tried to attack us he would be beaten. [The behavior Wataro describes refers to young, circumcised women, not the initiates.]

On the morning of *Irua*, we who were candidates were taken to the river by women of our clan to wash. The reason we were washed was to wash away *mũgiro*—the dirt the girl was coming to *Irua* with. That state of being uncircumcised was termed "dirty" and had to be washed away. Newly married women were singing songs as they washed me and then escorted me back home, where I stayed until it was about three in the afternoon and you could see the sun starting to go down. While at home, we were given small gourds of porridge and *ngima ya mũhĩa* made from sorghum flour]. These were fed to us with a spoon by our circumcision mothers. It was as if we had become children again.

We were eight girls who got circumcised together that time. The fields where we were taken was cleared of brush and was made of grass. It was the same place where other dances took place. There were so many people who came to the field to watch us. They were all ages.

The one who was my supporter was the one who told me how to sit on the *mathangu* [leaves] and what to do during circumcision. My mother brought castor oil to put on the wound after we had been cut. The circumciser was an old woman who was fat and very black. I felt a bit scared when I saw her. She had been paid money for the task—my parents gave her 3 shillings. To do the cutting, she used a *kienji*. My supporter, who was our oldest mother, held me from behind so I would not move about. The circumciser cleansed the knife with water and then smeared it with castor oil each time she circumcised a girl. Those who were brave did not feel anything—they just looked away. That is what I did—I just looked away when I was being cut. But those who were cowards started crying, even before being circumcised!

After it was over, castor oil was put on a soft leaf, and it was put over the wound to cover it until it was healed. If a girl bled a lot the parents would decide what to do, because it meant there was a dispute between her parents and her uncles, and before it was solved—by slaughtering a goat—the girl would bleed. So uncles were given in advance the number of goats given for the mother of the initiate when she was married—that way there were no problems.

On the way home, I walked slowly with no one to support me. There were so many people going with me, cheering and singing songs for me on the way to my mother's house, where sour porridge had already been prepared. But me, I was so weak and tired, I went straight to bed and slept.

After three days, a small girl came and shaved my head, and from then we called each other "*Wamathaga*," which means that as you have shaved my head, you are my mother, and so I can't call you by your name—only *Wamathaga*. It took me a month and then another to heal completely.

After it was over, I felt grown up and walked around proudly. When a girl got her ears pierced, then was circumcised, she was looked upon as a grown-up and was treated like one. No young boys would dare joke about with her or abuse her, for the boy's father would beat him. Circumcised girls were very respected, and those who went for *Irua* earlier than us, they were considered our mothers, and we would not disobey them or we would be beaten.

The girls who are circumcised together, of the same age, are *riika* [agemates] and are friends always. We used to go to sleep at our house and other times at theirs, working in the *shamba* together and cooking soup for each other. After going through *Irua*, we made beauty marks on our faces by rubbing ashes into cuts we made. We also made some on the breasts so that when dancing naked, the marks made our bodies more beautiful. That was our tradition. Later, some missionaries tried to stop traditions like this, but we said, "The one who puts on a dress and goes to school is a prostitute." My father refused to let me go to school, because he said I would become a prostitute. I never felt sad about not going to school. I was happy going to dances, because I was not alone.

When I got my first menstruation after *Irua*, nobody had told me about it. I was scared when I first saw the blood, because I had never seen it there before. I went to my mother, and she told me that it was normal and it was a sign that I'm a woman so I should start taking care of myself with men.

Nowadays, girls are getting pregnant when they are still at their parents' home. This is because they have no way of knowing when they are grown-up. Girls continue to joke around with younger boys even when they are grown. Now, a boy of my son's age [twelve years old] can abuse me and give no respect. It is not like long ago, when we refused to have any dealings with anybody who was not an age-mate. And now, young uncircumcised boys are being called "men" by girls, so they feel grown-up and can joke about with the girls. All this was brought about by school and when we threw away the traditional way of becoming adults through *Irua*.

* * *

I stayed for ten years before I met my husband. During that time I was going to dances and learning how to do things around the homestead and be responsible for the house. During the night, when we were sitting around the fireplace, my grandmother would teach me things I needed to know before marrying. Above all, she said, one should be obedient to one's husband without being stubborn. Also, one must cook good food, and she taught me how to do it. During the day, I was fetching firewood, washing the children in the compound, and helping in the *shamba*.

I would think about the kind of man I wanted to marry in those days. I wanted a good man who would not wander about, a person who was able to take care of things like the goats and cows at home so that eventually we would be rich and have many things.

I first met my husband when dancing—that is where people used to meet each other. The men would later escort the girls back to their homesteads—that way, a man came to know where a girl's home was, and if he wanted a certain girl he knew where to find her. That is how my husband came to know my place, because he lived far away from where we were.

My grandmother had told me that if a man was interested in you, he would come near the granary and start blowing his nose—that is just the way it happened. One day, the husband came near our granary and blew his nose, and I went out to greet him. After talking for some time, we agreed to meet again. We met at my home many times during the next few months, then I decided to have him so I went to my father for tobacco. Later on, the proceedings started for *rūracio* between our two fathers. I never knew what they agreed that my husband should give, but when we separated he still had not paid anything to my father.

On the day he came to get me, he came alone because I had agreed to marry him. When we got to his homestead, I found nobody there because it was at night. But in the morning everybody in the compound came to see my husband's new wife. You see, I was his second wife, so they wanted to see how I looked. Wangūi, the first wife, was there, and I could tell she was not happy to see me. That scared me. Right away she started screaming and abusing me. She had known me before, but now she had different feelings because she didn't want the husband to marry another wife. He insisted. I knew that I would be the second wife, but I didn't know Wangūi would be so bothered. But I learned she had had no say in the marriage when I went there to live. So she and I were not on good terms, and we just stayed that way, abusing one another.

One day, the husband's mother gave me a new *sufuria* [Kiswahili word meaning pot] to use, but Wangūi took it from me. I was angry, but I did not show it. I never allowed our quarrels to reach the point of physically abusing each other, but we did tarnish each other's names in public. Like she might abuse me by saying that I had poisoned her children—that's a very bad insult, because it's like bringing a false witness against another. In fact, that is the worst insult one woman can give another! But the older women in the compound would intervene when we were fighting, and so we learned to just keep quiet.

When I looked at Wangũi, I saw she was not happy, and after staying there awhile, I found I was not happy either and I began to hate the husband. Neither of us wives were happy. It wasn't just that he beat us, he was irresponsible. If you have a husband who is not caring about you—so that when the children are hungry or sick he's not bothered—then you feel angry. Even when we wives began to fight, we'd ask for his help, but we didn't get it. I began blaming him for bringing me to his place.

When I first went to his place, I was staying at his mother's house, but later he built a house for me. When I moved there, I found a big change because now I was required to fetch my own firewood. Before marrying, I used to cook, but younger ones would have already fetched the firewood. [One of the duties that Watoro mentions in an earlier interview that she had to do after *Irua* and prior to marriage was gathering firewood, which contradicts what she now states.] Now I was fetching my own water and washing my own utensils and keeping the house clean all by myself. I did not like being alone to do all that.

When disagreements came up between the husband and me, people in the homestead, especially his mother and father, would bring us together to talk. Sometimes I used to be beaten, and if it was me in the wrong I would try to change and never repeat that thing again. When a wife is beaten, it is because she has not made her husband happy, so she tries to change her ways. Do they beat wives in America? No? How do you know when you are doing something wrong?

So now I stayed about one year before I had my first child. I found I was pregnant when I stayed for two months without menstruating. I was feeling very sick, and my husband called his mother when the child was ready to be born. She came and assisted me and tied the umbilical cord and washed the child in a piece of broken pot because there was no basin then. She also called "*aririri*" five times to let people know that it was a boy-child. Later, I washed and rested.

Now that I had a chid, I felt a little bit light—and older, because I realized I had become a woman. It took me about three weeks before I came out of the house, and during that time women were bringing firewood, bananas, porridge, and other food. Those at home would cook for me and came to work in my *shamba*.

Who prepared me for motherhood? It was my grandmother who told us that we should feed a child bananas, arrowroot, sweet potatoes, and porridge. All these were roasted, then chewed and fed to the child. We would see Cũcũ feed the babies, and the children grew up very big and fat, so I knew that was the right way to feed a child. She also told me that if I got children I should never mistreat them and should shape their characters by watching the types of children they moved with, and if those children were not well behaved, I should prevent mine from moving with them.

After staying in my husband's compound for awhile, a third wife came and met me there. But this one finished only one year and then went away and left us. She left because of the same kind of mistreatment and lack of care and cooperation from the husband. I never felt badly that the husband was taking another wife. I had my own *shamba* at his place and my work to do. I didn't feel jealousy—I was not interested in who he was marrying next.

By now I had two sons to care for, and then a daughter came. After the daughter, I had two more sons. But when I think of my daughter, I feel pain in my heart. There was a time when she got very sick, and there was no help that the husband would give. After some time, she died. She was five years old then. When my daughter died—that was the time I made up my mind that I would leave that place. The problem of my husband not helping me, even when the child was sick, and other things made me realize I could not stay there any longer. He wouldn't even help me take her to the hospital.

That child—the daughter—disturbed me for three months. I was always taking her to the hospital, and she was getting three injections every time I took her. Then she was admitted and only spent one week in the hospital before she died. The doctors would never tell me what disease she had, so I never learned what was the cause of her death. When the child died, I felt as if I had lost direction, and I started feeling that now I could distinguish between bad and good. You hear, when I talked to my husband, he seemed not to care and started being uncooperative. He did not like to hear me speak of the child's death or sickness. I began to see him as bad. Now I had no daughter—her death left me very weak, with no energy. Then I knew I could never stay there. I did not tell anybody, but kept quiet to wait for a time when God would help me to leave.

Then one day my father came to visit us and he saw me unhappy, so he insisted on me going back with him to our home—that was when we were just released from the villages at the end of Mau Mau. Because I had been waiting for such an opportunity, I went with him back to my home, and my problems with the husband were solved. The husband could not insist that I stay with him, because when my father asked him for the part of the *rūracio* that he had promised, the husband refused. So I returned home and now I only get the ordinary problems here.

I left the husband when my oldest child was about eight years and the youngest was newly born. When I reached home, I felt my heart grow better because the problems I had known were gone. My father gave me my brother's *shamba* to cultivate, and after awhile I began to get food for me and my children. Then after the harvesting of the coffee, which we had just started cultivating then, my father would give me a share of what we earned and I could help my children by taking them to school.

One does not always know when changes are occurring, but realizes later on that the things she is seeing are different from what they were before. You see, after I came home and these children of mine started asking me for their life necessities, I noticed there was a big change. There was nobody else they could go to for their needs except me. If they had their own father, they would have somebody else to go to. But now it is just me. At times I feel sad, but I remove the sadness by knowing in myself that I'm not waiting to marry again. When I left the husband, I decided never to marry again or even to be good friends with a man.

* * *

When my daughter died, we were living in the village—it was during the emergency. When Mau Mau started [1952], I had just married. During that time, things were hard. We were put into villages, and all around us a trench was dug and spikes were put into it, so that if one tried to jump or if one fell in the trench, that person would die. The British were trying to prevent the freedom fighters from being fed by the people in the villages—that's why the trench was dug.

We were put into a village at Kibingo. After two years we came to another one here at Karaini. Our days were hard—I would wake up at four in the morning and walk up to where the trench was being dug and get there when the sun was just coming up. We would be given the number of feet to dig, and we'd work all day and come back sometime in the afternoon. While working on the trench, the soldiers would line up, and they beat those who became lazy and were not working as fast as they wanted us to.[1]

During that time, my husband was a government soldier—he was a Home Guard. He was one of those supervising the work on the trench. He was given his portion to supervise, and sometimes I could hear him using hard words to make people work. By that time, we were not friendly, and he would not treat me as a wife but just like any other woman. When we were released from the work of the trench, or other communal work in the afternoon, then women would go running to their *shamba* to work. First, one cut maize for cooking that evening, then cultivated in a small area, then came running back to meet the deadline [curfew]. When we reached the village, there were guards already there to prevent anybody from going out at night. Because the houses were built in lines, the Home Guards would start from the first house in one line and go from house to house looking for freedom fighters—Mau Mau—and they beat the residents of the house sometimes, trying to force out any hidden fighters they might be hiding. During that time, we were being beaten and told to show where the Mau Mau were. But at the same time, supporters of Mau Mau were coming and forcing us to take the Oath, and the one who refused could be killed. If a Mau Mau came and found me cooking, I would gladly give him food, but if one refused, one could be beaten and, we heard, cut up into pieces and locked inside the house. We were in great trouble then.

Finally, when freedom came, we rejoiced because we knew that would be the end of the beatings and mistreatment. When we heard about the fighting at Nairobi, we were happy because we knew the fighting would soon be over.

Uhuru changed things, because I started seeing new things coming that were different from the old. *Maendeleo* [progress] was beginning and soon we began to forget the old days, when things were so bad. As that was the time I left my husband, I found that now I could rely upon myself to buy certain things that were becoming available—such as corregated iron sheets—that I needed in life.

*   *   *

After Mau Mau, I was raising my children on my own. Caring for your children isn't easy. When you see your children trying to take others' things, you tell him not to steal because it is bad. If the child brings something strange into the house that you haven't bought yourself and you tell him he's stealing, he might say that he's doing it for you and that makes you feel badly. Then you take him to school and pay the school fees without delay. Going to school keeps my sons out of trouble. If I see one of them moving with bad characters who are influencing them to do bad things, then I talk to that one and tell him to stop moving with such people.

Boys should be taught to be obedient and hardworking. If they are working hard at either grazing the cows or working on things around the homestead, it stops them from going and spending their days and weeks at another boy's place—it keeps them from roaming. A girl should be obedient, too—doing what she is expected to do. And she should respect others, especially the elders, and be hospitable to everybody she sees.

All of my four sons have been to school. If one is schooled, it is a good thing because he can read signposts and know where he is. And after school, with the help of God, one can be employed and have a good job. My firstborn reached Standard Seven [seventh grade] and the next born reached Form Two [second year of high school]. But the younger ones you see here working with me in the *shamba*, one is in Standard Four and the other is in Standard Five. The reason the first-born dropped out after Standard Seven is because we had less money for school fees. Before there was school, we used to exercise our brains by playing games and singing songs and trying to learn from our parents the things they were doing. But now, children need school to better their lives. This is because a schooled person can read, so he knows where there are jobs by finding them in the newspaper.

Yes, I have observed that those who have been to school know how to get a job. Like now, if you and I walked together into a office seeking a certain job and you are schooled and I am not, you will be taken and, me, I will be left behind. Those who live in a place like Kagumo should finish up Form Two, because that is the level of education needed to bring progress here. If people want more money they can still go on to Form Four, but I think Form Two is enough. And today, it's just as important for a girl to go to school as a boy.

When we were children, all of the girls knew they would marry, and so we did not need school. But today a girl may get pregnant before she marries and have to get a job to feed her children. If she happens to get pregnant and there is no husband, she will have to depend upon her parents to feed and take care of her children, or she will find a job.

When I married, a woman got a *shamba* from the husband—not just one piece but several pieces in different places. One plot would be for maize and beans, another for sweet potatoes. Each kind of food needed a different soil and amount of water. But now women have only two or three plots, and women without husbands must depend on their parents to give them land to cultivate for their children. I grow maize and beans in two different places, but it is barely enough to feed my sons and their wives and children. No, the older sons do not cultivate at their father's *shamba*. They stay here with me. If my daughter had lived and she had no husband she would be living here, too. Sometimes I worry about how all these children will be fed.

* * *

During our time there was a big change when a woman's first-born got circumcised and there was a lot of feasting. The woman had her head shaved completely and became an elder. But today, there is nothing like that being done. No woman's head is shaved nor does she get *ngoni* in her ears. That ceremony for elders is gone. Awhile back, I finished with menstruation. I had a lot of headaches and chills for a time, but I felt happy because God brought menstruation to an end. I was not in need of it anymore.

Now that I am a grandmother, I find there is a difference between being a mother and a grandmother. Take this child here [grandson in her lap], I never chew roasted bananas for him and I can only give him the food left by his mother. If it is porridge, I feed it to him using a cup. If my grandchildren fall asleep, I take them to bed. A long time ago, you know, one used to carry a baby everywhere one went. I try and teach my grandchildren some things—like this girl here, she is learning how to peel potatoes by watching me. And if I happen to see any of these children doing something bad, I will stop them. They have to obey what I say. Their mothers are too busy working in the *shamba* to watch them all the time. When my sons—the ones in primary school—are home, they take care of the older children, but these two small ones need their mothers or me. And now one of my sons' wives is pregnant.

It is good to have many children, but we do not have as much land as we used to and this means problems. When there is a good harvest we have plenty of maize, but when the rains do not come we have to go and buy maize from the market, and then there is less money for school fees. Do I think my daughters-in-law should use family planning? No! I have heard a woman can bleed to death from taking those pills. It is God's will to have as many children as one is given.

* * *

When did I become a Catholic? When I was a mother with grown children. It was just recently when the old church was being reopened. The reason I joined is that my mother had joined, and she found her life better. As you know, "Where the goat goes, the kid also follows." Another reason is that my conscience convinced me to leave worldly things alone and join the church. I guess you could say that it is the Spirit that called and directed me there.

Before I started going to church, if I went along the road and somebody abused me, I would abuse that person back. If one started talking to me in dirty language, I would reply and not be ashamed. But now, if somebody comes and starts abusing me, I just let her continue until she gets tired without abusing her back. The church teaches good things—like we mothers are told to respect our children, and in turn they will respect us. When you do it, you see it's true. I never joined the Catholic Women's Group or any other women's group, but I did join the adult education class for a short time. Then I had to stop because the work at home got to be too much. That's the same reason why I can't join a women's group—I have too much work.

I first heard about the adult education class about eight years ago when it was announced by the government. When the teachers for the class came to Karaini, we learned through rumors that we were required to go. I finally joined last year so I could learn how to read and write my name. I went for one month only. If I had continued I would have learned how to write my name. But one is really helped only after completing something to the end. If one leaves it halfway, she does not get as much help from it—isn't that so?

The adult education class was just here in Karaini. If I had been coming from here at my home, it would have been a short distance. But I was coming from way down at the *shamba*, and it is quite a distance to walk. If I started class at four o'clock, then I reached home late.

When I get home, I go running to the river for water, then cook, and by the time I'm through, there's no time left for me to attend class. I can see that it has helped others because they are able to read books and write their names, but I didn't have time with all the work.

If I had to choose between joining a women's self-help group and the adult education class, I would choose the women's group because there one learns good things from one another and the money given each woman enables her to help herself by buying things she needs. If I had enough money, I would not always be worrying about school fees. I would also buy a cow so we would have milk for the children.

*   *   *

Six years ago, my father died—that was a big change for me. When I separated from the husband and when my father died—those were when I changed the most. My father never got sick. We had spent the day together here on the *shamba*, and then he went to take beer in Kagumo. When he came home, he started vomiting, and when he was taken to hospital he never recovered. He died the following morning. It was hard to believe that he died, because it had been my father who had helped me and it meant that now I would have to start helping myself alone. When he died, I started having many thoughts, especially when my children started growing older and needed clothes, food, and above all, schooling. Now there is nobody to help except me. I have been thinking a lot about these things lately.

Of all the roles I've had, the most important are cultivating, fetching water and firewood, and being a good mother. Next is being a good wife. After that comes being a daughter, then a student—that is least important, but it never ends.

My greatest accomplishment is that I have built an iron sheet roof for my house and have moved out of my grass-thatched house. This kind of roof is better because the gutters catch the rainwater and it runs into the petrol drum, so we don't have to make so many trips to the river. Also, a thatched house has to be repaired every year but *mabati* lasts longer.

At times I dream of coming to cultivate here and producing a lot of food crops. Other times I dream I'm holding bundles of money notes and I'm laughing. I normally feel sad when I wake from this dream and discover that I don't have anything. I like it that I am self-sufficient with the use of my *kibanga*, my *kiondū*, and my *mūkwa*. They help me to keep myself and the children fed. The only thing I don't like about myself is that if I abuse anybody and they abuse me, I find it difficult to ever talk to that person again. I see this as bad, but there is no way I can change it.

Womanhood means to me taking care of one's things at home and caring for the children. It means supporting the children and home together. Being Agīkũyũ means knowing that I generated from Gikuyu and Mumbi, the first man and first woman of the Agīkũyũ.

Now it is starting to rain, and we better run from here [*shamba*] to Wambura's before that machine of yours gets wet. It's always good when it rains after cultivating—like a blessing.

Note

1. Kenyan writer Ngũgĩ wa Thiong'o has described a similar scene in his novel *A Grain of Wheat* (1967).

An older woman with matū *and* mbuci *in her ears and a ridge left in the top of her head where the tumpline has been placed over years of carrying heavy loads.*

5

Wangeci's Story:
A Widow Among Women

Unlike Watoro, Wangeci has access to her husband's land because she is a widow. Her status allows her to remain on her husband's land, which she has increased in value over the years through tea cultivation. Her monogamous marriage to a man who encouraged her to be self-sufficient helped prepare Wangeci for widowhood. In addition, Wangeci is actively involved in two women's groups, unlike Wamutira and Watoro. My choice of a widow was based upon prior counseling experience in the United States, which led me to postulate that the death of a spouse among Gikuyu might be a transformative experience—one leading to new self-perceptions, knowledge, and skills. Wangeci's case is illustrative.

Of the four women in their fifties, Wangeci has achieved the most in developing her homestead. She began by building a timber house with cement floors and a corregated iron sheet roof. During the time I was there, she was having a well dug so that she and her daughters-in-law will no longer be dependent upon fetching water from a stream. Wangeci is proud of the accomplishments acquired through her own hard work.

The word that comes to mind in describing Wangeci is "industrious." She is a small woman with the boundless energy of a hummingbird. During our sessions her hands were never still—she was weaving a basket, peeling potatoes for the family's lunch, or pulling up buckets of mud from the borehole that would soon become the well.

Wangeci agreed to become one of my "teachers" because she felt that God had chosen her for such a role. Her narrative accounts were well organized and full of detailed description often told with a sense of humor. She illustrated particular events in her life by donning attire appropriate to the occasion and acting out the scene with whatever props she could find. To simulate the circumcision scene, she donned an approximation of the circumciser's costume and then staged my research assistant and me as initiates and demonstrated how the circumciser had leaped toward each girl with her knife three times. The effect was highly convincing!

Wangeci demonstrates a keen sense of self-awareness that enabled her during our sessions to view her own life-span development in relation to that of her cultural group. She perceives herself as unusual rather than typical of Gikuyu women, partly because of her status as a widow and partly as a result of her own personality. Of all the women, Wangeci is the most goal-oriented. She likes setting specific economic-related goals and then works hard to meet them. Halfway through the sessions she let me know that her next objective was to buy a sewing machine for a son trained as a tailor. She wanted my help in selecting one. I gathered the information and at the end of our sessions took her to Nairobi for the final purchase. This, then, is "the widow's tale."

—J.D.

I was named Wangeci for my father's mother because it was me who gave birth to my father. I was the firstborn and our clan is Ũnjiru. My father, Gacoki, was a brown man who was very hard working in the *shamba*. I can remember him bringing food to us children when we were herding the goats and cows. My father died when I was about ten.

My mother, Kaguu, who was the second wife of my father, is a jolly woman. Even now if you were to meet her, you would not think she is my mother—you would think we are of the same age. Besides my mother, there was my father's first wife, called Wambura. We shared everything with her children—it was as if we were all children of the same mother. And our mothers liked each other's children as their own.

Another woman who lived in our compound and was important to us as children was our grandmother—the co-wife of my father's mother—because I never met my real grandmother. We always called this woman *Cũcũ*, but her name was Wakarira. She was most responsible for me. You know, at that time, all children were left with the grandmother and older children during the day when the mothers went to the *shamba*. *Cũcũ* was a hardworking brown woman who was jolly with children.

I was the oldest child in my family. There was a boy who followed me, but he died when he was about four. Then Mwai, my brother, was born. My mother was pregnant with Mwai when my father died. Njeru, the next born, and my sister Muthoni are from relationships my mother had with other men after my father died. Mwai was about six years [old] when Njeru was born. I was responsi-

Figure 5.1 WANGECI'S FAMILY

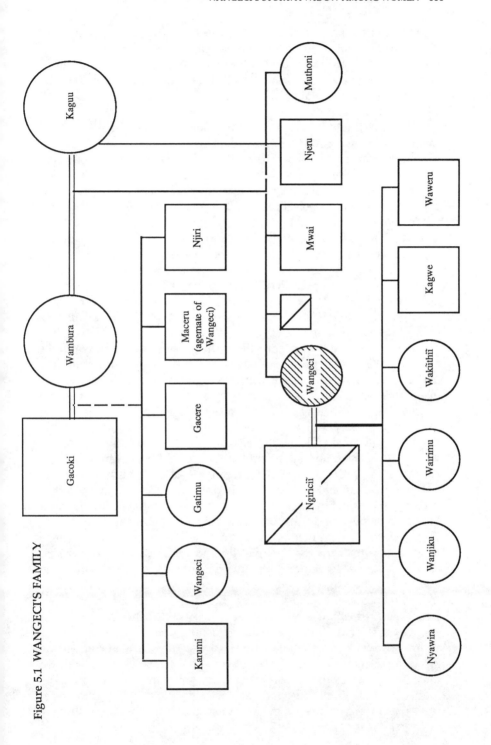

ble for looking after the younger ones. But Maceru, who was my age-mate and the son of my older mother called Wambura, would help because he had to look after his brother, Njiri. The older children of Wambura were all big by the time I can remember them. Karumi, the firstborn, was in the Italian war [World War II]; Gacere, the next, was working; and Wangeci was married.

My grandmother taught me many things growing up—like how to fetch water in a gourd and how to fetch wood. But it was my mother who taught me who I was related to. She would wake me up one morning and tell me, "Today, I'm going to take you to your Uncle So-and-so's." Then she would put things into a basket for me to carry, and we'd go to my uncle's place. When we reached there she would tell me how I was related to each person there.

Was I raised differently from my brothers? Yes. When you are small, everyone sleeps together in the mother's house. But as you reach a certain age, around five or six, your brother cannot sleep in your mother's bed anymore. Then boys go to their father's *thingira*. You, being a girl, stay at your mother's, learning what women do. When eating, the boy's food is carried to the father's house, but you stay with your mother.

When we were young, sometimes the girls used to wish we could be boys. We would pretend that we were *anake* [young men] and make beer from maize-stalk juices and then divide ourselves up—some being "men" and others "women," as the older married people did, and then we'd drink "beer" and laugh a lot. We would make small houses to play in, but we never did sexual imitations. Even if a boy came and tried to raise one's dress to see the thighs, one would run and tell her father and that boy would be beaten.

After my father died, I started staying alone quietly under the granary. Sometimes I would cry, thinking of all the things my father used to do for us. I thought that he would come to life again, but then I realized he never would. Now my mother and I were alone.

My father's death changed my way of looking at things because now I came to learn that people die and it's not that they are just asleep. Also, his death brought a lot of changes in my life because the good things he used to do for us children came to an end. He used to roast bananas and yams for us and chew them so we could eat them when we were small—that was good. He would bring clotted blood and cook it for us when the men had taken blood from the cows. When we went to herd goats and cows when we were bigger, he brought food to us to eat where we were herding. So after he died, we never went far to graze, for we did not have anybody to bring us food. Sometimes, the cows and goats would go and feed in other people's *mashamba* because we'd leave them alone when we got hungry and went to find something to eat. Then those people would become angry.

After my father died, I could see my mother with nobody to help her now. She would take a hoe and go and dig in her *shamba* by herself, take the cows to the river and feed them and other things. I remembered this later, and when I became a widow and I knew that I, too, would have to do things for myself.

* * *

As children, we had many games we used to play when we were not helping our mothers. There was one where we used a broken piece of pot and drew lines in a rectangle on the ground. We'd divide the rectangle into two smaller rectangles at each end, then draw two crossed lines [creating four diagonals] in the center part. [At this point in the interview, Wangeci got up from the stool she was sitting on and drew lines on the ground with a stick to show what the game pattern looked like.] Now, you take a stone or broken piece of pot and throw it into the first square and then hop over it with one leg. On the way back, while still hopping, you have a kick the stone out. [The game is similar to hopscotch.] Another game we played is *ciũthi*. We used to collect stones, then throw one up in the air, catching it with the same hand before it touches the ground. We'd start with one, then two, three, four, up to five. Then we'd try and throw them all up in the air and catch them on the backs of our hands without spilling any.

We learned riddles from our grandmother. "Catch a riddle," she'd say. And we'd tell her we were ready—here's one for you.

Mwarĩ mũtune rwarĩ.   A red daughter in the field.

You don't know? It is easy. If you don't know, you say, "Take all my cows," as a way of paying for not knowing the answer. Here's the answer:

Kirayo kia njahi.   Blossoms of peas.

[At this point, I had the uncomfortable feeling of a student in a classroom who has missed the answer to an obvious question. However, when given the answer, it was easy to see how beautifully the problem cast as a metaphor fit the context of peas in bloom.]

* * *

Usually when a child was about five or six, a ceremony to remove the child from her/his mother's bed took place. But for me, it didn't happen until I was about eleven, because my father had died so it was not necessary for me to have a *rūkoro*. A goat was slaughtered and its skin was dried in the sun to spread out for my bed. But I don't remember *mambura ma twana* as being a big occasion like *mbuci*. It usually happened when the mother wanted to get another child. It meant she could resume sexual relations with her husband. During those times, a woman would not have sexual relations while she was suckling a child, and we used to suckle our children for three to four years. It's not like now when women are having babies almost every year. We had our own kind of family planning then.

My mother and grandmother were the ones who taught me good behaviors as I was growing up. *Cūcū* told me, "Bad things have no product in a good life"—that is one of the wise sayings the elders gave us. Bad things are like standing on the road and abusing people or getting into somebody's house when they are not around and removing something from there. Good people are those who are obedient to their parents and grow up listening to them and the advice they give.

I remember one time, I removed a gourd from the granary and went to the river with it. I fetched water and on the way back I broke it, but I did not say anything when I reached home. So when my mother discovered the broken gourd she beat me because I had hidden it and not told the truth. That time I learned that hiding the truth can be bad. Among Agĩkũyũ we say that cheating somebody is like killing them, because if they found you had cheated them they could very easily stab you with a knife.

Cūcū used to say, "An obedient child eats his/her mother and father." By this she meant that when you obey your parents and respect them, all they have saved for you in the future will be yours. She used to send us to get something from a neighbor's house, and she would put saliva on her hand and warn us, "If the saliva dries up before you have returned, you will surely die." So we'd run fast. We learned to obey.

Sometimes *Cūcū* would tell us stories at night in her house around the cooking fire. We were never told stories during the day because hyenas would come and eat us—that is what we were told. If we happened to mention stories during the day, *Cūcū* would tell us to touch the three firestones that make the fireplace to prevent the hyenas from coming.

Though my grandmother taught us many things, I learned how to weave baskets from my mother. She used *migio* [type of bush] when I was very young, and then later she began using sisal. *Cūcū* made baskets out of *ngutwii* [stinging nettle fibers]. I would sit on the ground and watch my mother and grandmother carefully to see all that they did, including *gwokotha* [process of rolling plant fibers together to make strings]. But me, I started making baskets using banana fibers because they were easier to use. I collected those that were left after feeding the cows and tried making a basket. Then my mother would help me. She started the basket and I watched how she did it, then I did it just the same way. Sometimes, when the *migio* trees were pruned, we would peel off the red bark and make strings from it. The red strings were used as decoration. Sometimes strings were dyed with soot to make a black design. My mother showed me how to collect soot from a blackened cooking pot to decorate a basket.

We started to make baskets from *migio* strings just before we were circumcised. We used to spend a lot of time with a *migio* plant trying to get string from it, then drying the string for *gwothoka*. We learned how to *gwothoka* well and made small baskets that looked like a bird's nest. But in those times, women did not make sisal ropes for carrying things [tumplines], because our ropes then were cow's hide cut into thin strips and then joined to make a *mūkwa*. It was as we were growing up, learning how to weave, that we began to think about going for *mbuci* and *matū*.

*　*　*

When my agemates began to have their ears pierced *mbuci* and then *matū*, they told me not to follow them around. I went to *Cūcū* and told her what they had said. She said it was because I did not have my ears pierced, and she went and told my father to brew beer so I could take it to my uncle to get permission for *mbuci*. [When Wangeci refers to "father," she means her father's younger brother. Brothers to one's father are called "*Baba*"—father. "Uncle," in this case, refers to her mother's brother.] It was not the Agīkūyū tradition to ask permission for *mbuci* from where the child was born, but from the oldest uncle's home where the mother came from.

When my oldest uncle agreed and gave permission, I went to have my ears pierced *mbuci*. Before we had our ears pierced our heads were shaved with a knife—*kienji*—all around the edges, with hair left in the center. It was *Cūcū* who shaved me. At that time, too, our mothers' heads were shaven, but not completely because none of them had a child who was circumcised yet. It was another grandmother, called Waturi, who did the piercing at the top of the ear using a sharpened stick of an acacia tree. After the piercing, castor oil was smeared in the holes and sticks were put in. *Cūcū* would change the sticks about every four days for me until the holes were healed. I don't remember that the piercing hurt—it was just something one did to show she had reached another stage of life.

When *mbuci* healed, *matũ* were cut in the lower lobes. There were many children there watching us have our ears cut, but no grown people. By watching us, the younger girls would know what to expect when they reached our age. I didn't cry, but I squeezed my eyes shut. It hurt, but the pain has faded in my mind.

After *matũ* healed, big sticks were put in the holes. They were wider than your earring [over an inch in diameter] and made of wood or curved stone. Sometimes a cassava—when it was still fresh—was cut and kept and dried in the sun and put in. Once put in, the earplugs would shine from far away and one looked very beautiful and people would talk about how beautiful so-and-so's daughter looked. Another kind of earplug was black. These were called *ndebe*. They had holes in the center and were wide at both ends like a spool of thread. They were put in by rolling them over the drooping lobe of the ear so that when a girl danced, the *ndebe* jingled.

After piercing the ears, one knows that she has left the childish things behind. I began removing myself from the childish games and began acting more grown-up, because now the days were being counted for me to go for *Irua*. *Irua* was the most important ceremony among our people. Between *matũ* and *Irua*, I was not allowed to go to the forest to dance but could only dance outside the houses and was careful not to be involved in any sexual relations. You see, I was being prepared for the time when I would become an adult. There were so many of our agemates from the whole village who moved together, abusing [in this case Wangeci means "teasing"] one another and sharing our secrets. We were very playful. But then an elderly lady came and if she suspected we were becoming loose in our ways, she took us in a mother's house and made us sit down with our legs apart so she could look at us. I can remember her doing it once. She was investigating our private parts to see which ones were becoming sexually involved. Knowing that she would investigate us kept us from becoming active sexually. Even up to the time of marriage, after *Irua*, the older women would keep an eye on us like that.

After staying for some time, *Cũcũ* went to my father [father's younger brother, who was the head of the family] and told him that I looked suitable for *Irua* and asked if he could make the necessary arrangements. This was before I had begun menstruating. If your first period came before going to *Irua*, it was a bad omen, and your father would not be given the first goat during the *rũracio* negotiations when you married.

After eight gourds of beer were taken to my uncle, I went to his place and was given a goat and a cow. These were taken home by the women from my clan.[1]

I learned about *Irua* from my two grandmothers—the mothers to my father and mother. They sat down with me and told me that it was time I got circumcised before I got any bigger. They told me it was the Agĩkũyũ tradition—to mark the end of childhood and the beginning of adulthood. One had to undergo *Irua* to be separated from the other children. To Agĩkũyũ, nobody could carry out a sacrifice unless that person was circumcised. We say, "A goat which has not shed blood cannot offer a sacrifice." It means that, like the goat, the person has not yet shed blood.

After taking beer to my uncle's place to get permission, he told my mother and father [father's younger brother] to make some more beer so he could go to their home to drink it there. Then my father took over the preparations. He told the women in our homestead to go for sugarcane, and the following day the juice was removed from the sugarcane and it was used to make beer.

The way women prepared sugarcane for beer is that once the stalks were cut, they would be *gũkiro* [passed over a piece of hard metal that had percolations all over it], so that thin thread-like pieces of sugarcane were left. Then the thin threads were put in a skin bag filled with water and put in a hole in the earth. Young men would remove the threads and press them into a ball. They tied the ball with strings and started draining the juices from the sugarcane threads into the skin by tying the strings tighter and tighter until the threads became dry, hard, and white. The juice left in the skin bag was now ready to be put into *itumbi* [huge egg-shaped gourds]. The women strained the juice, using leaves from an acacia, as it was poured into the *itumbi*. I can remember women doing this. The *muratina* [a special bean pod that was a fermenting agent] from a tree was added to the sugarcane juice, and the huge gourds were put near a cooking fire—all around it—to cook. The heat of the fire helped *muratina* to release its juices, which mixed with the sugarcane juice. The women had to keep the cooking fire going all day so the juices would boil. It took one whole day, sometimes two, and by the next day the beer was ready.[2]

When the beer was ready, a boy was sent to tell my uncle. He called his clanmates, and they came to drink the beer. When they got drunk, they would start singing *Irua* songs as a way of showing that they were giving permission. Just before going home, the uncle set the date for *Irua* eighteen days from that time.

During the next eighteen days, you could hear women singing the *Irua* songs. These songs could only be sung at this time, and they were naughty. [At this point Wangeci burst into laughter, and when I pressed her for details, she described them in only general terms.] They were songs about intercourse and things like that, which you didn't hear talked about ordinarily.

When the day came for circumcision, I was told to go to my uncle's place for the blessings called *karathiro*. We went singing slowly to his homestead, and on reaching the gate, I was hidden in between the women of my clan so nobody would see me. So we entered the homestead that way and were singing.

When we reached the place in front of my uncle's house, I started singing:

Nĩndutangĩrũo	Bring out for me quickly
Ndĩwamathiĩ.	I am in a hurry.
Ndĩwamagendera.	I am on a journey
Na ngũndio iria	And give me some milk
Gũtihindi ciomire maitũ	For my mother could not have come from a place
Ita ciaraga.	Where cows never calf.

When my uncle heard me singing this song, he came out of his *thingira* holding a goat, and he gave it to me to take back home. He also gave me four shillings and his wife gave me two shillings. Afterwards, they brought sour porridge that they had made for the women of my clan who escorted me there, and, I can tell you, those women enjoyed it. After they had taken the porridge, we started the journey back to my home with all those who were at my uncle's homestead accompanying us. At home, the dancing continued all day up until the time we should go to the field.

Slightly before three in the afternoon, all the girls going for *Irua* were taken to the river to wash. We washed together with the women from our clan. Then one woman, who was a young bride with only one child who came from my father's family, carried me on her back so that I would not touch the ground back up to my home to dress for the ceremony. The reason a young bride carried me is that they had been carried by young brides of the mother's family to the homestead when they were married. So, during *Irua*, it was time for them to do it for somebody else.

Why wasn't I allowed to touch the ground after being washed? To keep me clean and pure—it was the clan's way of showing appreciation for one of their girls who is maturing. When I reached home, a *mũndũ mugo* was there, and he put a mark on my face from the forehead around to the chin and back up on the other side with *iria*—a white, chalklike substance that signified mother's milk, because it was as if we were being reborn—this time as adults. Then I was dressed with beads on top and a *thira* and two pieces of cloth called *retho* tied around the shoulders, so that when I was swinging the beads against my breasts on the way to the field where we were to be circumcised, the clan would be happy because I wasn't shaming them. During the operation, the *thira* and *retho* were removed, except where a girl had big breasts—then her circumcision mother would leave the *retho* covering her.

When we got to the field, it was crowded with people who had come to see the girls get circumcised. The men from the clan were chasing away those near the girls until a distance was made between the girls and the crowd. So the people were surrounding the girls with old women on the inside, then the rest behind them. Of course, children were there, but if any misbehaved they were carried away. At the center of the circle were the candidates for *Irua*, who made a line like we plant maize nowadays. Men, women, boys, and girls were all singing as the girls took their places in the center. They were songs like:

Aya yoi ĩĩ ndirĩ ndũgũ	I have no relations
no mũthuri ũnyitĩrĩire mwana.	only the old man who is holding my child.

I had been eager to go for *Irua* so I could become a mature girl like the ones at home and be loved like them. I also wanted to be able to wear beads and have my sheet smeared with oil and acquire a *mũthuru* [a skirt with slits] and finally be able to go to dances. So I was not afraid of the pains I had heard people say were experienced during *Irua*—I was excited and eager.

When the circumciser came into the circle, she was dressed in two sheets, one tied on one shoulder and the other tied with a knot in front. She came hopping and jumping toward us, holding her *kienji*. She would make the first cut, then go back again and come jumping forward again to make another cut. Each of us were cut three times—first one side of the clitoris, then the other side and in the middle so that a V-shaped [triangular] wound was left where the clitoris had been. By the third time, the circumciser would get set in her work, and those girls who were cowards were screaming and crying. Usually, a circumciser was given three shillings for doing her work, but the parents of a girl who screamed and shitted in the field had to give the circumciser a goat, too.

If a girl cried or screamed, the others in the line could beat her after the operation. And later, when we went home and were healed and started visiting each other, she was given the leftovers to eat. Each girl in our *riika* would leave some little food for her and after all of us had eaten we would put the leftovers together in a calabash and give them to her. She would never eat from a full calabash when visiting us.

Where I got circumcised at Karaini, there were only two of us—Wambaca and me. We were the first in our age group to go through *Irua*. When I sat down, after spreading my *mathangu* [leaves] , I was held by my two supporters. One was my older grandmother, called Ngunju, and the other was my "sister." I call her sister because she was a grandmother where I was born [one of Wangeci's grandfather's co-wives]. Among Agĩkũyũ, a grandmother can be your sister because your mother can have a daughter who is your sister and was named for the grandmother. So your sister and she have the same name. The one I call sister was like a mother to me—that's why I chose her to be one of my supporters. Both of those women held me while I was being circumcised—one from behind, sitting down with her legs over mine, and the other holding my hands. But when the circumciser came jumping toward me, I was not watching.

I had been told by my supporter to look away so I wouldn't see the circumciser and become frightened. So I was looking up at the sky. The first thing I felt was a sharp pain like fire—just like you feel when you cut yourself badly with a *kibanga*. Then I felt my body numb and did not feel pain again until three days after the operation, when the wound got pus. But when the circumciser was doing her cutting, I was brave and did not cry. I was the one circumcised first, and as I had been brave, the other girl braved herself and also didn't cry. She knew I would beat her if she did.

Though there were only two of us that time, sometimes there are many. Another day, at Kariko, there were eighteen girls who got circumcised and six others who were circumcised near where the primary school is now. At that one, two girls cried. So those who got circumcised earlier went out and started beating the two who had cried until we were bribed by the girls' supporters not to beat them again. They gave us a bamboo container containing castor oil, which was used for medicine in those days.

The two of us who were circumcised together, we never showed our pain—even if you met us you would never know. When you realize that men, boys, girls, and women are watching you, you make yourself brave and afterwards get up and walk home even though you are feeling weak. I would not want the people to see me as a coward. Not even my supporters were helping me walk home. I wanted to show people that now I was mature and could endure pain.

When I reached home, before going into the house, I was told to hold a goat by my mother, and she gave me six shillings. Usually it is the father who gives the girl a goat, but because my father was not alive then, my mother gave it to me. After entering the house, I slept first. Then I was given sour porridge to drink and ate potatoes and bananas mashed together. Later, I was taken behind the house by my mother, and a leaf that the circumciser had put on the wound was removed and I was washed with warm water. A piece of old soft blanket was smeared with castor oil and put on the wound. It took only one month for me to heal.

After it was over, I felt that now I was a mature girl. Then I started waiting for my first menstruation. Others treated me differently. Because I was growing big breasts and was circumcised, they started to respect me and treat me like a grown person.

Irua taught me how to move from childhood to womanhood. It helped me to leave my childish ways and start acting like a grown-up. There was nothing that was as important as *Irua* during our time, because after *Irua* one learned how to act and behave like a mature person. Today, one is born, but she does not pierce her ears like we did and she does not go for *Irua*. Where does she shed her childhood acts and behaviors? She grows with them, matures with them, and even marries with them. Her acts are childish. She is not clever, nor is she mature in her mind.

Irua was our tradition. There was the time for women to go for *Irua* and so we did. It had much meaning, as it was a way of doing what the ancestors had done. It was a way of staying part of them. *Irua* was a tradition and something one just did—just as we eat every day and never stop to think about it.

Irua has no meaning to Agĩkũyũ girls today because now they have become people of a different culture. The only important thing to them is schooling—to pass or fail. After marrying, they carry the childhood behavior to their new homes. Take this girl I have here [granddaughter, aged 14], she is now mature enough to go for *Irua*, but I can't bother to take her because her mother would not like any mention of it. I wouldn't want her to go either because it has no meaning nowadays—it is useless.

There is nothing that can take the place of *Irua* to help a girl make the transition from girlhood to womanhood today. Big girls who are grown and mature are playing with girls of their daughters' age. There is no separation of age groups. You can see a girl swinging her hips in front of her father and mother nowadays. During our time, when my father was alive, I could never bend to pick up anything or do work when he was around because I would not like him to see my thighs. Even when sitting in the kitchen, I would never sit in a way to show my thighs. I would pull down my skirt to cover my knees. Today [Wangeci goes into an adjacent room and comes out dressed in a short, tight-fitting dress], a girl is washing clothes or dishes in a basin, and she bends with her back to her father and does not feel ashamed to continue washing, showing her father her naked thighs!

At times, young girls come here and ask me questions that we would have never asked an older woman—like how one becomes pregnant. I tell them one has to wait and see for herself. And if a girl gets pregnant, the only thing I can advise her is never to take abortion tablets, for if you take them you will surely die. Now younger women are getting two or three children, but they come close together. Us, we would get the number one was able to get, but we never got another until the smallest one was three or four years and able to be a little independent—until it was weaned. We would space them out that way.

Even if we tried to change back to the old ways, everything would go up in the air—it would have no meaning. In my time, one's *riika*mates were important, but today *mariika* have no importance to younger women. For us, they still have meaning. Like the woman called Wambaca in Karaini that went for *Irua* with me, we still help each other. If I'm in any need I call her, and she gathers people and comes to help me in the *shamba*. When my daughter got married she paid for most of the photos taken, and when her sons get married I will help her with the same. She also came and helped me with preparations for my daughter's wedding—like what to cook and buying the gifts. Sometimes, we give advice to each other when one knows more than the other. Like after my husband died, Wambaca came and said, "Now that your husband is dead, if I were you, I would not have another child by any other man and would only look after the ones your husband left." So I felt advised. But now, a younger woman will talk and joke with a man—even a younger one. In our case, those who were younger than us, if we met with them, we had our own way of greeting them that showed the separation between our ages. Now, it is different.

*   *   *

After *Irua*, I stayed for only one year before I got my first menstrual period. Because I was not at my father's home, I got a handful of soil and went and threw it under my bed at home. *Cūcū* had told me that when one was expecting menstruation, her body would start feeling tired and lazy, and after a day or two one would see a flow of blood. If that happened at another girl's homestead and not ours, I should take a handful of soil from that girl's homestead and go throw it under her bed at her home to make it appear that I had started menstruating at home and not at another's.

Cūcū also told me to stay in the house while I was having *mambura* [menstruation]. So I stayed there, and when *Cūcū* noticed that I was not moving out she came and asked me why and I told her. She told me not to go anywhere until the bleeding had stopped. There was nothing we used to cover ourselves with—no cloth—so we just

sat on a stool, bleeding. The stool on which one sat while menstruating was not kept in the open where anybody could sit on it because it
was considered unclean [contaminated]. Because I did not have my
father, there was a hole dug for me to sit over as with other girls. I
was with my mother only, so the other children did not know what
was happening. When it was finished, Cūcū fetched some water for
me from the river and after washing myself and my clothes, I washed
the stool and then threw it under the bed where it was kept.
Afterwards, I was given oil to apply to my body, and that day I spent
at home. The following day, I could go out and visit my friends.

I started to take care of myself where men were concerned. Cūcū
and my mother had told me not to move with men, because now a
man might spoil me for nothing and then I might end up being a
mūkoma ndi [unmarried pregnant woman] if I got pregnant while at
my father's place. Then I would never have the chance of being someone's first wife.

It was during this time of being young circumcised women that
we began to make ourselves more beautiful. When we were younger,
we had had our two bottom teeth cut out with a knife and stick once
the new ones grew in. Now we would file the upper ones, curving
them to make them look better. We would also make these marks you
see here [short, dark vertical lines on the cheekbones—cicatures] with
a razor and then put in soot from a cooking pot. Also we put marks
on the breasts because we used to dance half-naked, and our breasts
were very straight and so they were beautiful when we danced. We
never thought of ourselves as "naked." Even now, women go about
naked because of the dresses they wear that show their legs.

The marks on our breasts were made using the inside of the
maize stalk that covers the kernels. A small piece was cut and one
side was covered with saliva to make it stick to the upper part of the
breast here. Then the other side was lit with fire and when it healed it
left a raised place. Yes, it was painful, but you did not feel it so much
because you wanted it done to look beautiful.

During this time we were going to dances. We would spend the
day dancing and even we could decide to spend the night at a thingira and nothing would happen. We would go to the thingira of a
mwanake kiumbi [a handsome, well-liked young man]. Before we went
there we would tie our clothes with a rope. We would get one edge of
the skirt at the front and tie it between the legs and round each thigh
with the rope—that way you were protecting yourself. We would
spend the whole night at this young man's house being turned over
by him on the bed. He would only touch our breasts and nowhere
else. At times, we would be so many on the bed that the man would
ask his friend to come and help. But if we disliked the friend, we

would not let him touch us. The *mwanake kiumbi* was the one who was a good leader in songs, who was the best dancer, had a nice voice, and cracked a lot of jokes, and was handsome. When we went to that man's house, we would never go back home until very early in the morning. The mothers would not see us at all—that was our way of giving them respect.

I kept going to dances for a long time before I got married. It is not like now when a man comes to a girl's place one day and the next day they get married—no, it took years. Many used to come and visit, and I would go meet others at dances. That is the way I saw my husband—there in the dances.

He did not know our home, so he asked his friends. Then he came near the granary in our homestead and stood there. Us, we were in the kitchen giving stories and cracking jokes—making a lot of noise. Then he started blowing his nose for the first time. My mother heard it and told us to keep quiet. When we did, we heard him blow his nose again. We kept quiet and he blew it a third time—like this [she covers one nostril with her thumb and blows loud]. Our mother told me to go and see who was there, because I was the only girl in the kitchen with the women.

I went, and after seeing who it was I asked him why he had come. He told me, "To visit." I asked, "To visit whom?" Then he told me, "To visit you." He thought I would not mind. Because it was the first day he visited, I did not ask him a lot of questions. I told him to go in peace and that he should not be abused—meaning that he was welcome to come again.

He stayed for three days without coming back and on the fourth day he came again. He did the same thing, blowing his nose. Because I knew who it was, I went out to see him. We talked awhile, and then he left. After the fourth time of visiting me this way, my mother asked, "This man who is always coming here, who is he and what does he want?" I told her about him.

The next time he came, I asked him who he was—his mother, his father, and his clan, all the particulars, even if I knew them already. I knew that if he was really interested he would come another day and tell me what he had been told by his parents, and I would tell him what I was told by mine. Then the friendship [relationship] would be established. When we had done that and he had gone and told his parents about my parents and clan, he came back and said that our clans intermarry.

From then on, he began watching my steps—when I was cultivating, he would send a group to come and see how much I could work to know if I was hardworking or lazy. He even watched to see if I stayed at home and did not wander. He did this until he learned about me fully. Finally, he came one day and asked for tobacco. I went for it from my father [father's younger brother] and gave it to him. If I had not liked him, I would have told him to go away. He took the tobacco to his father, and his father told him to make some beer to take to my father to pay him back for the tobacco. That is how we used to get married—not like today when a boy loves a girl, they go to his home and she starts cooking for him right away.

Before I met my husband, I had an idea that I wanted a man who took good care of his father's things. He had to be productive in the *shamba* and know how to take good care of a person. Knowing a man sexually was not in our thinking until the time when one was official-ly married. But if he turned out to be sexually inactive at that time, we would not hide our displeasure—we would leave the man in broad daylight and return home. The reason is that as you are a woman, you would not want to stay married to one who is a woman like you. Sometimes, a woman would stay for the first year after marrying and then tell her mother if her husband was sexually inactive. The mother would tell her daughter to wait, and the second year, if there was still the trouble, the mother would advise the girl to come back to her own homestead. So she would go to her father's compound and take back all the goats and cows given for *rūracio*, returning them to the hus-band's father. The husband would be left holding his head in his hands, because he knew he could never marry again now that every-one knew his state.

The purpose of having sexual relations is to have a child. If the husband was inactive, it meant that you would not get a child. Any other time, sex was just like eating dirt. After you got a child, your husband would not have any sexual relations with you until after you had stayed for four years—he would not even sleep in your house during that time. Until the child was big and old enough to have a *rūkoro* put on him/her and was officially removed from the mother's bed, the man could not have sexual relations with his wife. If you look at a man of my age now, he is still strong because he did not use up all his sexual energy. Look at young men nowadays—they are tir-ing easily and growing old fast because they think all the time they are enjoying sex, but they are not. The girls, too, are growing old very fast using up a lot of sexual energy for nothing.

Now people are doing what they feel they have the right to do about sex, and they do it in their own way. A young girl marries today and gets a child year after year, and after five or six years she looks older than her mother and dies early because she is wearing out. In our time, one waited for four years before getting another child, giving time for the body to build up strength, all the time eating good food like green vegetables. One can go to the river and fetch water, but can you fetch blood and energy from a river? We knew these things, and we had our own kind of family planning. People had only the children they needed, and there was plenty of time for the body to heal between children. Nowadays, people talk about family planning with pills and medicine, but we didn't think about such things. I would not like my daughters to take the pills or other things because we hear stories about them. But I hear that some women who have had all the children they need go to Tumu Tumu to the clinic to get fixed so they don't have any more children.[3]

Some of our men take other wives—it is true. Then they have more children. But some, like my husband, only had one. A man would wait until those four years while his wife suckled the children were over and be patient, because if he went and had sexual relations with any other woman he would be called *githaria* [adulterer], and a song would be composed about him and it would be sung openly by his *riika*mates and those of his wife. They would shame him.

During the time my husband and I were coming to know each other—when he came to visit—we had to be careful. When I escorted him from the compound, I would throw his walking stick to him at the gate and come back running. When walking to some place, I could not go alone but would always be with my mother or *Cūcū* or a small child. Even if Ngiricii saw me and accompanied us partway, he would not talk to me.

It was three years after Ngiricii first came to visit that the negotiations for *rūracio* started. Finally, the men from both our clans met and settled the number of goats that Ngiricii would give to my father. In the morning, twelve goats were brought to our compound, and right behind them were the women of Ngiricii's compound carrying six large gourds of beer.

On the day Ngiricii came for me, he was accompanied by somebody named Kabuu. Ngiricii came saying that he was coming for a visit. I welcomed him and gave him food. After that he told me to escort him to the gate. When we reached our gate, the other man held my hand and told me that I would have to go with them now that all the *rūracio* had been given. I did not scream. I just went with them to Ngiricii's father's place without trouble. When we reached the gate, though, I refused to go in. A woman from the compound came and escorted me in.

During the old days, we were married when our parents still wanted us, so the man would have to find a way to take the girl without her parents realizing it. My mother was not left happy. But the following day, when she guessed that I had gone to Ngiricii's homestead, she cooked food and sent somebody with it to my husband's place. At that time, I could not eat anything cooked in his homestead, because I would be considered greedy if I did. I had to wait until a goat was slaughtered and I was officially welcomed into a new house built by my husband later.

It was a women called Wanjira who welcomed me that first night. She was my in-law now, because her husband's father and Ngiricii's father were brothers. After Wanjira welcomed me, she took me to Ngiricii's mother's house. Ngiricii's mother lit a fire, but I went into the room where the bed was and never came out to warm myself at the fireplace. The reason I went to the bed was to show that now I had become her child.

The following morning, Ngiricii's mother asked me to come out to the fireplace. She went and brought sisal threads for me to make into strings for a basket. She gave me threads, because if I didn't start making my baskets then, when I went to my own house later and needed to get food from the *shamba*, I would have nothing to carry the food home in. It was not until three years later that I moved into my own house. The mother loved me because she didn't have a daughter and I was a companion to her. You see, Ngiricii went to Nairobi short-ly after I went there to work as a sweeper in a European's store. During the three years I stayed with Ngiricii's mother, she treated me well and taught me many things—like when a married woman starts menstruating, she should not sleep in the same bed with her husband.

Before Ngiricii and I moved into the house he built for me, his father—who was a *mūndū mugo*—blessed the house by sipping some beer, then spraying it from between his teeth into the house. Then he poured some of the liquid near the fireplace in the center of the house. But during this time, I was told to go the *shamba* so as not to inter-fere—I was told about it later. After that, Ngiricii's father could never enter the house again, because now I was one of his children and a father does not enter his grown child's house.

Ngiricii's mother went to the river and collected three good stones to make the fireplace in the new house. Then she went and got some *ndoma* [arrowroots] and bananas. She lit a fire in the fireplace and placed a pot of water on the fire over the three stones she'd brought. Then she put the *ndoma* in the pot to cook. She peeled the bananas and started to roast them. So now I was put in my own house, and I stayed in that house for three days without moving any-where. It was like getting married again, so I had to hide my face from people. But now I could have sexual relations with my husband.

Another thing, during those three days, *ndoma* was not given to any outsider, because we believed that if it was given to somebody outside the compound, the new house would be contaminated. After Ngiricii had stayed with me for a few days in the new house, he went back to Nairobi. I was given a *shamba* to cultivate. At that time, a

woman's *shamba* was not all in one place. I had two pieces of good
land down by the river and four up here, where I planted maize and
beans, sweet potatoes, and millet. I would get up very early while the
ground was still wet and cook some gruel for Ngiricii's mother and
me, then sweep the house out and hurry to the *shamba*, where I
worked until the sun was going down. I liked working hard—even
then. Sometimes a letter from Ngiricii would come, and his brother
would read it to us. Then I missed seeing him. But usually I did not
think about him with all the work to be done. A few months after
Ngiricii left, I found I was pregnant.

*   *   *

I first learned I was pregnant after staying for three months without menstruating. When I noticed I had missed three times, I went to
my home and asked *Cūcū* what could be happening. She asked me
whether I had had any sexual relations with my husband before he
went back to Nairobi, and I told her yes. Then she told me I was pregnant and now I should stop greeting the *anake* [circumcised young
men] I had danced with before I was married, for they were known to
cause one's pregnancy to abort due to jealousy. You see, if you had
refused one of the young men who had tried to woo you, he might
take some herbs called *ngunga*. He would drink some of them in a tea
and hold others in his hands so that when he came to greet you, the
ngunga would cause an abortion. So I had to avoid those *anake*.

During that time of being pregnant, I could only eat certain foods
like green vegetables, and, at times, I cooked bananas. When it came
time for the birth of my first child, I had spent the day comfortably,
cultivating in the *shamba*, and I had carried one and a half *ndebe* [large
containers] of potatoes home with my mother. When we got home,
my mother told me to go and light the fire—by that time I had gone to
stay with my real mother because my husband was in Nairobi, and
when I felt my time was near, I moved in with my mother because I
could not figure out how I would tell my husband's mother when the
time was reached. As my mother was cooking for others at her fireplace, she asked me to go and make a fire for my cooking in a house
where she used to store things. After cooking my greens and eating
them, my mother came and we stayed together. She fixed porridge,
and instead of carrying it to her house, we just took it there. Then we
went to sleep, each in her own house.

At around midnight, I called my mother and told her that I was
having a stomachache. She told me to go and take some water. At that
time, I didn't know what labor pains were. I told her the ache was
severe and it couldn't be stopped by just taking water—it felt as if it

was way inside near the backbone. She told me to sleep on my back and not to lock the door. So I did what she told me—she knew what was happening.

When I tried to sleep again, I couldn't, so I called again and told my mother I was going to sit up and warm myself by the fireplace. She woke and came and lit a very big fire and told me to get a mat from my bed. When I tried to get one, I couldn't. I was in too much pain. My mother went into the bedroom and came out with a mat and placed it on the floor and told me to lie down on it and sleep on my back. I told her I couldn't sleep. Then she decided to send for my husband's mother. I told my mother I felt like my abdomen was swollen, and I had to push hard. My mother began pushing on my stomach and the baby just came out. My husband's mother arrived just in time to cut the umbilical cord with a razor. Then my mother washed the child. It was a girl, so the two women called "ariririti" four times.

When it was daylight, my mother sent my brother to go and call other people from my husband's homestead. They came with bananas, potatoes, porridge, and firewood. The women from my husband's homestead didn't take me back to my husband's house immediately but told me to stay and get a little strong and then we would go back there. I stayed for some time and then left to join my husband in Nairobi because that's when Mau Mau first began [1952].

* * *

I was still a mūhiki [bride] with only one child when I heard a rumor that there were Mau Mau people giving the Oath, which consisted of eating the meat of a dog. At that time the baby was sick, and my husband heard and told me to bring her to the hospital in Nairobi. So I decided to get away from the oathtaking and go to Nairobi. After taking the child to the hospital, I stayed on in Nairobi during most of the fighting. What happened is that we received a letter from here telling us not to come home, for people were being killed and it was not safe.

During the time we were in Nairobi, my husband was working as a cook for one of the many Europeans that lived there. I used to stay at home in the place where Africans stayed, locked in the house the whole day while my husband worked. I did not like it. If it was cooking I needed to do, I cooked with a jiko [charcoal cooker] instead of using a fireplace as at home. It was hard to get things like food. Ngiricii had to have a passbook, which was like an identity card but was carried in the pocket. He had to carry it always wherever he went.

Ngiricii never told me whether he supported Mau Mau or not. He never wanted to tell me his secret thinking—he kept that to himself. So we stayed in Nairobi without problems for some time. I do not remember our stay there as being a big change, but a temporary one, because I knew when the fighting stopped we could go home. When we heard that things were better here, we decided to come back—that was a year before *Uhuru*. Then, soon after, we heard that Kenyatta was released from Maralal, where he had been held in detention, and we were being granted our freedom—*Uhuru*.

On the day of Jamhuri [Independence Day], we watched for Munyao to climb Mount Kenya and raise the flag. During the night before, we watched the fireworks being shown at Kamuruana Hill and guns were fired. In the morning we started singing, cooking a lot of food, and slaughtering chickens to celebrate, because it was a holiday. I felt so happy that day because now we were free. Some tried to tell us that *Uhuru* was just for the rich Africans, but I realized that it was given to everybody who had any brains and was hardworking. We had just planted tea here, and I knew we would not be cultivating tea—as much as we wanted—if *Uhuru* was only for the rich. The government would have told us that if you picked tea you could only pick one kilo like the British used to tell us before we got our freedom. So it was the lazy ones who said that *Uhuru* was only given to the rich.

*   *   *

I first learned to pick tea before *Uhuru* when Brook Bond Tea planted it at Kianjagi. That was just before the Mau Mau trouble started. We had not planted any tea here yet, so we used to go there and were taught how to plant and cultivate tea by a *muzungu* [white, European] and his workers, who had come from Britain. We also learned how to pick—two leaves and a bud—and how to use the old leaves to make new plants [cuttings] for more tea.

Then, when we returned here from Nairobi, we decided to plant our own tea just before *Uhuru*. Everyone was beginning to plant it, and we thought we would try it. We learned that people could earn a good profit with tea to buy some of the new things that were becoming available in the shops—like iron beds, wooden tables, and clothing. Government extension workers came to our *shamba* to see our tea and show us how to make it better by pruning and picking it using a long stick to make the tea bushes level with each other on top. Where did we grow it? Up here. Before Mau Mau, part of the *shamba* was planted in maize and another part in yams. But it was not well kept during Mau Mau, so we cleared part of it for tea and kept other parts for maize and beans. And we cleared some new land.

At first I picked only 3 kilos [6.6 lbs.] of tea a day, then increased to 4 [8.8 lbs.] or 5 [11 lbs.] and finally got so I picked 10 kilos [22 lbs.]. When we pick maximum is when we have picked 11 [24.2 lbs.] or 12 kilos [26.4 lbs.]. But young people can pick up to 40 [88 lbs.] or 50 [110 lbs.] kilos a day. Us, who are old and our bones are getting stiff, we cannot afford to pick faster than 12 kilos [26.4 lbs.]or so.

I'm always learning new things about cultivating tea and developing my land. I've learned to put manure around the tea bushes and how to trim the edges. I use manure either from the goats, cows, or chickens and mix it with rubbish from my house to increase growth of the bushes. Fertilizer is necessary to yield better production of the tea. I have learned all this from the *baraza* [outdoor meetings] held by the KTDA—Kenya Tea Development Authority. I also use manure on the gardens where I have maize and potatoes growing. And now I am planting cabbage and *skuma-wiki* [kale], too. Before, we just used to collect wild spinach.

When did I become a Christian? I started going to church before Mau Mau. Neither of my parents were Christian, but when some of my agemates and I saw others going to Sunday Service at the church in Karaini, we decided to go, too. We were already mature girls by then who had gone for *Irua*.

Then I saw that the sister to my mother had become a Christian, and I could see her staying peaceful and having good things that I longed for, like cleanliness and being able to take care of one's home and a good relationship with the husband. I began thinking that I should join the church, too.

Becoming a Christian changed my life—even my soul—because in the days before I became a Christian I used to cook and drink liquor. I would cook *njohi* and sell it to people. But after becoming a Christian, I stopped cooking *njohi* or drinking it. Before, I would abuse anyone who tried to abuse me—like if they came demanding something that was mine and I refused to give it to them, they would abuse me. But now, even if somebody comes and abuses me or tries to fight with me, I will not fight back. I believe there is only one who fights for me—that is God. That is why I say that Christianity is good.

I did not get baptized until I was a married woman. I had been going for catechism at the Anglican Church, and after mastering those lessons of the Bible, we had been told to learn the Apostle's Creed and know a prayer before being baptized. So I learned those things, and a day was set for our baptism. I can remember that day. We went to church very early in the morning and sat in the front seats with our baptism "mothers." We got up then and made a line around the basin of water and each baptism mother would give the Christian name of the woman who was her "daughter" to the vicar, and he would baptize each of us, saying our new name and putting drops of water on us. I was the one who chose my name, "Peris," and told it to my baptism mother.

After staying for twenty years married the Agĩkũyũ way, my husband and I renewed our vows in the church. Then I became a member of the Mother's Union. I find that going to church now feeds my soul with words and prayers that help me forget about doing something wrong and console my soul when I am feeling badly.

Shortly after the renewal of our vows, I went with other women from the church to Mutira, and we were initiated into the Mother's Union group and were given certificates to show our membership. The Mother's Union helps in teaching about good home care and how to bring up one's children by giving the women advice. The teachings of the group show us how to advise our children and to correct their mistakes in a good way. We are also taught how to stay in harmony with our daughters-in-law by not interfering with their affairs and not desiring the things our sons have bought for them. We are reminded not to abuse one another and to be obedient and keep our Christian beliefs.

Sometimes the teachers in the Mother's Union are the wives of Bishops. These women are trained to deal with family problems. I can remember one called Gathoni who came from Nairobi and taught us to refrain from desiring other people's things. She said the minute you ask to borrow something and you are given it, if the owner comes for it and you refuse to give it back, it will cause a fight.

Every year the Mother's Union has a rally at Embu where members from all the churches in the area go, and we are given teachings by trained people from Nairobi and other places. The lessons are on how to keep harmony in the home and how to use Christian teachings to solve our problems. Through the Mother's Union I learned how to be self-sufficient without desiring other people's things.

I joined the Mother's Union first, then later I became a member of the *Uritu wa Gatwe* Group when it started about three years ago. The Mother's Union and *Uritu wa Gatwe* are sort of connected, because it was members of the Mother's Union that started the women's self-help group. "*Uritu wa Gatwe*" means "Power of Gatwe." Both the self-help group and the Mother's Union have helped me save money for my needs. Since I joined the Mother's Union, I no longer waste money on going to buy beer for myself and my friends. In the self-help group, we all contribute so much each month and at the end of the month that contribution is given to one woman—a different woman each month. If your child is sent away from school because he lacks school fees, then you can use the contribution money to pay that child's fees. With money given to me by the group, I have built this house you see, fenced with barbed wire, and am now digging this well for water.

Sometimes, the government sends extension workers to teach us new things in the self-help group—like how to raise pigs to make money. We are also part of the *Maendeleo ya Wanawake* [Development of Women] Organization. Maendeleo sent an extension worker to show us how to raise pigs. We have a male and a female and after the male mates with the female, we will slaughter the male and sell the meat. In the future I would like to see us build better sheds for the pigs and a trough for food and water. Pig raising is our main project.

Today, the sub-chief is coming to talk with our group about a plot of land that we would like to purchase. You can see that our group is doing a lot to help us improve our lives by making us more self-reliant. The group has been important to me, because now that I am a widow I can only depend upon myself, and the group helps me get what I need.

* * *

I became a widow when Waweru, the last-born, was twelve years of age. [Wangeci has four older daughters, who are married and living away. The two youngest children are sons in their early twenties, both married and living with her at the homestead. She lost one child before it was a year old but does not consider its death significant to her life history.]

I think I was about thirty-seven when my husband died. He had been sick and stayed in the hospital at Kerugoya for a long time. But the doctors never told me what disease he had—they never said. I can still remember well the day he died. It was the third of March.

I was at the hospital, visiting him, and he was saying, "Wangeci, the only thing I can tell you is to take care of yourself, the children, and the things you have that are enough to help you. I feel now that my time has come." He said this softly.

I asked him, "How should I take care of myself?"

He told me, "A widow has a lot of advisers. Take care not to be deceived out of what you have—the cows, the tea, the *shamba*, and the children. If you are not watchful, somebody may try and take them from you by force.

"Who is the one who will dare to take them from me?" I asked.

He said, "Wait, and I will think." He said this slowly and then he was quiet. So I kept quiet and waited for him to think. But when I looked at him, I saw that there was nothing—he had died. I was shocked because I had been waiting for his answer. That was the last time we talked.

Now I felt cold at heart and my body shook. I lost appetite and felt very thirsty in my throat, like sand. For the next few days, any-time I took water or tea, the thirst was never quenched. I was shivering even though it was hot outside. I was scared, so I prayed. There and then I just decided to stand on my own with Jesus without thinking of anybody else to help me. Yes, my faith helped me to see that.

When I came to tell my children that their father had died, I did not know what to say, because they had loved him very much. I told them that I had left him in the hospital. They asked whether he was feeling better, and I told them that he was not feeling well and was not getting better—I told them this the morning after he died. When I went back to the hospital that morning, I found they had kept him in refrigeration. I never told the children what was happening, because one was only in Standard Seven and the other in Standard Five—the two boys. I felt that the news of their father's death would affect their learning at school. After three days—that's when I finally told them. The children cried and cried, and they looked changed, too. They felt very sad and found the hole in their lives deep to try and cover.

The hardest change for me was to refrain from moving with women who had their husbands, and learning to stay alone with my work. When I made friends with a woman who had her husband, and the wife would tell her husband that I was getting a good house and he should build a better house for her, he would tell her that it was me, Wangeci, who told her to say this—putting the idea in her head. He'd tell her, "I can see you want me dead so that you can own a cow" or "You want me dead so you can be talking with your children like Wangeci." The husbands thought that I showed their wives that I was having better things now as a widow, so I had to take care there. I also refused to move with married women because I realized that I might be beaten by women who had their husbands, because they might think that I was moving about with their husbands. So I decid-ed to keep to myself and be self-reliant.

I stayed for about four years, still thinking about my husband before I began to get used to his absence. I changed then and stopped thinking about how he had helped and began to forget about his good work. It took me those four years to learn to do all the work myself.

It is different being a widow, because there are some things you cannot do when your husband is around, but then when you are wid-owed, you are forced to do them and you discover for yourself you can do these things. For instance, trapping moles—women leave that to their husbands. But a widow has to do it to stop moles from eating up the tea plants. So she learns how. If a married woman finds a banana tree falling down, instead of finding a post and putting it in the ground to hold it up, she calls her husband to do it. A widow has to do it by herself. Feeding the cows is usually the husband's job, but I have to do it myself. And I milk them as well. Yes, the learning is different for a widow.

When I was married, if a child was sent home from school for some reason, I could tell the child to go and tell his/her father why she/he was sent from school. This is normal. But now, being a widow, I have had to take care of my children and their school fees so they wouldn't be sent home. A widow, therefore, has a lot of work and a lot to think about.

What advice would I give to a woman recently widowed? I'd tell her to stay self-sufficient, taking care of her children and the things at home. I'd say, "Don't wait for outsiders to come and advise you on how to run your affairs. Do not follow what others are doing blindly. Make yourself a *mūtumia ngatha*" [a self-sufficient woman]. Another thing I would tell her is, "Do not join forces with any woman who has her husband, for you might lose a lot. If you go to help her with her work, your work is still there waiting for you when you get home, and nobody is there to help you." Like now, since I started digging this field, if my husband were alive he would have dug up the rest. But now the field has to stay the way it is until I get time to finish it. "One cannot defend and at the same time fight." So being a widow, one needs to do her work first, single-handed, slowly by slowly, before she can help others. That way, one will win the respect of the people in her area. This is the advice I would give.

Nowadays, in our society, widows do not get help. They say each has his mother. It means that even the father's [deceased man's] brothers can't help, as they are interested only in their children. It is the mother of the child who takes care of the child, and a man helps only his own children today. But long ago in Agĩkũyũ society, if there was a feast somewhere, a share of meat would be brought to the widow, and the father's brother took over the dead father's role—like my father's younger brother became my father after my real father died. But nowadays, the brothers to my husband have never even thought of buying a kilo of meat to bring to my children. They say they have their mother to care for. Even in the community, people say that you, a widow, are rich with all the things left to you by your husband. So they never think to help someone like me.

What do I remember best about Ngiriciĩ? I am happy when I remember how he brought me here to his place and told me that if I worked hard I would be able to support myself. I also remember that he was very hardworking in the *shamba*. He liked, and took good care of, the children. At times, when I had a new baby to care for, I would not cook. He would be the one to cook or, at times, hold the child while I was cooking. He showed me that women can also plant bananas. So whenever we went to the *shamba*, he would plant one and then force me to plant the next. He taught me that I could also do things that men normally do, and I am grateful because that way he helped me to be self-supportive and stand on my own after he died. He was a good person, and that's why I'm always proud to say that I was his wife—*mūtumia wa Ngiricī*.

*   *   *

When my children were growing up, I taught them to respect their elders. I told them, "Any woman married to somebody of your father's *riika*, respect her and call her "mother." Respect should also go to the father's brothers and the uncles.

A child that does not do what he/she is told to do is wrong. A child should be taught that his/her parents are there to be obeyed and respected, for they are the people who have given birth to the child. I tell my grandchildren this now. I say, "Obey your parents, for they are the ones who have given birth to you and are caring for you while you are growing up. They are wiser than you who are small. You are their child, and you will always be so until they die. Obey your parents so that days may be added to those which you are going to live on this earth."

Now, I raised four girls and all are married. The important things to teach a girl are how to cultivate, to clean the homestead, sweeping the house, and not throwing the rubbish under the bed. Rubbish can be saved and mixed with manure and put around the tea bushes for fertilizer. I showed my daughters how to cultivate, digging the soil with a *kibanga*, how to plant, and when the plants grew to take care of them, weeding and turning the soil. That way I was taking them to high school.[4]

It is important to show a girl how to respect people anywhere she goes, to teach her that when she goes and marries in another place, she should show those parents she meets at her husband's home that they are just like her mother and father and so need respect and obedience. It is also not good to laugh while other people are talking, because they will think she is laughing at them and become angry. Finally, she should not forget God—always pray for the good food given before eating.

A boy needs to learn that he is the cornerstone on which to build a homestead. He should be taught to cultivate cabbages, carrots, and potatoes, as well as maize and beans. He should go to school, and as he gets more knowledge, he should bring that knowledge back home. For instance, he can get himself trained as a mason or carpenter, and those skills will help him develop his home and will provide money to bring up his children well. He can also help his parents when they are old that way.

Now, when I was growing up, our mothers and our grandmothers in the kitchens and *mashamba* were our teachers, showing us what to do just as we show our sons and daughters. The *shamba* and homestead were the school. A woman would wake up early, cook whatever she had to cook, then sweep the outside around the house and inside, collecting the rubbish and throwing it in a certain place to be used as fertilizer later on. The young girls near her would learn that it is good to keep the compound clean and the rubbish swept and saved for fertilizer. If the mother was cooking, the girl would learn how to make *irio* and the right mixture of maize and beans for *githeri*.

The bigger and older girls were our advisers, telling us how to behave with people younger than us, how to take care of ourselves in front of men, and to respect the elders. We'd learn certain ways of behaving, just as young girls learn these things in school. Even nowadays, girls are still learning from their mothers and grandmothers at home.

Even though school was not important when I was growing up and our parents thought that if a girl went to school she would become loose and a prostitute, today it's important for girls to go to school, so they will learn how to become self-sufficient and not depend, when they are grown, upon their parents or others. The highest grade any of my daughters achieved was Standard Seven, but the son who was supposed to go to Standard Seven refused—he got malaria, and so he said he could not go to school again.

I thought I would try to learn how to read and write so I could become more self-sufficient. I decided to join the adult education class at Gatwe—I was looking for more knowledge and how I could develop my land better. If I could learn how to read and write, then when going to withdraw money from the bank, I would no longer have to put my fingerprint on the bank slip in the place for a signature.

The class was held at the school—it was not so far away from here. The first day, I did not know what time the class met, so I went very early, before four, and stayed there waiting for people to come. Then I only saw letters written on a blackboard, and looking at them made my eyes water. The following day, as I had been too early, I decided to stay home and work a bit longer. When I went at five o'clock, I met the class ending. I was told that the class meets everyday, Monday through Friday, at 4:00 P.M. But by that time, I decided it was better to stay home and cultivate and forget the adult education class. The reason is that I could go and cultivate a piece of land or even cook during the time of the class—to go and waste time at the class and not understand anything seemed useless. Well, I decided just to continue putting my fingerprint on the bank slip.

If I had a choice of going to either adult education class or the women's group, which would I choose? The women's group! In that one, we do work that helps us—like building the pig's pen or buying their food or even contributing money to each other. That's not like being told to learn letters that are hard for me to see. I dropped that class because I did not understand what was being taught, and not understanding, I decided it was better to stay home doing something else to help myself. But there are some women who have gone, and they say they can read letters and are never cheated at the shops because they know how to do maths. But me, I do not care.[5]

The way I learn best is seeing how other people do things. I will attend *baraza* like the one for tea growers held at the biggest factory at Kagozi. By going to the *baraza*, I learn better ways of increasing my tea yield. By being taught new ways of doing things and using my own head, I try to do things that will improve my work and my way of living.

*   *   *

Which of my roles in life is most important to me? Now, the most important is cultivating my farm and doing the work of the homestead, because those are needed before all else. Then I would say being a member of the Mother's Union and Uritu was Gatwe, because the women's groups help me a lot, as I've said. Being a mother or grandmother is next most important. Then the one of being a wife to my husband, because the role of being a daughter was a long time ago.

Long ago, before the missionaries came and started changing things, the role of an elder was important, too. During my mother's time, when a woman's firstborn went for *Irua*, her head was shaved and a *mūkwa* was put on at night, and she got *kirira* from the other women. But when Nyawira, my firstborn, went for *Irua*, it was after the missionaries had come, so the ceremony for elders was not observed.

I have not gone through menopause yet, but at times I stay for three months before I menstruate. Sometimes I get headaches and hot spells, but I never experience chills. I think menstruation will end soon.

Of all the transitions in my life, I think the death of my husband changed me the most. I started keeping to myself, as now most of the work in the homestead was all mine. I could not move with other women for marketing or other things, because by the time I came home, I'd find the cows not fed, there was no water, and I had to cook. Also, I was having to learn how to do new things I never had to do before when my husband was alive. So I changed the most when he died.

My greatest achievement has been to build this house of timbers with a cement floor. I don't really dream of the future. I know that someday, some hour, I will die. But I don't think about that. For now, I am satisfied with my life the way it is, except for getting the sewing machine I want to purchase for my son who is the tailor. At times, I feel that the headaches I get are due to thinking so much about how to buy this son a *kibanga* or a *jembe* [hoe] and that one a sewing machine.

My strongest character is that I like people and I'm hospitable to all—even when calling you to come and eat my food, it is with a clean and happy heart that I do it. I can't think of anything I'd like to change—I feel satisfied with myself. Being a woman means being able to keep things to myself, to go ahead and do them but not talk about them.

I think of myself first as Mũgĩkũyũ, because I was born in the Agĩkũyũ tradition and brought up in it. I had *mbuci* and *matũ*, then went for *Irua*—those were part of the tradition. After that I think of myself as Kenyan.

I have given you this knowledge freely—and given a lot of it. Now I hope you will help me go to Nairobi and buy that sewing machine for my son. [We went the following week.]

Notes

1. Wangeci is the only informant in her age cohort who relates being given a cow in addition to a goat. According to culturally recognized "experts," a goat is the norm. When I asked about this later, Wangeci insisted that she had been given a cow. My suspicion is that she was exaggerating a bit.
2. As taking beer is an important aspect of any ceremonial occasion and because women are largely responsible for beer-brewing, they perform an important function related to Gikuyu ceremonial events, and their skill as beer-brewers is recognized and appreciated by their male counterparts who depend upon them for the supply.
3. Wangeci refers to tubal ligation, which is fast becoming an accepted form of family planning among older women of childbearing age who have had the number of children they desire—usually six to seven—and want to prevent additional births.
4. Another woman I interviewed referred to this as the "shamba school."
5. Five months after the interviews were completed, I made a follow-up visit to the adult education class that Wangeci referred to and found her in class, squinting at the letters on the blackboard as she tried to sound the words—she had decided to give the class a second try.

*Two older married women dressed in modified traditional dress for a
circumcision ceremony.*

6

Wanoi:
The Many Facets of a Midwife

Wanoi typifies Mutira women in their early fifties who converted to Catholicism shortly after Kenyan independence. Similar to other Catholic women, she persuaded her husband to remain monogamous. She participates in both the Catholic women's group and a self-help group. In addition, she attends adult education classes. Her uniqueness stems from her role as a midwife. The only woman whom I met in her early fifties practicing midwifery, Wanoi has fewer opportunities today to apply her skills because more women seek hospital births.

Wanoi is a creative woman. Whether pursuing midwifery, weaving a basket, or composing political lyrics to be sung to a traditional Gikuyu song for a campaign rally, Wanoi demonstrates an exceptional ability to innovate. Her peers refer to her admiringly as "clever." Said the leader of Wanoi's self-help group, "If Wanoi was of the age when she could have gone to school, she would have learned very fast. She is somebody who is teachable, and even now with the adult education class she has been able to learn a lot quickly. She is the leader in our singing. She is one who is clever and creative."

In basketry, Wanoi's ingenuity is expressed in the elaborate patterns she weaves and in color combinations that remind me of a Guatamalan cloth applique. She is also experimenting with new basket shapes using banana fibers. Not afraid of change, Wanoi is willing to take risks to try innovative ways of doing things. As openness to change and willingness to risk are both dimensions of creativity, Wanoi's life is, indeed, creative.

Physically, Wanoi is a beautiful woman with sharp, chiseled features and high cheek bones accentuated by piercing, intelligent eyes. She has two short, dark slashes (cicatures) on either side of her long, straight nose that enhance her beauty. It was Wanoi's beauty and self-assurance that first attracted my attention in an adult education class. She appeared an experienced student who was willing to help other women with the skills of writing and mathematics. I approached her at the end of class one day to schedule an interview, and she invited me to her homestead.

It turned out that Wanoi was as intrigued by me as I was by her. Not only was I of a different color and culture, but she saw in me a means of learning about a world that lay beyond Mutira Location and Kenya. We discovered similarities: Our oldest children were born in the same year, and we had both been teachers—I of high school students, she as an "expert" in traditional Gikuyu culture for University of Nairobi students, who visited her once a year.

Wanoi is a self-assertive extrovert, eager to teach anyone willing to learn. At the same time, her role as a teacher complicated our work at first because she thought I was interested in a generalized picture of Gikuyu women rather than her personal narrative. It wasn't until the third interview, when we began to talk about circumcision, that I was able to communicate successfully that I wanted to know about her life as an individual. Even then, there were times when I felt that Wanoi was idealizing her roles—presenting a facade of the person she felt she ought to be. During our initial interviews, Wanoi was direct and clear in her explanations, but as I delved more deeply into her life, contradictions arose that, at first, confused and frustrated me. For example, in the initial survey interview, Wanoi stated that all her children were living: thus, she was counted with the women who had lost no children. During the later interviews, I discovered that she had lost her first three children—two as infants and one as a boy of seven who died of disease. Such a revelation amplifies the hazards of quantitative research. To a stranger, particularly from another culture, an individual may protect herself by revealing only what she wants the social scientist to hear. Only through long-term interviews and observation is one able to scratch beyond the surface and learn about other dimensions of an individual's personality. Although in general Wanoi is self-assured and assertive, in some situations in which there are other self-assured peers or older women, Wanoi demonstrates a lack of assertiveness.

Another form of confusion arose from my inability to fit events together as a chronological sequence rather than as conflicting stories. When I asked Wanoi how she had learned her skills as a midwife, she told two different stories over a three-week period. It wasn't until several weeks later, through probing, that I discovered both stories were true but for different periods in her childhood.

Wanoi's apprenticeship as a midwife did not occur in isolation. Rather, her exposure to her mother's profession as a midwife was an integral part of the rest of her indigenous education, just as her continuing education as a midwife is only one aspect of her many-faceted adult life. Nevertheless, for purposes of clarity, I have chosen to present Wanoi's experiences as a midwife in a sequence of events beginning at one point in her life.

Of all the women whose life histories I collected, it was the most difficult to end the sessions with Wanoi. Often in the process of collecting a life history, a transpersonal relationship develops that resembles both a counseling relationship and a friendship. In such cases, the informant is apt to feel a sense of loss when the sessions terminate. It was critical in Wanoi's case that I prepare her for the end of our formal weekly sessions. When I introduced the subject prior to the last session, she became agitated and wanted to know if termination meant the end of our friendship. I assured her that it didn't. In succeeding months, after the research had ended, I made sure that I visited her whenever I went to the research site, up until the time I left Kenya.

—J.D.

My name is Wanoi. When I was born my mother named me after my mother's mother who came from a place called Inoi. Mary is the name I was later baptized in the Catholic Church. I am of the Ũnjiru Clan.

My father, Gataie, had two wives. The first was my older mother called Wakaitheri, who was co-wife to my mother. She had four children. The first was a boy called Nginyĩ or Maina, and the other three were girls. The older two, Kagũre and Muthoni, used to smear us with oil and plait our hair. Kagũre was beautiful, and men used to like her, but she had loose morals. Muthoni was a good girl. The last born of my older mother was Wanjira, who was my agemate. My mother, Kerũ, which means "brown," used to take care of Wanjira after her mother died, so we were raised together.

My mother was a widow when she married the man I called "Baba" [Father]. I never knew my real father, because he was killed for stealing someone's millet shortly after my mother married him. My mother was pregnant with me when she went to live at Gataie's—the man I knew as my father. Gataie and my mother had five children together, but the first two—Nginyĩ and the girl Kagũre—died when they were very small. The others are Mugo, Karani, and Muriithi, who are my three younger brothers. My mother did not have another girl apart from me.

My father was first a big man in the village, then he became an elder, then a chief and retired only recently before he died at the age of a hundred and twenty. I never knew him much because he was always away on government business.[1] My older mother died before

Figure 6.1 WANOI'S FAMILY

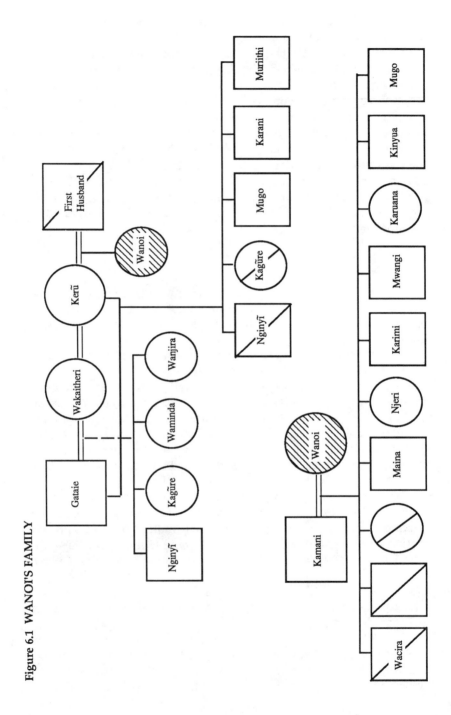

I was a mature girl—I can still remember when she died. We were getting arrowroots at the river with her, and a big bird came and sat on her head. She was so scared that she never survived that day. But my mother is still alive. You will meet her. She is a small, jolly woman who likes people.

My mother was a circumciser and midwife. She was very good at her job. She was a woman who worked fast, without delay. But nowadays, she no longer is a midwife. When I was growing up, she never used to nag, though she was talkative. My mothers and my grandmother—the one who was my mother's mother—were my teachers. My grandmother did not live with us in the same compound, but I would visit her. She did not live far away.

My mother would often take us to stay with our grandmother while she did her work. During these times, our grandmother would show us how to make porridge, cook *irio*, peel beans, and fetch firewood for the cooking fire. She did not say much, but we could see how she was doing these things. She would also advise Wanjira and me. Once I remember her telling us how one sits when she goes to get circumcised, and how one takes care of herself after circumcision.

Those *wazee* [Kiswahili term for "old people"] like my grandmother, sitting around the fireplace at night, would teach us a lot of things. They told us stories about giants, but I can't remember those well. There was one story, though, that I remember about a greedy wife. Let me think.

Once there was a girl who when she got married and went to live in her husband's compound, a goat was slaughtered and the meat was hung inside the house where she was staying with her husband's mother before being officially welcomed into her own house. She got hungry and went and cut a piece of the meat and started eating it in bed where she had to stay. This was before she was allowed to eat meat, and while she was still eating the piece, somebody came into the room where she was in bed and saw her. She dropped the piece of meat right in the bed. People were angry when they heard about her greediness, and so they took her back to her parents, because nobody wants to marry a greedy wife.

There is a song that is sung with that story that I will sing for you. It is called "The Greedy Wife Who Showed You the Meat in the *Itara* [rafters of the house where firewood is kept to dry]."

Mūhiki mubio,	Greedy bride,
Mūhiki mubio,	Greedy bride,
Nyama iriitara wonirio nu?	Who showed you the meat in the

| | *itara?* |
| Ĩi, *wainaga.* | Yes, we sing. |

That story was important because it taught us that we should be patient when we went to live at our husband's home, until his parents were ready to welcome us officially with a goat. The song was sung if any bride showed she was greedy. I would have sung this song to my brother's wife, because when she was newly married, I met her stealing chicken meat from our house and also ripe bananas. If it was long ago, she would not have remained married. She would have been sent back home for being so greedy. It is only recently that this tradition is not followed, or I would have sung the song.

What was I like as a child? I was one who never used to stay at one place but moved around from place to place. As children we were not naughty and we liked each other, but we used to fight sometimes. We would fight with a blunt *kibanga* and if somebody provoked me I would fight that one with my teeth and scratch him/her with my nails. I had so many friends I wouldn't be able to count them. I was always looking for those who were like me—those who were talkative and daring and did the things I wanted to do. I remember once when we were jumping with huge poles over a huge fire outside. Then one of us fell and got her legs badly burned. From that we learned that fire can be dangerous. Also, when you are smashing food in a cooking pot, if you bend down to look inside you can be burned. Another time, when we were roasting maize, the seeds [kernels] started popping off and burned me on the chest. So I learned that being so near roasting maize is dangerous.

I used to want to make porridge as a small girl, but when I cooked nobody ate it because it was always undercooked. I was teaching myself how to cook by watching my mother. I used to cook over the fire with small pots bought for me in the market, and I broke so many. Later, when I was old enough to be left with the young ones—my small brothers—I used to take some maize and beans, mix them together in a small pot and put it on the fire to cook the way I'd seen my mother do. All this I did with the smallest child tied to my back. Then I would go and fetch green vegetables from the garden. I would chop them, then peel potatoes, called *kahuro*, and chop them, too. After the *githeri* cooked for a while, I'd put in the potatoes, then the vegetables. While these cooked, I'd sit down and take the baby on my lap—just to train myself—and squash some food in a calabash using a *mũiko.* Then I'd chew a bit of the smashed food, spit it out onto my first finger, and feed it to the baby.[2]

Some days, I would not cook. On those days, I waited until my mother left to go to her *shamba,* then I would go into the granary and get millet and grind it on a big stone with another smaller round stone, with the baby tied onto my back. If the child started crying and stopped me from grinding, I would pinch him. After grinding the millet, I went for water, which we kept in a gourd, and mixed the millet flour with water into a paste. Then I mashed the paste and put it in a cooking pot with more water over the fire. I was told by my mother never to put the baby down when cooking because he could crawl to the fireplace and get burned, so with him on my back, I stirred the porridge until it cooked and then put it into a gourd and hid it under the bed where we slept with my mother, so it would sour. It would sour [ferment] in about three days.

During that time, we never had our own beds. Children slept with their mother until they were quite big. I was taken from my mother's bed at about the age of seven. At that time, a goat was slaughtered and a piece of its skin was put across the chest called *rũkoro* and the rest of the skin was spread on the floor after it dried to make a bed for me. The ceremony is called *mambura ma twana* and means that the parents can have sexual relations again. But I do not remember much about this because it was a long time ago.

The first important change in my life was when I pierced my ears—something my oldest brother, Maina, never wanted me to do. You see, he was a Christian by that time, and he wanted me to go to school and not pierce my ears. He was the firstborn of my older mother, and when he came back from the Italian war [World War II], he forced me and my brother to go to the missionary school. He bought me a dress and took me to sub-A, which was like today's nursery school. I never reached sub-B, which is like Standard One. When coming from school one day, I was beaten by some girls of my *riika*—age group—who were all about ten years old, because I had not had my ears pierced *mbuci* and *matũ*. During those times, anybody who did not have her ears pierced was termed still a small child, no matter how big she was. So I vowed to get my ears pierced, but my brother was against it. One day, I ran away from school and threw the dress my brother had bought away and tied on a sheet. I pierced my ears myself with an orange-tree thorn, but the holes never got so wide because anytime I went to my brother's *thingira*, he would remove the sticks and throw them away. Then I would take cow dung and smear it into the holes to prevent them from disappearing. As soon as I got home to my mother's, I'd put other sticks in. I had watched my mother pierce girls' ears, so I knew how to pierce my own. And nowadays, I pierce a girl's ears if she wants it.

* * *

[Wanoi relates two different accounts of her experience with *Irua*. When I questioned her about the discrepancy, she explained that the story of going with one friend, without the knowledge of her parents, is her own experience, whereas the other relates to the normative experience of most Agĩkũyũ girls of her generation.]

It was my grandmother who told me how one sits when she goes for circumcision and how to take care of oneself afterwards. She told me that the first thing to do after *Irua* is to check to make sure that the *ithangu* [soft leaf used as a bandage] has not been put too far back so as to cover up the hole where shit comes from. "When one is healed," she said, "you must begin to watch for blood coming from between your legs."

Before I was circumcised, I was taken to the river by many women of my clan where they washed me and threw me up in the air. Then I was carried to the big field of grass near the marketplace where we were to be circumcised. There were fourteen girls that got circumcised together. We were dressed with skirts of green colors and had hats with feathers like your hair. There were many people—men, women, and children—there that day. The women and girls were singing and dancing. The circumciser wore a cloth, and she used a knife that looked like a small axe that was very sharp called a *kienji*. After we were cut, castor oil was put on, then *ithangu*. By then the sun was going down.

[A week later, Wanoi gave the following version of what happened to her, personally. The account was so atypical, I was unsure whether to believe Wanoi or not. Her mother confirmed later that Wanoi's father was not anxious to see Wanoi circumcised and that she had not even received the uncle's permission. It seems likely that the account is fairly accurate with some exaggeration.]

When time reached for circumcision, I was a herdsgirl, looking after the goats. My friend came and told me that she would be circumcised. I did not want to be left behind. Because I was grazing the goats in a place far away from the field where the circumcision was being held, I decided not to tell anybody, but to just go, because I knew my parents would not allow it. The reason my father had refused to have me circumcised up to that time is because by body build was small and he was afraid I would be beaten by *irigũ* [uncircumcised girls].

When I saw people going toward the field, I sent the goats into the bush, then gathered *mathakwa* [leaves] because I was told by my grandmother that a girl being circumcised sits on such leaves. After collecting them, I went to the field and reached there just when the other girl—my friend—was being circumcised. I quickly put down the *mathakwa* leaves and sat down on them with my legs spread. I didn't even have a supporter! After being cut, women took me home.

I went home slowly, slowly, with women of my clan on either side of me, holding me and dancing and singing. When I got home, I found my mother had gone away somewhere to drink beer where people were celebrating the *Irua* season. But I met my father's eldest brother, whom I called *Baba*. He told me that as I had braved the ceremony without a supporter, he would give me a goat. So you see, my bravery is not recent. I was brave even a long time ago.

When I entered the compound, people remembered that my father had never beaten my mother, so they went to look for her. You see, it was the custom that a mother should be beaten on the day that her first child gets circumcised if she had never been beaten before. So when my mother finally got home, my father found some *mukenia* [type of plant], and he beat my mother before I was allowed to go into the house. My mother and father were surprised to find me circumcised, but they did not show it.

I did not stay long in the house before I was taken outside behind, and the clotted blood was removed from the cuts and they were washed with warm water. Then castor oil was put on *ithangu*, and it was put over the wound. I stayed for three days, and then my head was shaved, and as I was the first daughter of my mother, her head was shaved, too. It took me three months to heal.

How did I feel after going for *Irua*? *Irua* was like being given a degree for going from childhood to womanhood. One became mature. It was very important in those days, because when one got circumcised, one would not joke about with uncircumcised girls and they would give us respect. If I got circumcised a year earlier than you, you would not be able to abuse me. If one refused *Irua*, she was beaten by others, abused, and would not have anybody visiting her home looking for her to marry. But the minute you got circumcised, no one would stand in your way—you were ready to marry.

Once circumcised, a young woman could talk and joke with young, uncircumcised men, but we did not move with them sexually until one got married. But now, my small daughter Karuana [aged ten] knows things about sex, and even Njeri [daughter, aged twenty] knows, even though she is uncircumcised.

And another thing, there are no *mariika* today. The girls who went for *Irua* stayed friends and would talk until dark, asking each other questions about the day and joking with each other. People knew which age group they belonged to and what behaviors were good for their age group. Nowadays, there is no difference between age groups. That is why children are so naughty—there is no way they know when they are grown up, because circumcision is no longer practiced among the girls. *Irua* meant becoming a member of a *riika* and learning Agĩkũyũ traditions, but after *Uhuru*, people started saying that Mary in the Bible was not circumcised, so why should we? That is when *Irua* started losing its meaning. I would not like to see girls circumcised now, but if the old people are to be believed, *Irua* would come back.

* * *

I wasn't full grown when I delivered my first child as a midwife, but I had had my ears pierced and was circumcised. I was almost Njeri's age. This is what happened.

One day, I was up on a wooden tower, frightening the birds away from the millet field when a woman came by carrying a basket and sat down near a sugarcane plant. She started calling to me. Now me, I assumed that she was a lunatic, so I came down from the ladder and started to run away from her. But she called me again, telling me that she was giving birth. I started wondering what to do and was feeling a bit scared, but a voice deep within me told me to go back and help her. So I went and saw that she was sitting with her legs apart. She told me to take the sheet she was wearing and put it on the ground to catch the baby. Then I saw the baby's umbilical cord after the baby came out but had nothing to cut it with. So the woman asked me if I took snuff and told me to take the string from my tobacco pouch and use it to tie the umbilical cord. She told me to cut a piece of sharp stem from the sugarcane plant and peel a thin thread and cut the umbilical cord with it. From then on, all my fear disappeared.

How did I first learn about being a midwife? It happened that my mother was a midwife, as I have told you. She used to circumcise girls during *Irua* and helped women give birth, even removing the afterbirth by pressing on the ribs of the mother. As I accompanied her everywhere, I saw all that she was doing.

A long time ago, there was a woman whose children used to die. The last born, the one who survived, was always carried about on the woman's back when she was going to do any work. My mother was like that woman, and as I was the only child for some time, even when I was big she used to tie me on her back, and I was able to see all that she did when she went to help a woman give birth. I would see that she did not wash her hands when she delivered a baby. She just took some *migio* string—the one that's used to tie the *igoto* [banana stem cover used for a case for carrying ground tobacco used as snuff]—and used the string to tie the umbilical cord. Then she'd wash the baby with cold water in a broken cooking pot. She would go for the fern that grows on top of the *mukoigo* tree, and when she got back the fern leaves were chewed and the liquid given to the baby so it would not get a stomachache.

Later, what happened is that any time a woman was to give birth, I would follow my mother at a distance and watch her. You know, in those days the houses had walls only on the side where the bed was. The other side walls—the ones on either side of the fireplace—were moveable and were called *rigi*. One of these blocked the view from the entrance of the hut, so you could not see the fireplace and the mother's bed, where women gathered for a woman's birth. So I used to hide behind that *rigi*, just inside the doorway of the hut and peek around and see what my mother was doing. There was nothing done in that house that I didn't see, but I wasn't frightened. I would watch and then go and tell the children my age that so-and-so gave birth—the way the woman was breathing hard, pushing hard, sitting on the stool with the other women telling her to push hard. I saw my mother pushing on the woman's stomach with her fingers to get the baby out.

From watching my mother, I saw that soon after the child comes out, she told the mother to kneel down and hold the child on her lap. After the mother knelt, my mother would tie the umbilical cord and cut it with a sharp piece of sugarcane thread or razor and then take the baby and wash it. Then she would wrap it in blankets. The afterbirth was taken outside and buried away from the place. But the mother of the child never used to wash herself in my mother's time. She just wrapped herself with blankets for about eight days, then took them off and washed in the river. Right after the baby was born, I used to hear the women give the ululations—"*aririri*," five times if it was a boy and four times if a girl-child. So I saw all my mother did, and I told myself that someday I would be doing like her.

My mother did not know I was sneaking and watching her, but she realized that I knew everything after I first helped that woman in the sugarcane field because I came and told her what I had done and how I went about it. She was surprised and asked how I knew what to do. I told her, "At so-and-so's place, I saw you give five ululations. At another place you gave four and washed the baby in a broken piece of pot." She was happy and told me not to stop what I was doing but to continue being a midwife, because now I would be able to help others. I don't know how my mother came to know midwifery—maybe from *her* mother. Knowledge is passed on that way.

My second time to deliver a baby was when I was going to Kerugoya. I met a woman in the bushes struggling very much, so I went and asked her whether she was about to give birth and she said, "Yes" and told me to call any woman who was passing by and could help her. I told her that I could help. She was surprised and asked me whether it was true. I told her, "Wait and see." So I helped her deliver and meanwhile sent a woman to borrow a razor blade from a nearby homestead and I used it to cut the umbilical cord. That woman never went to the hospital, so I took her home, and when a goat was slaughtered for her, I was given some of the meat and I carried it home to my family. So now I was a midwife.

I was delivering women when we were in the concentration camp. [Wanoi refers to the enforced villages set up by the British beginning in 1953, after the Mau Mau Rebellion a year earlier. Her depiction is accurate because the Gikuyu, who were formerly living in scattered homesteads, were now forcefully concentrated in the temporary villages.] I was newly married then. Later, just before we got *Uhuru*, I was about eight months pregnant with Njeri, when a woman and her husband came from Nairobi in the evening to visit our relatives who were from the same home village. The woman was very pregnant, too, and she happened to deliver that evening in the house of our relatives. But the afterbirth got stuck up inside her.

My brother's wife came and told me that the woman, Kabuchi, had given birth and the afterbirth refused to come out. I felt badly when I heard the news, because Kabuchi had already given birth and left me behind—still pregnant. I went to see if I could help. An old grandmother had been called who was a wise midwife, but she had not been able to get there yet, so the women encouraged me to try. I thought for a few moments, then I asked for a razor blade and cut my sharp nails and removed all the dirt and washed my hands. I asked for Sunlight soap to apply on my hands and make them slippery. The woman's stomach had swollen by now, as it had been several hours since she gave birth. I slipped my hands up inside the woman's body and pulled out the afterbirth. Everybody got astonished—even my mother when she heard about it. By the time the old midwife came, it was all over. After I removed the afterbirth, I washed my hands and went straight home, full speed without waiting, because I was feeling badly, as Kabuchi had given birth and left me still pregnant. I had helped her, but I was still pregnant.

So after that, people started talking about what I'd done and the skill that I had, and the news traveled wide. For that skill of removing the afterbirth that way, I learned it on my own—maybe it was God that gave me the knowledge, because I had never seen anybody remove stubborn afterbirth, nor had I been told how to do it. After one month, I gave birth to Njeri and the afterbirth refused to come out. My mother said it was because I had removed Kabuchi's afterbirth while I was pregnant. That same old midwife was called and she removed the afterbirth in me.

From then on, people preferred to have me help them with a

birth. I can help my own cow give birth, and if the afterbirth gets stuck, I can remove it just as I did with Kabuchi. For learning how to press on the ribs and deliver a baby, you can say that I stayed with somebody who knew something—my mother—and then copied what she did. But for removing the afterbirth, I did not copy from anybody, as I had not seen it being done at any other time. The knowledge of what to do just came from my own discovery.

Then I learned things from other midwives as I went along—like if a woman is bleeding, maize cobs are roasted and then put in a container with water and stirred. The black solution is given to the bleeding mother to drink. It stops the bleeding. But usually, mothers don't bleed.

Another thing—I was told by an old midwife that if ever I attended a woman who shits while delivering, I should tell the people nearby and hide the shit with clothes. After that I should fetch a climbing plant called *mukengeria* and take it and some *mugumo* tree leaves and hold them together with the umbilical cord, then cut them together as a sacrifice, as shitting while giving birth is a bad omen and not normal. But nowadays, there is no such thing. Even if a woman shits while delivering, nothing special is done.

When somebody comes for me to help with a delivery, I can't go without those people giving me something in return, as going has made me leave my own work. I can remember one day, two women came for me to go and remove the stubborn afterbirth from a friend of theirs. I told them to take her to the hospital, but they didn't want her to go there. So after I had removed the afterbirth, I was given 30 shillings [equivalent to 2 U.S. dollars] and then taken back home.

One day I went to Wanyuki's Maternity Clinic [a private maternity home in a nearby town], and Rebecca, the trained midwife, was not there. A pregnant woman came to the clinic and was just about to give birth, so I helped her deliver and washed the baby with Dettol [a disinfectant] and wrapped it in a blanket and laid it on the bed next to the mother. When Rebecca came, I told her that she should share her salary with me for I had done her work. She is the one who made me go to the midwifery course at Wambugu Farm in Nyeri. She knew that I could be a trained midwife and help in the clinic because I used to visit her there and watch how she did things. Sometimes, I would help her tie the baby's umbilical cord. The only thing I didn't do was to weigh the baby—I left that to her.

When we went to Wambugu Farm for midwife training, we taught the medical officers the things I'm telling you about and how, if a woman has a threatened miscarriage, we would give her honey and her pregnancy would be saved. If the honey didn't work, the woman was taken to a *mūndū mugo* to have banana leaves and other traditional herbs applied.

It used to be that if a baby was coming out feet first, there was nothing we could do except press on the mother's ribs and try and help her give birth feet first. But many babies used to die, as the head would get stuck in the mother's womb. A child born with the umbilical cord surrounding its neck was believe to be a *mŭndŭ mugo* if it was a boy-child and a circumciser if a girl-child. Certain kinds of plants were collected from the forest, and before the umbilical cord was removed from the baby's neck, a goat was slaughtered and a *mŭndŭ mugo* splashed *tatha* [contents of a goat's intestine] on the child, because it was believed that such a child was God's work, so the child was blessed.

Occasionally a child was born still in the placental membrane such that you would not know it was a child until the membrane was removed. When this happened, people used to say that the child was born without *rugwiki* [sexual intercourse]. So a goat would be slaughtered, too. Then I would pierce the membrane, and the whole thing would come away from the baby. If a baby's head is very big, I have to cut the mother's vagina with a razor blade to make the birth easier.

A few times I have delivered twins. There is a woman who is a neighbor of mine, and I was helping her deliver. She was very big and gave birth to twins. But they were not old enough, so one stayed alive for only four days and the other for seven days and then died. Maybe if she had gone to the hospital, the twins would not have died. But the problem was that she was giving birth in the middle of the night and she was far away from any road.

Nowadays, when I am called to assist a woman, before doing anything, I put the razor blade and piece of string for the umbilical cord into a *sufuria* [aluminum cooking pot] to boil over the fire. And I use Dettol when washing. I learned these things at the training course. After the course at Wambugu Farm, the health officers are interested in our progress as midwives, and they said they might bring us the materials they promised last year—things like scissors, cotton wool, thread, and big bottles for keeping our things in.

At Wambugu Farm we went to learn more about midwifery and how to keep records for every child born in the area—with the name of the child, its mother and father, when the child was born—and then to take the record to the headman or chief. Our teachers at the course were health officers from the government and nurses from the hospital. There were even some whites with their interpreters. After learning about different types of problems during a delivery, we were taken to the hospital. We went to the maternity ward and then, four women at a time, were taken into a room for our lesson. In the room was one woman who had her baby lying crosswise in the womb, in an astride position, another with a child coming out feet first, another one with the baby's head at the vagina in a normal position. We were given rubber gloves and told to put our hands in these women's wombs and feel the positions of the babies. The first two were to show us the kind of women we would not be able to help deliver easily at home. Then a woman who did not have enough blood [anemic] was brought in, and we were told you can tell such a woman by the color of the inside of her eyes and color of the palms of her hands and nails. We were told *never* to try and deliver such a woman at home but take her to the hospital.

The problem with some private maternity clinics is that the midwife does not check the health of the mother she is assisting. I've learned now that it is important to check to see if a woman has enough blood, the position of the child in the womb, and if the woman is big enough to have a normal birth at home.

After looking at the births at the hospital, we were shown a woman who had given birth two weeks earlier. We were given gloves to feel that her womb was not completely closed and saw how one could put in a coil [I.U.D.] when the woman is ready. We saw another woman who had stayed for five weeks and saw how the womb was getting closed. We were told that a woman cannot have a coil put in until after her first menstruation has resumed. All that knowledge we got from Wambugu Farm, and I still have it here, stored in my head. You see, I did not know how to write at the time. But when I came back from there, I went to the adult education class to learn how to read and write, so after one year, when the medical officers came back to see my work, they saw that I had written the things I had learned at the course and had kept a written record of the births I had delivered in the area. Only now I have lost that book with the births recorded in it.

The difference between what I learned from my mother and what I learned at Wambugu Farm is that today I cut the umbilical cord with a clean pair of scissors and before we used to use a razor blade. At times, the razor blade would be rusty and would have been used for shaving a number of times. We did not have any cotton in those days or any Dettol to sterilize the instruments. Now it is better, because I can help somebody deliver without the danger of the baby contracting tetanus—though that never happened to me. So, you see, I have kept on learning and improving my skills.

*   *   *

Long ago, when I was *mũirĩtu,* we did not know about sexual matters before we were married. Even if we knew our parents were sleeping together, they would tell us later that they were "eating tortoise honey"—by that they meant that they were tasting the sweetness of sex—but we did not understand. We were told by our grandmother that if we had sexual relations with young men, we would be given a bunch of bananas to give the child we had been looking for by our husband when we got married. If a man discovered that his wife already knew about sexual intercourse, he would go and tell his parents. Then his mother would cut a bunch of bananas and give it to the wife to give the child she had looked for earlier. So we were careful about our behavior before we got married.

Even before I started menstruating or had any breasts, I used to go to dances once I was circumcised. There was one kind of dance I remember called *mweretho*, where young men and women would hit each other against the chests, then the girls were thrown up in the air by their male partners. I liked watching that dance, but I did not have many girls to participate with me. By that time, some girls were beginning to go to school, and the missionaries told them not to dance—that it was bad.

There was another dance where young men and women met called *kiruri*. A young man would hold a girl and she would twist and whirl around. Even young men from school would sneak away and spend the nights dancing, and then in the morning they would sneak back to school without having eaten anything. Then such a young man spent most of his time dozing in class—that's what we heard.

During the night, after dancing, we would sleep there in the bush next to the dancing field, each with her man, and we would not do anything under the blanket. In the morning, we would separate. I used to attract men because I knew how to crack jokes. They liked to sit near me and feel good. There was always one handsome man, we called *kiumbi*. He was the one who was clean, good to talk to, and a good dancer. We girls would go to his place and all of us spend the night there. He had a very big bed. It would hold twenty girls with him alone. So we'd spend the night with him embracing each girl in turn. He would do nothing to us, as our skirts were tied to keep him from having sexual intercourse with us.

It was during that time, after *Irua*, that we put these cuts on our cheeks for beauty and others on our breasts. The ones in the cheeks were cut with a razor blade and soot from a blackened pot rubbed in, but the ones here [on the breasts] were made with a hollow bamboo stalk. We'd press and press until the upper skin come off, then smear in oil. [Wanoi describes a different technique of scarification than described by Wangeci.] We found it beautiful to make designs on the breasts, and later when one got married and was suckling a child, the breasts were decorated.

Those years after *Irua*, before I got married, were my happiest years, because I didn't have much work in the homestead then. I would wash and dress well, fix my hair, and go to a dance. I would come home and get food—I did not have all the work I have now. *Haiya*, when you are married, what kind of happiness do you feel? It is nothing but work. Like now—all the work I have in the *shamba*, worrying about the children, their school fees, where the husband is, and where I will get the money for the radio I want.

I first met Kamani at one of the dances. When we went to dances, we didn't have much chance to talk with a young man—we just danced. Talking came later, when he came to visit you at your home. A man would come to woo you, and if you liked him, you would arrange to ask your father for tobacco. Otherwise, you might tell him you are not ready for marriage. With Kamani, I wanted him. So I went and told my father that there was a young man asking for tobacco. My father told me to go and find out which clan Kamani came from and about his family. If the clans are ones that intermarry, then your father gives you the tobacco. That is what happened with us. Then Kamani's father brewed beer to take to my father. After that came the negotiations for *rūracio*. I found out that the number of cows that Kamani agreed to give my father was two cows that hadn't calved, a bull, and thirty goats. Four of the goats were to be slaughtered for me, and Kamani's relatives promised to cultivate the *shamba* I would get when I moved to his place.

Kamani's relatives dug up the grass with sharp-pointed digging sticks, and women from my place were called to do the work of cultivating and planting. During this time a lot of beer was being brewed. I was still at my mother's house, and on the day the women from Kamani's place came for me singing and ululating, I found the *shamba* nearly ready for harvesting and a house almost completed. That day I did not wear anything special, just a string of beads and a white sheet tied at one shoulder. My head was shaved clean and I went with it shining. I liked the women singing, but I felt sad to be leaving my mother's house.

I lived for the first two months at the house of Kamani's mother, but during this time we did not look at each other. I could not go out at all, only stay in bed. The mother would cook food like porridge and pass it to me in bed to eat. After the harvest, Kamani announced that the house he was building was completed, and some beer was brewed. Then a *mūndū mugo* came and took me to the river to be cleansed. He poured *tatha* from a goat's intestine over me and then in the house to bless it.

Kamani's mother went to the river and got three smooth, round rocks and came and put them in the center of the house to make a fireplace for cooking. Then she went back to the river and collected some arrowroots and put them in a pot to cook over a fire she had made. As the bride, I could now enter the house, and I cooked the arrowroots and shared them with Kamani's mother, my own mother, and the other guests who had come to watch the ceremony of me going to my own house. Now I was free to stay in my own house and cook for my husband. However, as a bride I still could not eat meat until a goat had been slaughtered. Even as girls, we would not eat when we saw men nearby, nor would we want them to catch us chewing because it did not look nice to see our teeth or us swallowing. So we used to eat away from our husbands after we cooked for them.

It was just at the time the British declared the emergency that I went to live at my husband's home and we could not get a goat because the British would think we were going to give it to the Mau Mau freedom fighters. So it was some time before I could eat meat at my husband's home. When I moved into the house with Kamani, I started to cook for him, warm water for his bath, and even wash his body if he wanted me to. Once you are married, you are governed by somebody else, so there is a big change from when you were living with your mother.

My mother had told me that the best way to be with the husband is to be obedient. When you are told to do anything, you do it without asking questions, because if you refuse, you will be beaten by the husband. "If you try to run away from your husband's home," she said, "you will be returned, and if your husband accepts you back, you have to pay a goat and a gourd of beer to appease him." I learned that a good wife is the one who stays at home, cultivates her own food, and after selling some, buys some goats. At that time, wealth was measured by the number of goats and cows a person had. A woman who was hardworking and was able to buy many goats was called *ngatha* by people, because she had her own wealth and took care of the home. But nowadays, *ngatha* only means a wife who is not wandering about.

I used to be told by my grandmother that a wife who does not obey her husband is called *mbura matū* [deaf-eared]. Even when dancing with the women, you would hear us singing, "Look at the sun, so you may have time to go and cook for your husband and children." Nowadays, we have songs that we sing at weddings about being a good wife. At that wedding you were at with us, you heard us singing the songs about being a good wife to the bride—to love only her husband and children, be hospitable to the people of the village, and everybody will know she is good and she will be praised.

* * *

I was lucky to get pregnant with my first child before even a few months had passed after Kamani and I moved to our new house. I did not know I was pregnant until the baby inside was about three months old and I missed menstruation. I went and told my mother that I was feeling something kicking in my womb and at times it would kick hard. She told me I was pregnant and to not tell anybody. So I waited.

Then the time came when I felt sick and my stomach was aching. I did not know what kind of disease I had, and I started screaming to my husband, telling him that I felt as if somebody had poisoned me. I was scared and was not sure what was wrong. When my husband came and saw me in pain, he went and called four women who came and stayed with me. They lit a very big, bright fire. We stayed at the fire for quite a long time with one or another of the women coming and feeling my stomach after each pain to see if the baby was coming.

When the child was ready to come out, there was not much pathway for him to pass out, so one woman took a razor blade and made a cut to make more room for him. When he came out, she tied the umbilical cord as I have described to you before. I was kneeling down, holding the baby, and the cord was cut and tied. Then some parasitic plant from the *mukoigo* tree was brought to me and I chewed it and the liquid from it was given to the baby to prevent him from having stomach upsets. The women called *"aririri"* five times, and the child was named Wacira.

I did not move around much for about three months. During that time other women were bringing food and fetching water and firewood for me. The tradition is called *itega* and is still practiced. Nowadays, though, we go with bread and sugar and sometimes money, instead of just bananas and porridge.[3]

I felt a big change after Wacira was born because now I was a mother. I was happy because I'd jumped to the next stage. You see your *riika*mates who have not passed to motherhood, and you know, now, that they are yet to face the birth of a child. Now you are looking to your children, not just the husband. And also, now one is wide enough so that other births coming afterwards are without difficulties.

* * *

Wacira was born just before we were put into a concentration camp at the beginning of Mau Mau. What happened is that the British put Kamani and me in a village with a lot of other people from this area. Later, a big trench was built to keep Mau Mau fighters from the forest from coming down to the villages. Bamboo spikes were put inside the trench, so the freedom fighters wouldn't get access to the people in the villages who were feeding them—that way, the British thought the Mau Mau would starve.

We got food to the freedom fighters anyway. Like me, I was one of the women who used to take food into the forest for them. I would first tie the food with banana leaves, then put it up beneath my normal wearing sheet, tie a belt around myself to hold it, and go to the *shamba* outside the fenced village. I would always take a *kibanga*, a *mūkwa*, and a *kiondū* as if I were going to cultivate. Nobody asked me where I was going, and if asked, I would tell the Home Guard I was going to the *shamba*. Then I would walk idly for some time and start collecting firewood in bushes. Finally, some scout for the Mau Mau would come out of the bushes, and I would give him food. I felt more excited than scared. I wanted to help because my brother was one of the freedom fighters by then.

There were quite a few scouts for the Mau Mau—even girls and small boys like Mugo, here, who would sing, *"Itho, Ingoritho, Itho, nī politho"* [Father, you are met, Father by the police]. This was to alert the Mau Mau that the police are coming. The child would sing, beating his vocal cords at his throat to distort the words being sung enough to fool the Home Guards. The Home Guards did not know what the boy was singing, but the Mau Mau knew what the words meant.

During Mau Mau, women were also fighting. Some even went into the forest to help. Women in the villages fought by singing. It was authorized by the British that each village should catch freedom fighters and hand them over to the Home Guards. When we found some, the Home Guards were very happy. Once one came in his jeep, and he seemed very happy that some Mau Mau were captured. To show him we were happy, we began singing and dancing, but then we grew mad, and as we were dancing we started cutting the tires of his vehicle with *ibanga* [machetes], still pretending we were happy. It was ironic. We were destroying the vehicle—almost him—but he still thought we were happy. Because so many older women's sons were fighting, we used to sing:

Mūka ūciaraga ihīī   Women who gives birth to boys
  riua rīkuuma naī.   the sun has risen badly.

There was a big change when we went into the villages because we could not move about without a Home Guard watching us. We could not do a lot of cultivating either. At times, we would just stay there, waiting for the authorities to let us out. One could only wait and pray to God to take care of you. What one had to do in the village was to make sure she did not meet with either the Mau Mau or the government police for fear of being killed. We took a lot of care and were obedient to the orders issued by the British, otherwise there was trouble. Sometimes we were removed from our houses in the middle of the night, even beaten like slaves. We were forced to work during the day digging the trench, even though it was not our wish to do so. When we heard the droning of aircraft coming to bomb the Mau Mau in the forest, we'd run a lot until it was over. The British planted bombs up near the forest and some are still buried near Gatwe. A few years ago, some children playing uncovered one and, thinking it was a ball, began to play with it. It exploded and killed one of them.

When I began to act as a scout for the freedom fighters, I took the Mau Mau Oath—I would not have failed. I had long hair that I could plait at the time, and it was cut with a blunt *kibanga*. Then I became the one who used to beat the girls who refused to take the Oath, and I cut their hair with a blunt *kibanga*. It was a way of making sure that people were loyal to the Agĩkũyũ traditions and to the freedom fighters who were working to liberate us from the British. I knew my brother was fighting, but I only saw him once. Then he looked very tired and hungry.

When we finally got our freedom, we had something to rejoice about. There was much happiness and singing. I can remember one of the songs we were singing that day.

Kamatimu, mũhoe Ngai	Home Guards, be praying to God
Riria nyakeru akiĩnaka	When the British go back home
Mũgatwika nyama cia nderĩ.	You will be fed as meat to the vultures.

On the day of Independence, *Jamhuri*, I was with Njeri, a child born one week earlier. People from here had gone to watch Munyao raise the flag on Mount Kenya. There were so many fireworks the night before, and that morning the Union Jack Flag was lowered and the new Kenyan flag was raised at Kerugoya. On that day, Maina, who was in nursery school by then, broke his hand because of shaking those small flags given to them at school so hard. So I watched the celebrations at Kerugoya while taking Maina to the hospital for treatment. Yes, those times—one can never forget them.

* * *

Soon after the British declared emergency, I got my first child,

Wacira. Then I got another who only lived for six months, and then another who died at the age of one year. So there were three children who were born before Maina, but only one was alive when he was born. Then Wacira died when Maina was only about seven months old. What happened is that he was sick with measles. He was feeling pain, and I had taken him to the hospital to be treated. The next day, when we were at the garden cultivating for the short season's crops, I told Wacira to hold Maina while I cultivated. He refused, telling me that I had refused to take him to the hospital again and he was still sick.

When we came back from the garden, he said he was going to sleep outside—to rest and ease the pain. Suddenly, I heard him produce an "ah 'aaa" sound, and then he kept quiet. I got scared and took him back to the hospital. He spent three months there before he died. After he had been there awhile, wounds began to develop because of urine infection. The children were never removed from their beds or turned over, nor were their sheets and clothes changed, so Wacira would urinate and it would cause the sores.

The day I took Wacira back to the hospital, the heavy rains of 1961 started, and he died when it was still raining. It rained hard for many days. Later, I realized that Wacira died of tetanus—it had come from the measles. That boy's death changed me. If you have something and it is taken from you, you would not feel so happy. Me, I started to get thin, remembering I'd never see Wacira again or the things he used to do. I stayed a long time before I got used to his absence. That was just before *Uhuru*, and it was not long after that that I became a Catholic.

*   *   *

My mother became a Catholic while we were in the villages during Mau Mau. She used to tell me about going for catechism classes in order to get baptized. She advised me that being a Catholic helped one to leave bad behaviors like abusing people, singing and dancing during *Irua*, and drinking beer.

I joined the church after *Uhuru* because I wanted to continue making my name clean and to learn to leave behind bad behaviors. I decided to join the Catholic Church because it was the first denomination here on earth—it was left by Jesus. And the Catholic Church does not discriminate. Even people with clothes that have lice are found seated together with clean, smart people. What the church emphasizes is to like everybody. It wants to have unity and peace among all people.

Once, before Mau Mau, I went to church, but I did not understand what was happening. I only saw a white man preaching. I was told he was a priest. But I do remember one reading from the Bible. The priest read that "Nations will fall against nations." I asked myself, "How are they going to fall against each other?" Then one day during Mau Mau, I went to harvest millet and I met my oldest brother called Maina. The first thing he asked me was whether I knew him. I thought that strange, but answered, "Yes." He slapped me. I was surprised. He asked me again and I said, "Yes" again, and he started to beat me until I denied that I knew him. My brother was a Mau Mau, and the reason he slapped me was because he was afraid that I might reveal him to the Home Guard and he was testing me. But I didn't understand that at the time, and I thought about the prophecy of that priest and realized that it was coming true—"Nations will rise against nations;" fathers will deny their own children, and a brother will deny his sister and she will deny him.

That same day I went home and my mother asked, "Do you know me?" and I said, "Yes," and she started to beat me until I said I didn't know her, then she stopped. She explained about my brother. In fact, it happened that during Mau Mau times, a son could kill his father and vice versa.

That priest had also told us that after some time, things that fly like birds in the sky would come, and during Mau Mau I saw airplanes for the first time. Then I really believed the priest. Another time it was prophesied that *amemenyi*—destroyers—would come. Before, maize kernels stored in the granary used to be infested only by weevils. But now, if you go into a granary, you can see moths destroying the maize completely into flour. Aren't they the destroyers we were told about?

So I joined the Catholic Church and that's when I got this name Mary. I changed when I joined. Before, if I was abused by anybody, we would fight and I would never keep quiet about it. If I heard that people were gossiping about me, I would go and ask them about it. I could stand outside my house and abuse anybody hard without caring. But now, if someone came and started beating me, I would not return their beating. Even if one were to come to my homestead and start cursing me, I would just ignore her. So there is a big change. I am able to humble myself now to follow Jesus's teaching that even when he was abused, mocked, and saliva thrown at him, he only humbled himself.

When I go for the Sunday service, the reading from the Bible and the interpretations help me in straightening out my behaviors. At times, a reading can be concerned with how wives abuse their husbands and so in return are beaten. If I have abused Kamani the night before, I go and apologize and make good our relationship. My husband is like one organ of my body. We two make one body, and when hating him, I am also hating myself and vice versa. The church taught me that.

I can remember a time when I was very sick with a high fever for three months. It wasn't malaria. I had a bad stomachache as well. All those months, I never cultivated my *shamba*. The church members came and cultivated the whole *shamba*, collected firewood, fetched water, and washed the clothes. They cooked for my children and my husband every day. The members have helped on two occasions like that when I was sick. Now I'm having my renewal wedding, and the women will help me with money and cooking for the guests. So in our church, we help each other.

We have a group that teaches us to be better wives and mothers. It's called Catholic Church Women's Action Group. I have been a member for five years. Its work is to help every woman to love her husband's parents, the people of the community, and her people at home. It teaches us how to treat our husband well and bring him closer to God. At times, my husband might come home drunk. We are taught how to deal with him, touching him all over and asking him why he got drunk, so that when he sees our concern, he will not feel like beating us.

When we first started the group, we were only 20 women. Now we are 370 women. We go helping the poor—like if somebody does not have a house, we contribute money and build a house for that person. We help each other when we are sick, like I told you, and encourage women to renew their vows with a church wedding. Anytime there is a wedding, like mine next month, each member of the group gives a contribution and then they go and sing songs and dance and make the people who have come to the homestead after the wedding happy. We also visit schools, giving advice to girls about how they can be better women of tomorrow by not being loose around men and staying in school. Some of our girls now are becoming pregnant while they are in school, and then they are forced to leave and come home. It is not a good thing. Our group also goes into homesteads preaching and teaching good morals. We have found it necessary to compose songs and go singing as a part of our teaching, because that way the people listen.

It was members of our church women's group who decided to form Winyeriĩkia Women's Group. But Winyeriĩkia is commercial, because we make money from our projects. Like this one of weaving banana fibers—those women from Nairobi who came and taught us how to make the baskets are paying us 20 shillings for each basket. They also gave us 1,500 shillings, which we divided amongst ourselves, each woman getting 50. But we were counseled to give our husbands 20 of it, so they will know that the place we go each week is productive. Our group raises pigs, as you know, and slaughters them and sells the meat to raise money for the group.

Long ago, when I belonged to neither women's group, I always waited for that time when my husband would give me money, and when he didn't I remained poor. Now I am able to take care of myself with the money we contribute each month. Like the granary I'm adding here at this homestead, I will not ask my husband for a cent, even though he got his coffee harvest money just the other day. If I rely on him to give me money, the day he misses I will have a problem. So the women's group really helps me financially, and I'm learning how to do new things like these baskets.

Even though the women's group helps me in many ways, I still have to cultivate the coffee to raise money for school fees. We started growing coffee in the villages just before *Uhuru*, and we planted it here afterwards. At first, we were afraid the government might just take our coffee away from us, because the British had not allowed us to grow it. But when the first yield was ripe, extension workers came and paid us for the harvest. Then they came around and showed us how to plant seedlings, digging the hole, then filling them with manure and putting dirt around the seedlings. We plant coffee trees in straight rows with the help of *conti*, which is a sort of line measure. Picking has not changed since we began. What has changed is the way we take care of the coffee. We plant with less manure now. At first, agricultural extension workers did the spraying for disease, but now each farmer sprays his own coffee. Nowadays, we know how to prune back the branches of the coffee trees in such a way that there are more berries in the next year.

Coffee is only harvested twice a year, but we get more per kilo than people who plant tea. I am always learning something new to improve my *shamba*—look down there, all that maize I have planted and the tomatoes you see here. When the passion fruits and avocados are ripe, I will take them to the market and sell them. Though we don't have much land here, my *shamba* is good because I work hard.

* * *

I do not forget anything I learn. For instance, when I was at Wambugu Farm, I learned that when a male pig is made sexually inactive, it grows fat quickly. I learned how to circumcise [she means castrate] the young male piglets so they can be fattened. When I came back here, I taught the Winyeriĩkia members how to do it. I learned that when the mother pig gives birth, we have to watch it carefully so that it doesn't eat the first piglet, which is something a sow normally does. Now we raise the pigs with the knowledge I learned when I went for the course.

I also teach the Winyeriĩkia women new ways of weaving baskets. Another woman and I were the supervisors on decorating sisal baskets with woolen thread for designs. We taught the rest how to make the designs. And these banana-fiber baskets, mine was "number one," and I even made a big tray that was given to Vice President Kibaki when he came for the *harambee* fund-raising for the secondary schools. That is why the woman from Nairobi told me that I have my own kind of blessings, because I learn many things quickly, then I am able to teach others the same things. And I like learning new things, too. That is why after I returned from the course at Wambugu Farm, I decided to join the community adult education class so I could learn to read and write.

I first heard about the class when it was announced in church that the president was giving free adult education classes and that old people should go to school, too, and learn how to write their names and read the names of places—like that sign on the road that shows the way to Kamuiru. Before I had not known what it said, but now I know. I can read anything written in Kikuyu and written in large letters.

I first joined the class a long time ago because Mugo [last-born son, now age six] was not born yet. We used to pay 6 shillings and were taught by a man called Kamenyi. When I became pregnant with Mugo, I became lazy and stopped going until 1982 when President Moi announced that it was important for adults to go.

I joined because I wanted to know how to write and read without anybody's help. Like now, my daughter at school at Mwea, she writes a letter in Kikuyu, and after reading it I know that she is asking for cotton wool or something else. We can also talk our secrets in letters. Now if Kamani is in town working somewhere, I never tell somebody to write him. That somebody might abuse him in the letter without my knowledge, and then he would accuse me for nothing. Now, I write my husband and say what I think is important, and he writes back.

Because I know writing and some maths, I was made the clan's treasurer, and when we went to put the money in the bank, I was happy to be able to put down my signature instead of a fingerprint. And I know the amount of coffee I pick and keep a record.

Sometimes at the adult education class a community worker comes and teaches us things that are good to know. You remember the day last week when a woman from the family planning clinic came and taught the women in class about different food groups and what is the best combination to feed one's children. And she even asked the women with babies if they knew about family planning, but some of them were shy. I think family planning is a good idea, and I'm training to be a community educator so I can teach other women how to go about it.

What do I like best about the class? I like reading and would like to know how to talk in English because if I knew, we would be talking together in English. The hardest part for me to learn is maths and especially when we were having thousands. But adding smaller numbers is easy. Reading and writing Kikuyu are easiest because they are my language. Sometimes there is a newspaper printed in Kikuyu called *Githomo* ["Reading"]. I enjoy that newspaper.

I would like a newspaper in the class, but the visitors [guest speakers] give information, too—like about raising chickens and cows. A cow like this one here [she points to one of the family's cows], now that it is hot and there is not enough grass, I learned we must buy extra food in the shop for it. I also learned to boil water for drinking and to keep it in a pot. But we do not follow that practice because what I do is go to a spring that produces very clean water and fetch water there for the homestead. But some women with very many children do not have time to fetch water and then boil it. Usually we boil water when we make tea—that way it is clean.

If I had to choose between attending the adult education class and the women's group, I would attend the women's group, because it is the one that gives me financial help. The adult education classes teach good things, but it does not help us with school fees for our children or to get a new granary.

The way I learn best is by comparing myself with other people and trying to work better than them. The Agĩkũyũ says that "a woman never challenged does not give birth." We also say, "Going wide is seeing and learning much." The one who just stays in one place is a fool. When I move outside, I learn something new and when I come back I try to use new methods I've learned.

* * *

Long ago, when a woman had a son as old as Maina, she could become an elder and was made a member of the *kiama* if the woman wanted to. But these days there is no recognition when a woman's child gets circumcised. Some children are even circumcised without the knowledge of their parents. The old customs are not followed now. The only change I felt when I stopped menstruating was feeling sick with a lot of heat and sweating sometimes. That was about four years ago. Now that it's over, I'm happy. I am not very interested in wanting my husband sexually either.

Of all the changes I've told you about, the one that changed me the most was when I gave birth. That's because I knew then that I had become a woman entitled to some duties and respect. But when I stopped menstruating I was happy, because now I'm like a young girl again because I'm not always having to wait and wash clothes and cook for everybody. My daughters help with those things now. If I spend the night anywhere, nobody can ask me about it, and I do not have any small child who is crying—that makes me happy.

My biggest role is working at home in my *shamba* and in the homestead. Then next is being a mother. Third most important is going to the Women's Church Group and Winyeriĩkia, because there I'm taught how to stay comfortably at home. Leave the work of midwifery to last—I can only do it when it is there to be done. Before that comes the wife's role, because it means that I am able to keep my home whole, as the word *mũtumia* means "one who can mend and seal and make whole." The role of student is more important because then I learn a lot of new, good things that I did not know were there before. The role of teacher should come between the role of student and midwife.

What am I proudest of having achieved? I know I have achieved a lot of things—like making that granary there. It is me who thought how to make it. My husband never asked. I also know that I'm able to cultivate my *shamba* well and get a lot of yields from it. That is because I am a hard worker. But I use my brain a lot, too.

I always dream and pray that before I die, I may see my children grow up to support themselves, with the boys marrying and having good homes, because I see that it is me who supports them now. The boys should finish school and also the girls. Long time ago, when I was a child, parents used to say that they wouldn't take their girls to school because they might become prostitutes. But now, girls can help people at home as well as going to school. Some even go further than their brothers—look at Njeri. She has gone further than Maina, who stopped in Standard Seven.

My strongest character is loving people and never discriminating between them. Anybody who is friendly to me becomes my friend. I do not choose whom I make friends with—they choose me. My weakest character is that if anybody makes me annoyed, I feel frustrated that I can't shout back and tell that person my mind.

What does womanhood mean to me? It means taking care of the home so that where there are loopholes, I mend them, and when my husband comes home drunk and furious, I try to cool him. Agĩkũyũ means that I have gone through *mbuci* and *matũ*, then *Irua*. These things make me pure Mũgĩkũyũ. You can never be a pure Mũgĩkũyũ, but if you stay around us long enough, you will learn a lot about our ways, because now you are my friend.

Notes

1. Local chiefs were appointed by the British colonial government during the period to which Wanoi refers.
2. I often saw the ten-year-old daughter in the compound where I lived feeding her small sister in the same manner, using her first finger and shoving mashed food into the baby's mouth.
3. There were a number of occasions during my year and a half in the field when I participated in *itega*. It was always a joy-filled event, when women sang and danced as well as providing food, firewood, and, today, shillings for the new child and mother.

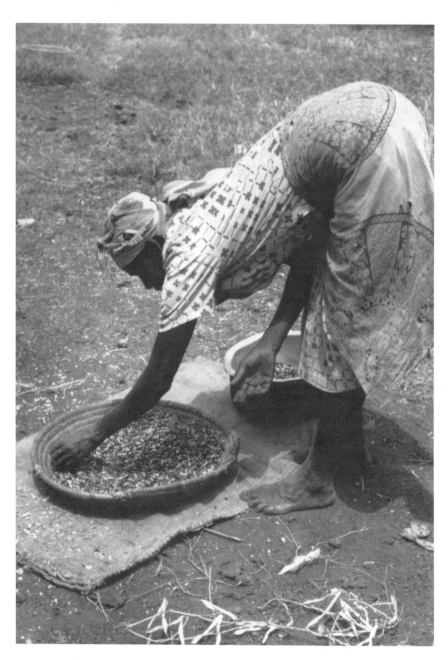

Preparing beans for githeri, *a Gikuyu staple dish.*

7

Lives and Schooling: Nyambura

Whereas most women in their early fifties had little or no experience with formal education, schooling has had a major impact on the lives of those in their twenties. The mean average number of years of school that women in this age group had attended in Mutira was 5.8. Only three in our sample reached the secondary level, and none reached university. Though a very few women do reach the tertiary level, they are exceptional cases. The majority of young women in rural areas do not have the opportunity of attending secondary schools, which requires a financial investment on their parents' part. Others attend *harambee* (self-help) schools, which are usually less well equipped and where teachers, often hired by the local community, are either less well trained than those in government schools or not trained at all.

What kinds of changes does formal schooling imply for the lives of the younger women? Do these women, born on the eve of Independence, have greater socioeconomic opportunities than their mothers and grandmothers? What are their major life concerns as young mothers? How do they view their roles as women?

Nyambura and Wanja represent two different possibilities for rural women in their twenties. Nyambura was formally educated through Standard Five (fifth grade), when she dropped out of school—she represents the average. Wanja is one of two women in the sample population who completed Form Four (four years of high school). She represents an increasing number of young women, who, armed with a secondary-school certificate, return home to search for wage work and a better life.

Nyambura typifies her cohort group because she is married with two small children. She lives at her husband's homestead. She depends economically upon her husband's salary as a postal clerk and the money she earns from picking tea. Nyambura is Catholic and is an active member of her church.

I had opportunities to spend time outside of the scheduled interviews observing Nyambura, who lives at the homestead of a family I had known previously and often visited. She has a cheerful disposition and is extremely hardworking. She delighted in teaching me the rudimentary skills associated with fetching water and cutting wood for the cooking fire. During our first few interviews she was shy. As the sessions progressed, she began to reveal her feelings and candidly talked about significant events that had occurred in her life.

—J.D.

I was born at Kamuiru, the last born of Kimere and Kagūre. My father, Kimere, was a tall, slender man—slightly taller than me—and he had a quick temper like Kinyua, my brother. Kagūre, my mother, is a cheerful woman and hardworking. I was named Nyambura for my mother's mother, who was born during the Long Rains [*mbura* refers to rain]. I am of the Unjiru Clan, and my Christian name—the one I was baptized in the Catholic Church—is Meri. There are three brothers—Magondu, the firstborn, then Karimi, and Kinyua, who is eight years older than me. Magondu is talkative and polite. Karimi is also talkative, but in a different way. I really cannot remember too much about them because they were already big and were married when I was still little. Kinyua, I remember. He was a good, young boy who didn't know how to defy order, but he did have a quick temper. There was also a sister, Margaret Kaiira, who was cheerful, as I remember her when growing up. She follows Karimi and was a big girl of eighteen years when I came to understand things.

Margaret and Kinyua were the ones who took care of me, but Margaret loved me the most. I could tell she did because she would bathe me, make up my hair, wash my clothes, and give me food. At times, she would carry me around tied to her back. Because there were no other girls in the family, she used to knit nice cardigans for me.

Margaret and Kinyua were the ones who used to tell stories and riddles around the cooking fire in the evenings. I can't remember any of the stories right now, but here's a riddle:

Gwata ndai.	Catch a riddle.
Ndagwata.	I am ready.
Wathiĩ na njira wathekio nũ?	Who smiled at you as you walked along the road?
Mwatũka wa thi.	A crack in the earth.

I was a child who liked to hear riddles and try to figure them out. I also liked to try new things. If people went to the *shamba* to cultivate, I would not like to be left behind—I wanted to go, too. I learned how to cultivate with a *kibanga*, go for water, and wash clothes from my

Figure 7.1 NYAMBURA'S FAMILY

mother. If she went to the river, I would be given a small gourd, and she would go and tie it with a *mūkwa* to my back after we had fetched the water. I learned most of the things like washing clothes with soap and scrubbing them to get them clean by watching my mother, then doing what she did.

I learned about all my relatives from both my mother and father. We would go to visit some relatives—like when my mother carried me on her back to visit my uncles and aunts. When we met them, I was told who they were and how they were related to me. It was important for us as children to know which people we were related to and who were clanmates.

How did I learn good from bad characters? My mother would advise me. If I was visiting or moving with a girl with bad characters, she would tell me never to visit that girl again. Like the girl who is lazy or does not respect the elders—that one is bad. I also taught myself, because I would know when I made a mistake and stop doing that thing and never repeat it. I can remember once I was sent somewhere by my father, but I refused to go. Then I was beaten. So I learned that it is bad to refuse when one is sent somewhere, and since that day my father has never beaten me.

When we were little girls, we used to play games like *mbiya*, where children try and hit each other with a ball made out of strings. We'd also play *ciūthi*, which is played with five stones thrown in the air. First, one throws one stone up in the air and at the same time tries to get another from the ground. Then she throws again and gets a second, third, and fourth stone. Finally, one throws all the stones on the ground and this time, she has to collect two at a go, each time, then one. The last time, one would fold the hands and throw up all the stones, meanwhile turning the hands, palms down and flat, to catch all five stones together on the backs of the hands. Then we'd throw the stones again to start over. We liked that game. We'd also sing songs and jump, using a rope. Sometimes we made toys out of maize stalks and string or bottle tops.

* * *

I can remember the first day I went to school, because it was Magondu, my oldest brother, who took me. His children were like my agemates, so he took all of us together. We spent the first day there trying to reach our one hand over the head, like this, to the other side of the head, and anybody who was able to reach her hand over and touch the ear with her fingers on the other side was big enough to go to Standard One. As we were chosen, we entered the classroom. We spent the day like this, then it was time to go home. On the way home, we chased each other and talked about the class and the teacher.

My home was at Kamuiru and I went to school at Mutira. We would start the journey to school at 7:00 A.M. and reach school at about ten minutes to eight. On our way, we'd go playing on the road and sometimes running instead of walking—racing with each other. We never wore shoes to school, but we had a uniform—a green tunic with a light pink blouse. The tunic had pleats with a belt behind and the blouse had a round collar. I used to hear my sister Margaret complaining about how dirty I got those uniforms while she scrubbed them in a *karai* [metal basin rounded at the bottom, used for washing clothes].

In the first year of school, we learned how to draw, make toys, and solve some math problems—like counting and subtracting maize and bean seeds. Also, we made pots out of clay. We were given homework—like making baskets—and would have to take the basket to school the next day for inspection. My sister showed me how to make the basket and prepare the threads into strings for weaving, as I wasn't able to do it yet. I was smaller than Muthoni [a niece in the compound, aged nine] when I learned how to make baskets. My sister and mother knew which plants had the best threads for weaving, so they would collect them for me. At first we used *migio*, then later we began to use sisal. It was hard to learn the patterns. My sister would show me how to weave the threads in and out of the main strings. Then I would try as I saw she had done, but sometimes I would make mistakes, and she would tell me, "No, that is not the way it's done, here watch me again." Then I would try again until I learned. About the same time, my sister was beginning to knit cardigans with knitting needles, and she could also crochet, so she used to teach me these things.

The school I went to was made of mud bricks. Only the two Standard Seven classrooms were built of stone. We used to sit on long benches, and we wrote on cut pieces of blackboard. Later on, we started writing in notebooks. If a child forgot her notebook, the teacher would punish her with a beating. By my last year of school—in Standard Five—I was going very early in the morning to sweep the classroom and then pour water on the floor to clean it [most classroom floors are polished concrete]. After cleaning the floor, I'd go for parade with the rest of the children, where the teacher on duty inspected us. Anybody who had lice on her hair was shaved over a portion of her head and sent home. Those who were dirty were pinched hard by the teacher and sent to the river to wash.

I can't exactly remember which lesson we used to start with, but we would go to class at 8:00 A.M. By the time we had reached

Standard Four, we got each lesson [subject] from a different teacher who would come into our classroom. But the first three years we had only one permanent teacher for all the subjects. There was a break time at mid-morning. During that time we used to play games and chase each other around the yard, then back to the classroom. Each lesson was about thirty minutes. The break came after the fourth lesson, then there were two more hours of lessons, and we'd have a break and go home for lunch. We'd come back at 2:00 P.M.—after about an hour and a half—and have three more lessons, then a break, then back to the classroom to collect our books before going home at 4:00 P.M.

The way math was taught is that the teacher wrote numbers on the blackboard, and we copied them down into our exercise books or on our small blackboards. After solving the problems, we took the book up to the teacher who would mark the problems we'd done. When we were learning numbers or words, after the teacher wrote them on the blackboard, she would call someone's name and that student would wake up and read what was on the board with the other students repeating after her.

Sometimes we had plays, songs, and dances that were in Kikuyu or Kiswahili. We sang songs like:

Ĩi wakĩthonjo gikura	Yes, you are noisy, making noise.
Thonjo kiratũ kiega nĩ kia mwalimu.	The best shoe is that of the Teacher.

We had plays that usually had something to teach us—like respecting the elders or working hard at our studies. Once I remember a child was beaten because he had been fighting with other children. And another child was beaten when he came late to school. I was beaten once, too. The teacher used to use a stick against a boy's back—that's the way he was beaten—but a girl was beaten on the palm of her hands.

After school, I would run home to help my sister go for water at the river or to collect maize stalks for the cows. On Saturdays, we helped in the *shamba*, weeding the vegetables, or during the harvesting of coffee we'd pick coffee berries. My sister would give me a small *kiondu* to carry to the *shamba* and I'd pick the berries on the lowest branches. We used to see who could get the most. On Sundays, nobody worked. We'd get up, bathe and get dressed in our best clothes. Then my mother took us to the Sunday School at the Catholic Church. We'd have Bible lessons and singing, and afterwards, on the way home, we'd visit our relatives and neighbors. We were always fed well on those visits.

I stopped going to school in Standard Five. What happened is that at that time, the local brew called *karabu* was on the increase, and my father used to drink so much that he was unable to take all his children to school. We used to be sent from school often because the parents had not contributed to the *harambee* fund for building another classroom or because we didn't have writing materials. I could spend the whole term without going to school. I never lacked the school fees but my father was a drunkard and never viewed education as something very important; there were so many of us children who were school age that with the drinking, my father could not afford to keep us all in school. I felt badly about leaving school, but there was nothing I could do.

* * *

Soon after leaving school, I went to live with the Mwais, who are relatives. Ever since I was little I was used to going to visit the Mwais, and I liked the place. So when they wanted me to go and stay with them, I was ready to go. [At this point in the interview, Nyambura's husband's mother entered the cooking hut where we were having the interview and, on hearing the exchange, explained, "Sometime back, people used to ask for young girls to help them in bringing up their own children. Usually, the girl was a relative. She became an *ayah*. So Mrs. Mwai went to Nyambura's mother, who was a relative, and as Nyambura was the last born and the mother did not have another child, she asked to be given Nyambura. Nyambura agreed and stayed with the Mwai family until she got married."]

I went to the Mwai's home when I was a child of about ten years. There I was taught by Mrs. Mwai things about how to care for the children, to cook, and to keep the house clean. This was a change because at my house I had never had to do much work, being the last born. There weren't any big differences between Mrs. Mwai and my mother, though, because Mrs. Mwai used to treat me just like one of her children, and we were related. Mwai is son-of-Kibuga, who is son-of-Ndegwa, who is son-of-Kimere, whom my father was named after.

The children I looked after at the Mwais—one was very small and the other was about the size of Mwangi [Nyambura's three-year old son]. The baby was put in a woven baby cot, and my work was to put the cot outside and, after some time, to bring it inside again. I remember how Mrs. Mwai used to wake earlier than me, and she would go and milk the cows. Then I would wake, and as she was preparing to go to school—she was a teacher—I would help her by putting tea into her thermos flask to take to school. After she left, I would start preparing the lunch, peeling the potatoes and carrots carefully so as not to cut myself. After preparing lunch, I would wash the baby's nappies [diapers] and other clothes—that took the rest of the morning. Then everybody would come home for lunch, and afterward I would wash up the dishes and look after the baby.

In the evening, Mrs. Mwai came home, and we would prepare supper together and then do the dishes together after dinner. Then she used to correct students' notebooks by the kerosene lamp. It was my job to keep the lamp full of kerosene and the glass clean. I remember that Mrs. Mwai and the husband never used to fight—if he said something that annoyed her, she would just keep quiet, but he knew that he had done something that made her annoyed and would apologize to her. They never argued with one another.

*   *   *

[An interview with Mrs. Mwai revealed the following about Nyambura's years with their family.]

When Nyambura came to live with us, she was very young. She was about ten years old. She worked for me as a maid. It is me who asked her to come because I needed somebody to take care of my children while I was teaching at the primary school. Her roles here were to take care of the children, cook, and care for the home. I taught her how to take care of the home—keeping it neat and clean—how to do the laundry, ways of cooking, and care for the children. I also taught her how to knit, toward the end of her stay, and bought her a knitting machine. She has it now and knows how to knit cardigans for sale. With the cardigans she sold while living here, she used to earn her money for clothes and other things I did not provide. No, she was not paid here. I taught her by talking to her—giving instructions—and showing her how to go about things. I was not sad when Nyambura was old enough to be married, even though I was not so happy to be left without a maid. I would have liked her to stay longer, but as her time to marry had come, I would not have denied her. A girl must one day get married. Wacera, whom as you know Nyambura eventually married, used to come here and visit. I knew him, and he did not seem a bad man for Nyambura to stay together with.

*   *   *

Did I go through *Irua* before I was married? *Wῖ* [you], those days are over! You know I am a Christian, and we do not believe it is a good thing. Why? Because it was a thing of the past. Going to school and learning some things helped us see the difference. We learned that we no longer needed *Irua*—that was for the old people. You know the president made it against the law. There are some who still do it, but not many. No, I didn't get my ears pierced, either. That was for our mothers. Some of those old women used to hurt each others' ears when fighting. I once saw a woman grap another's *matũ* [hole in the earlobe] and pull it until it ripped. That woman was screaming very hard from pain. No, I would not want *matũ*.

How did I meet Wacera [her husband]? Well, while I was staying at the Mwais, I used to go to the post office down at Kutus to collect the mail for them, and that is where Wacera worked—at the post office. So we used to see each other that way. Then one day he asked me where my home was, and I told him, and he promised to pay a visit.

When Wacera first came to the Mwais to visit, I ran away from him. But then I came to like him, as he visited me. That continued for some time, until I noticed he was not coming to see me as much and maybe had found another, better girl. After he stopped coming so much, I found I was two months pregnant. I went home and told my parents what was happening. My mother was unhappy. Wacera was called by my parents, but he refused to go. I have never had such mistreatment. He didn't deny that he was responsible for the pregnancy, but he didn't say anything about marrying me either. What defeated my understanding was that although he used to visit me every day after work, now that I was pregnant, he ignored me completely, and even when I tried to approach him about the pregnancy, he showed no sign of interest. To me, it seemed that everything was over between us. I was really angry with him.

Mwangi [Nyambura's firstborn child] was born while I was staying at my parents' home, knowing that there was no relationship left between Wacera and me. Even though everybody knew about the relationship—both our parents—it seemed to have died. I felt badly that I was having a child with no hope of getting married. I decided I would just have to raise the child alone. When it came time to deliver, I went to Tumu Tumu Hospital. The pains began about one in the afternoon and lasted up until nine that night. Mwangi was born that night, and I stayed in the hospital for about eight days, then went home to my parents' place.

Things really changed for me after I had Mwangi because I suddenly became conscious that I was totally responsible for this tiny human being and what the future holds for him. I started thinking about how I would bring Mwangi up, and when he grew bigger, take him to school. I started my knitting business so I would get money to take him to school. Now I knew I was a *mũtumia*—a full-grown woman. When you are a girl and then give birth, you find that you are changed. Your body features change, too—the breasts drop, and the features show that you are no longer a girl. And you change mentally, too, because you are always thinking about your children. So you have gone from girlhood to womanhood. Even when walking with a young girl my age who is not a mother, I would not call myself a girl anymore. The woman with a baby on her back signifies that she is a mother. When I became a mother, that was the biggest change for me.

While I was at my parents' home, my father gave me a piece of land to cultivate. My mother helped me plant maize and beans and some *skuma-wiki* [kale]. I worked hard to keep my mind off my problems and to get plenty of food for those at home. Sometimes my mother would look after Mwangi so I didn't have to work in the *shamba* with him on my back. Then I would make sure I returned to the compound in plenty of time to suckle him.

By that time, my sister was married and living down near Embu. Sometimes we would go and visit her. We would take a *matatu* [a station wagon or car, privately owned, used as a public means of fee-paying transportation] from Kagumo to Kutus and then another one to Embu. We'd stay there the afternoon, eating and even dancing with the women of her husband's homestead, then return home by dark. My sister had three children by then, and they liked to see my child. Margaret's husband is a teacher. He has planted a lot of coffee and even hired some workers to help with the harvest. He is saving some of the profits for building a stone house. Margaret is lucky to have such a good husband. When we visited her during that time I was separated from Wacera, it made me sad to think I had no husband.

At times during the period when Wacera and I were separated, he would come to my home to visit, and I'd realize that there was no love. So other times when he came, I just ignored him and continued with my work without becoming involved. During this time he married a girl, and they were staying together at Kutus—in fact, she and I were pregnant at the same time!

I tried to be happy on my own, but it was hard to find happiness because I was still young and to be a mother, without marrying—that is something I never imagined. I was feeling sick sometimes and would go to the hospital to be treated, only to be told that I was not sick. Finally, I learned to swallow the bitter pill and stay alone. Sometimes Wacera and I would meet on the way to Kutus, and he'd tell me a lot of nonsense—how he's coming for me. I ignored his words and began teaching myself how to use the knitting machine by watching a neighbor of the Mwais. Toward the end of 1982, I went to Kutus to start my knitting business there.

I set up my knitting machine in the *nduka* [shop] of one of Mr. Mwai's friends. I was making sweaters and jackets. People liked what I made, and I began to sell the sweaters. During that time, I stayed with my sister and her husband in Kutus. While I was there, Wacera started visiting me. By this time he had chased his wife away and left another girlfriend. He was staying alone and wanted me to come and stay with him. I told him to go and talk to my parents. He persuaded them that he wouldn't repeat his bad behavior, so I decided to take Mwangi and go and live with him. Mwangi was about two and a half years [old] then.

We stayed in peace for a few months, then I found I was pregnant again, and the mistreatment began—he even started beating me and slapping me around until I couldn't eat anymore. I felt that I couldn't leave him, because now I was having two children by him.

Finally, I decided that I should come here to Wacera's parents' place and tell them I was leaving after all. When the parents found out about the problems, they called Wacera and talked to him about the other girls he was moving with and whether he wanted any of them for his wife. The father said to Wacera, "I have known Nyambura for some time now, and I say that she should stay here with us, and if you have anything to say, then say it." Wacera kept quiet. He was going for a course in Nairobi, so I came here to live with Mwangi. When I got here, I found the father had recently died and Wacera's mother was very sad, with nobody to fetch water for her and the cows a pathetic sight. When I came, Wacera's mother was so happy that she didn't want me to leave, so she talked to Wacera and he cooled down and vowed not to mistreat me again.

At the time, Wacera had another woman friend, and he found me to be a barrier because I was stopping him from enjoying himself with other girls. Because we are here and not in Kutus, he has his freedom to do anything he wishes down there. Now he's not so angry and acting like a lunatic. When we have a problem, I go tell his mother. Things are much better now, and I only pray to God to help me to be strong.

At the time that Mwangi and I went to live with Wacera in Kutus there was no *rūracio* given, but just recently, when Wacera decided to come and live here with us at his parents' home, he took a thousand shillings to my father. Nobody asked him for it—he just chose to take it. The tradition of *rūracio* has changed from long ago—today's men who want to take it to the girl's parents can and those who choose not to, nobody forces them. But good men, they follow the old customs by giving the number of goats or cows that were given for the girl's mother. If the *rūracio* for your mother was ten goats, that amount would be calculated in terms of money, so the young man would give the amount in shillings to the girl's parents. People here negotiate in both goats and shillings. The more schooling a girl has, the higher the *rūracio* asked, because the father has made a big investment in her education.

*   *   *

Now that I am a mother with two children, I think about how I can teach them good behavior. First, a mother should teach her children to respect elders, to have good manners, and to obey the mother and father. I have two boys, but if I had a girl I would want her to be hardworking—like farming, washing clothes, and cleanliness. Also, hospitality to visitors is important and caring for one's things. I would teach the girl how to cook, and when I go to the *shamba*, tell her to accompany me and see the way I do the cultivating. When she is young, I would tell her to make sure she goes straight to school without passing through other children's homes. And I would watch her to see which friends she moves with—whether they are good or bad and counsel her. If she went to secondary school, I would tell her that after school she should not get in the habit of sneaking away from school like some girls and going to visit boys, making endless journeys moving from place to place. After she is mature, I would tell her, as Mrs. Mwai told me, not to have sexual relations until the time she is married. I would advise her to be firm on it, for a man who is really serious and not just after sexual enjoyment will wait for her until she is ready.

I am teaching my sons to be obedient and to work hard at things like farming and taking care of goats and cows when they get older. Boys of five or six begin to care for the goats and sheep, so these sons of mine are still a bit young. Another thing—they should learn how to cultivate the tea.

You have seen me picking tea here. It is only recently that I learned—in May 1983. At home we only had coffee. It was *Cūcū* [husband's mother] who taught me. She told me that one picks two leaves and a bud, and not to leave a big stalk but to pick close to the leaves. I used to pick very slowly, like a child. The first time I picked 5 kilos [11 lbs.]. Then I was able to pick more kilos as the days went by. Now, when I start after my morning work of the homestead, I can pick about 25 kilos [55 lbs.].

When I am not picking tea, I am working in the *shamba*, cultivating the maize and beans or sweet potatoes. We plant maize and beans together, but *waru* [European potatoes] and *ngwacĩ* [sweet potatoes] are planted separately in another plot. We plant kale and cabbage in one plot together with carrots and tomatoes at the border.

We have maize and beans planted up here and down at the river where the soil is best. Altogether, we have about six different plots, but some are very small. Most of the land on the hillsides is planted in tea. I think there must be about 5 acres [2 ha] of tea here. Does *Cũcũ* own it? No. Now that *Mzee* is no longer alive, it belongs to Wacera and his brothers. But Wacera does not have much to do with it unless it needs pruning.

Does Wacera ever help me in the *shamba*? Yes. When the soil needs to be prepared for planting, you will find him here working. Also at harvest time. But by the time he reaches here from Kutus on Saturday afternoons, all he wants to do is rest from the week's work—so I don't count on him. But when he comes, he usually brings some meat and bread or some other thing we might be missing here. Last month, you remember, there was a shortage of sugar. Not even the shops down in Kagumo had any. But Wacera found a shop in Kutus that had sugar so he brought some home to us. The same with *unga* [maize meal]. Six months ago, during the dry season, there was a shortage of *unga*. When that happens, people start buying it up and hoarding it. Then you miss *ugali* [maize-meal porridge cooked to a hard consistency] for a few weeks. Wacera knows where to buy *unga* when there is a shortage.

During the dry season, there are no vegetables to find up here. Then potatoes mixed with green bananas and *ugali* are our main foods. But I know it is good for children to have vegetables, so on market day, I go to Kagumo or Kutus and buy vegetables we no longer have here. The old people—they are happy without vegetables like carrots and tomatoes. They prefer *githeri* or millet porridge. But we who are young like vegetables—especially carrots.

I want my children to grow up healthy. Right now I am worried about the baby. The doctor at the clinic says he has a problem in his lungs. I see him breathing hard and wonder what is to be done. I want to take him to the hospital in Nairobi, but I'm told one needs to be recommended by a doctor here. Sometimes I become fearful, wondering if this baby will survive. Then I pray to God for an answer.

I would like to have as many children as God gives me. I do not like these family planning ideas. It is not good to put chemicals into the body. My husband would not allow it either. Children are a blessing to the Agĩkũyũ.[1]

Being a farmer and doing my work here are my most important roles, because without them I would have nothing to feed us. It's also important to keep the home clean—I learned that from Mrs. Mwai. Next most important is my role as wife to Wacera, then my role as a mother. My role as a daughter is less important, because I am now married and living at my husband's homestead. Do I ever cultivate the *shamba* at my parents' home? Sometimes I go there for a visit, but my brother is taking care of the *shamba*.

I do not belong to any women's group because I don't have time—there is too much work to do here. You have helped me fetch water—it takes many trips [I counted five on an average day] down to the stream and back again at the end of my work in the *shamba* to have enough water for cooking supper and bathing. The only day I take a rest is on Sunday or when I go down to the market.

Have I ever experienced the death of someone close to me? I have never had a child who has died, but there was an old woman who was staying near our home who died. She was a neighbor to my parents, and she liked me and Mwangi. When I was going anywhere, she would take care of Mwangi for me and she enjoyed staying with him. When I went to the market, I would bring her bread, and she would be very happy. When she died I was sad. She got sick, and as she was old we never took her to the hospital. Even though she was sick and old, I was very shocked because I liked her very much. I came to learn, then, that the body is just like a flower and will die sometime, somewhere. I know that I will die one day. I see life as just something short—"*toroni kĩndo kĩnini.*" A person must work hard during this life so at least she will leave those who stay behind without many problems.

* * *

The things I'm proudest of are that I'm now able to pick tea, I cultivate and cook well, and look after my children. At times I keep quiet and know that if I work harder one day I will be rich. I do not think I will die poor. My strongest character is being hospitable to people when we meet or when they come to visit me. When they come here, I cook food or tea for them—they cannot stay long without eating. But my weakest character is that I don't like moving out and going to visit other people much. I don't feel free to do it—it's just not me.

Being a woman means one who has her children and a family. Also, it means doing women's work like cultivating, feeding the cows—all those things. Being Mũgĩkũyũ means following the customs—like the things the clan does. It means going to clan meetings, attending its ceremonies, such as a marriage or burial. But today, I think of myself more as a Kenyan, because we are a nation now, not just Mũgĩkũyũ, or Kamba, or Maasai. Just last month we celebrated our twenty years of independence as a nation, and I was born just before independence, so we who are younger know that we are all Kenyan now. We have a new country and new ideas.

Note

1. When I returned to Mutira a year later, Nyambura was nursing a new baby, and the second born, having survived his first year, was toddling around the compound. Since then, a fourth son has been born.

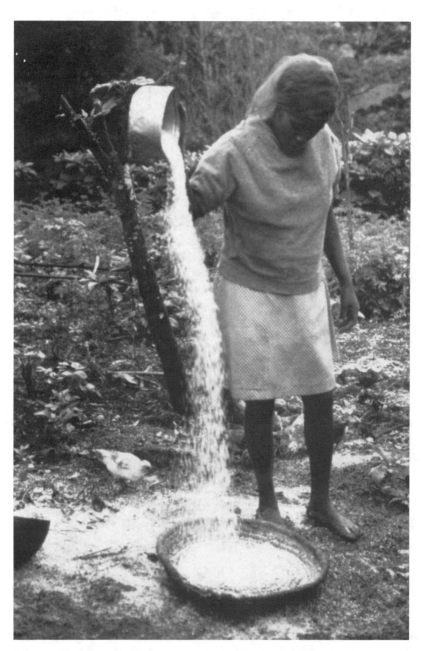

Winnowing rice traded for tea from relatives in lowland Mwea.

8

Lives and Schooling:
Wanja

Wanja lived a greater distance than Nyambura from the compound where I lived. She was often away teaching during the day. This made it more difficult to observe her everyday activities. Our relationship was largely confined to what we shared during interviews and seeing one another at the local Anglican church on Sundays. At the same time, I found Wanja's descriptions—particularly of her childhood—full of insight. She has a keen awareness of what it means to be Gikuyu, and at the same time her dreams and aspirations are tied to a Kenya of the future—one that recognizes educational merit and awards its citizens on the basis of ability rather than age and sex.

Wanja is a single mother with three children. She lives at her parents' homestead and depends upon her father for access to land for cultivation. She earns a small salary as a part-time nursery school teacher, but would like to be fully employed. She has the advantage over Nyambura of more education, and life in a boarding school provided her with new skills and her first taste of independence from home. Because she has completed secondary school, Wanja believes that she deserves more than the tedious job of picking tea. She yearns to become a business entrepreneur, opening her own shop. She views her present position as a teacher as merely a stepping-stone to the goal of becoming a shop owner.

As a single parent, Wanja expresses the hope that one day she will be able to support her children without the help of her parents. If she were able to obtain her own land, she reasons, it would enable her to become financially independent. Land of her own and a shop are the substance of Wanja's dreams.

Similar to other women in her age category, Wanja has difficulty in answering the question, "What does it mean to be a woman?" She agrees with Nyambura that motherhood is a key factor. But beyond this, she is uncertain. The old Gikuyu norms are changing, and women like Wanja are seeking new definitions of what it means to be a woman in the midst of rapid social change.

—J.D.

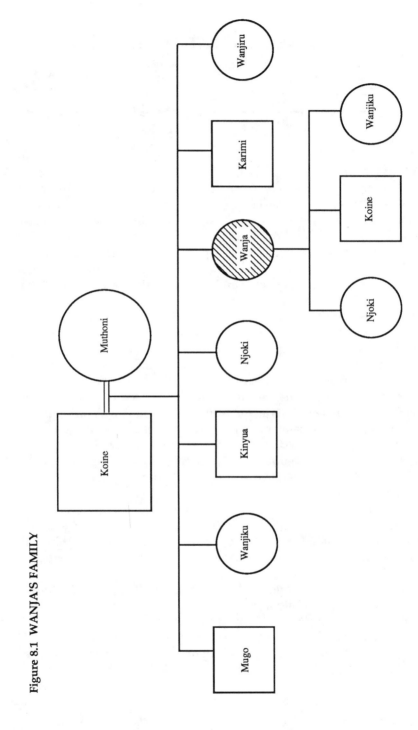

Figure 8.1 WANJA'S FAMILY

My father is Wilson Koine and my mother is Mary Muthoni. Everyone in my family has both a Christian and a Gikuyu name. I grew up going to the church at Gatwe, where I am still a member as you know. Wanja is my Gikuyu name, but Nancy is what I was baptized in the Anglican Church.

I am the fifth born. There are seven children, with Mugo the oldest, then Wanjiku, Kinyua, and Njoki just ahead of me and Wanjiru and Karimi behind me. My father has always been a good person—patient and merciful. My mother, too, is patient with her family and faithful spiritually. She is a member of the church choir—you have seen her there singing on Sundays.

Besides my parents teaching me as I was growing up, my older brother called Kinyua was also a teacher to me. He is eight years older than me and patient like my parents. When I was old enough to go to school, it was Kinyua who helped me with schoolwork. He was employed in Nairobi at the New Stanley Hotel, but he came home every weekend and that's when he used to help me with reading and maths.

When I was young, my parents used to tell me about my clan, Ũnjiku, and our nearest relatives. According to our family, we used to celebrate certain occasions together. For example, if some relatives wanted to slaughter a sheep, they'd call all the members of the family and they would come and share the meat equally. They would slaughter when there was a birth, for a circumcision, or when a girl got married. When the relatives came together, my father would introduce me to them—"This is your aunt who is your mother's sister. This is your uncle who is her brother." The brothers to my father I called *Baba* [Father] when I was growing up, because they were like fathers to me as we lived at the same place. But my mother's brothers, I called them "uncle." I call the sisters to both my father and mother *tata* [aunt]. As for my grandmothers, I never saw them. So slowly I got to know who my relatives were.

My clan refers to where my father came from. Even my oldest sister is called Wanjiku, which means "of the Ũnjiku Clan." My sister is named for my father's clan. The clan is still important to the Agĩkũyũ, and sometimes, when something has to be decided—for example, about land or even bridewealth—the members will call a meeting.

My mother told me that when I was small I loved my oldest sister very much and I often cried anytime I saw her go somewhere, so she rarely left me behind. She would tie me on her back and do her work of gathering wood and fetching water and cooking during the Mau Mau time, when we were in the village and my father had been sent to a British prisoners' camp and my mother was away digging the trench. We were left with my sister during much of that time, because both of my parents were away.

There was no difference between the way my parents treated the boys and the girls in our family. Long ago, the boys—when they got to be about six years [old]—were sent to graze the cows or goats, but now they are fetching water and firewood just like the girls. When I was young I never wished to be a boy, but now I sometimes wish I was a man, because when I'm staying here at home with my parents, if I were a son, I would inherit some property from my father—a piece of land after he dies. But being a woman, we cannot inherit land or property.

I was shown how to do the work of the homestead by my older brothers and sisters and by my mother. If my mother wanted to go to the market, she would go and tell my sisters to go and fetch some water or go to the nearby bush and gather firewood while she was away. I would take a small *sufuria* [metal pot] and follow my sisters to the river, and when I had filled the *sufuria* with water, I would put it on my head and carry it carefully up the hill to our home. But a lot of it spilled out. When I was a small girl, I did not collect firewood until I was a bit older, when I would go with my sister to the bush and start gathering the small pieces. Then she would tie them for me with a *mūkwa* to carry back to the homestead. Sometimes, we would go to the big forest with my mother. We would see a tree that had been cut and she would tell me to gather the small branches but to stay close to her because there are animals in the forest, such as elephants, hyenas, and leopards.That used to scare me. Once, later on, when I was alone with my sister and two other girls, we went into the forest to gather wood and when we reached there, we heard the voice of an animal. We turned and ran out of the forest as fast as we could.

When I was bigger, I started cooking for my baby brother, Karimi. I would make *gitero* [soft food cooked for a baby], using a *muiko* [wooden spoon flattened at one end for mashing]. I'd mash the potatoes and bananas together for Karimi just as I'd seen my sister do, then I would take some that was stuck to the *muiko* off with my finger and put it in my mouth and chew it until it was smooth. I'd put a bit from my mouth on my first finger and push it into Karimi's mouth while he was sitting on my lap.

About 1961, when I was almost nine years [old], I began to pick tea. I can remember this because I was in Standard One at the time. I used to go with my mother to the tea fields, and I would care for my small brother while she picked tea. I would stay at the side of the field, playing with Karimi or feeding him under a tree. Then, when he fell asleep, my mother would call me to come and start picking. While she was picking, I could see that she picked two leaves and a bud. I first started picking with one hand, slowly, putting each stem I picked into the other hand to hold until I got a bunch. Then I put the bunch into my mother's large tea basket, called a *gikabu*, that she carried on her back. I continued that way, picking with one hand at a time. Then, later, I saw that people were picking with two hands, and I tried it because you can get a speed in picking that way. Each is a different way of picking, and I learned both by watching what my mother and others were doing—they didn't have to tell me how to do it. I just saw for myself. On Saturdays and during holidays—that's when I would pick tea, because during the week I was in school.

I can't remember the first day I went to school, but I know I went alone with my older sister Njoki. When we got there, we were introduced to the teacher and went out to play. We were not taught anything that first day. But later, we learned to write by practicing on the ground with our fingers what we had seen in the class. We began number work by using maize kernels, beans, and pieces of stone to count.

What was a typical day in Standard Five? Well, I went to school at Kiamaina, so we'd start for school from here at 6:00 A.M. and reach school at around 7:00. There were morning studies for one hour until 8:00, then we went for assembly. We used to sing songs during assembly, and some passages from the Bible were read to us. Then we had a prayer and went to classes at 8:15. Depending upon how the timetable was arranged, sometimes we'd start with maths and other times with English. During the morning break we would go to the field and play with balls, beanbags, or we'd play *ciūthi*, tossing stones up in the air and catching them on the backs of our hands. Another game we played was called "rounder." The children would divide into two groups. One group made a circle outside and the other group inside. Then spikes or sticks would be placed in a large circle. There was a ball and a stick shaped like a *muiko*. One person from inside the circle would throw the ball to the one outside who was holding the *muiko*. The one outside would aim and hit the ball very far and then drop the stick and run round the circle and when the ball was caught, the person running would stop at the nearest spike. Each time the ball was hit, that person would run round the spikes until he/she had completed the circle and won.

After the last class of the morning there was a time for lunch. I did not go home—I carried a packed lunch. In the afternoons, we had handywork or subjects like geography or history. The teacher used to write on the blackboard, and we children would read the lesson from there and copy it in our notebooks. We would start for home at 4:30 P.M.

Sometimes after school, we would play games when our work was done—games like *ciuthi*, rounder, and *nginyangi*. *Nginyangi* refers to false walking legs—a pair of poles with a support for each foot [stilts]. The person would get up on the supports and try and see how far she could walk without falling.

When I was in primary school—in Standard One—the teacher told us to make a basket and bring it to school. I didn't know how to go about it, so my mother showed me how to make one. She taught me by showing me how she made the circle weaving of strings that would later support the basket. Then she showed me how she took the threads and wove through the main strings being sure that the threads were tight. At first it seemed very hard. When she finished a basket, I took the short strings left over and made my own small *kiondŭ*. That was my first basket, and I took it to school. But my mother did not know how to knit, so I taught myself later how to do that by watching a friend knit.

Before there were books, children used to learn from stories, riddles, and proverbs told by the adults. Stories were given at night and sometimes riddles, too. But proverbs could be given anytime. There's one proverb I remember—"*Kahora, kahora karĩ indo,*" ["Slowly, slowly gets things done."] There are two others I remember. One is "*Kaihu gacanga cangi gatigaga kwao gŭgĩthĩnjo,*" which means "One who moves about and never stays at home, leaves a goat being slaughtered there but never eats it because he/she is never around." My mother would also say, "*Rurigi rŭrĩ nja rutiagaga gĩakŭoha,*"—"A string outside does not miss anything to tie." She would use this one when one of us children had just thrown something outside that might be useful sometime.

Before our mother told us a story, she said, "*Itho a.*" This meant that a story was beginning. Those listening would reply, "*Itho.*" Then a story, like this one, would begin:

Long ago, there was an old mother bird and a young bird. The mother bird was very old and could not even go to the river. One day, she told the young bird to go for water so she could have a drink. The young bird refused, saying that it was going to dance kibata. The mother bird grew very thirsty and, at last, died because of thirst. But before she did, she cursed the young bird, telling it that it would never be able to take water from the river again, but only water from rain. And so, until this day, that bird takes only the water that drops on the leaves of plants.

What did I learn from the story? It taught us not to ignore our elders, to do what we are told unless we want something bad to happen to us. Even today, I remind my children that they must respect the elders and always obey what they say.

These were the kinds of things we were learning at home from our parents while we were learning other things from the teachers at school. By the time I got to Standard Seven, we had a lot more work to do, because it was the last year of primary school and we were busy reviewing and preparing for the C.P.E. [Certificate of Primary Education Examination]. It was also during that year that I got my first menstrual period. I remember the day because I was in school, and I started feeling aches along my backbone and in my lower abdomen. I came home that afternoon, but I never told anybody. I knew what had happened, because I had learned about menstruation from other girls of my age. They had taught me what to do when the time comes. My mother never told me about it.

The morning of the examination, I woke very early and took my pens and went to school. I went into the room where we were to have the examination and took the seat I was assigned. The examiners came and gave us the papers, and we worked on them the whole day. Some were difficult. During that day, our parents and relatives were saying prayers for us so we might pass. I was very tired when it was over and just prayed that I had passed. But it took a whole month before we heard the results. I was lucky and found I passed, so I could qualify for secondary school.

We found out the results in January, and I did not go to secondary school until that September, so I had some months home to pick the tea and help with my young sister. Because Wanjiku was married by then, it was my work to fetch water and to wash the clothes. This took me about three hours. Also, I had to sweep the compound and cook the lunch while my mother was working in the *shamba*. If I finished that work, then I helped pick tea leaves.

My father got a letter telling us I was accepted by a school down at Mwea—where the rice scheme is. I left home in September. In Kenya, most of our secondary schools are boarding schools, so we live at the school. When I got to the school in Mwea, I found so many girls from all over Kenya—Kiambu, Murang'a, even Kisumu. In primary school I had worn a smock with a blouse, but in secondary school we wore a uniform that was a dark blue skirt, a white blouse and a blue sweater. We also had to wear black shoes.

At first when I got there I was a bit scared, but I gradually got used to the place. During the weekdays, we'd wake up at 6:00 A.M., I'd go to the bathroom and bathe, then dress in my uniform. Breakfast was at 7:00 and was usually porridge. Then we had to go back and straighten up our bunks and clean the dorm before going to classes. The dorms were long rooms with rows of metal bunks on each side. Each girl had a box that she kept her things in at the end of the bed. We had to keep the dorm clean by washing the floors regularly. And in the dorm we were not allowed to speak Kikuyu. We were required to speak in English because that is what our lessons were in.

At 7:30, we would go in to study for half an hour, then there were morning prayers. At 8:30, we started the lessons of the day. We stayed in classes until 10 and then we broke for morning tea, which everyone liked. Then back to classes until 12:30 P.M., when we went for lunch in the dining hall. Lunch was usually *githeri* [maize and beans]. There were afternoon classes beginning at 2:30, and later, after classes were over, we'd go for general cleaning of the classrooms and compound, games like netball, and, at times, club meetings like the Young Christians Club or Young Farmers Club. I joined the Young Christians Club.

From four to six o'clock was the time for personal cleaning, like washing our clothes. At six was supper—usually *githeri* with some vegetables or *ugali*. After supper, we went for preps—preparations for the next day's classes—and were in bed by nine o'clock. I can remember one time, when I was in Form Two, during prep time, one of the girls switched off the kerosene lantern. The teacher on duty came and asked who had done it. When she found out, she wrote down the girl's name, and the following morning the girl was taken to our headmaster and was beaten. But usually when somebody did something she was disciplined by talks.

The curriculum for our lessons was to prepare us to take the O-levels (ordinary secondary school examinations] at the end of Form Four. We had English and Kiswahili, and some girls took French. We also took history and geography, and health science because we did not have a laboratory for other sciences at the school. If a person did well on the O-levels, she could go on to high school for two more years and the take the A-levels (advanced level examinations). Only those who do very well in their A-levels have a chance at the university. I finished Form Four, but I did not do well on my O-levels, so I stopped there.

I found secondary school very different from primary because we had new subjects like biology and commerce that we'd never had before. The teachers were different, too, because they gave us a lot of tests and were more educated than primary school teachers. Most of the teachers at our school were men, even though we were all girls.

After I finished Form Four, I came home here to live. By that time I was nearly twenty. It was that year I became pregnant by a man from here. When that happened, I knew that I was no longer a girl. I started to think of what course I would take or where I would be employed. When a girl has her first child, she becomes a *mūtūmia* regardless of whether she has a husband or not.

I have not gone through any of the traditional transitions like

mbuci and *matū* or even *Irua*. But I have heard of other girls being circumcised, though it is against the law now. I was a young girl when I
saw a group of girls being circumcised, one after the other. That was
sometime in the 1960s. But today one would not know if her agemates
are circumcised or not—we don't talk about it. Sometimes one reads
in the newspapers about a girl dying because she was circumcised
badly. That is to let those who would try it know it is unsafe. Most of
these old traditions I do not see as important, because they only take
people backwards, not like Christianity, which came to take people
forward and brought development. Even *mariika* [age groups] are not
important anymore. A Form Two girl and a Form Four girl are no different because none of them is yet a mother. But if one of them has a
child, then they cannot be of the same *riika*. Before, *Irua* made the difference, but now that it is no longer practiced, the only division is
when a girl becomes a mother. Then she finds herself with a new kind
of responsibility.

*   *   *

After I finished school and came home here to live, I was cultivating and picking tea. I had my first child—my daughter—in the
hospital. Most younger women today prefer hospital births. Then I
began living with another man down at Kerugoya who I thought
would be my husband and had two more children by him. But things
didn't work out and I came back home to my parents. I felt very dis-
appointed that after completing my education I wasn't able to find a
good job. I hoped to find a job as a primary school teacher, but there
were no openings. Finally after staying here for awhile, I got a job
teaching old people like my mother at the adult education class. It
was not easy teaching there because those women didn't know how
to read, but they were older than me. Also, they never came regularly.
Sometimes, I was not paid on time either. I taught there for two years,
and then the class stopped, so I was home here again without a job.

During that time I was helping my mother pick the tea leaves and
cultivate the *shamba*. We have about one and a half acres of tea and
other small plots for cultivating food crops. But the money from tea
cultivation goes to my father. Then he gives some to my mother and
me. My father helps prune the tea bushes, but he does not do much
picking. He is usually away on some business. He is on the church
committee, so he is busy.

The only food crop my father cultivates is yams—that is a man's
crop. Sometimes he helps by preparing the land for maize, and he
helps with the maize harvest. My mother is very clever. She saw that
women in Mwea were earning good money with their pineapples, so

now she has planted a small field to see if they will grow up here. She also grows a lot of garden vegetables like cabbages, tomatoes, garden peas, and carrots. Though my father has given me a piece of land, I usually plant maize and beans. I would like to have a big enough parcel of land to grow tea. Then I could make a profit.

About a year ago, I was invited to apply to the nursery school near Gathũthũma. They wanted somebody who had some teaching experience, so I was taken. I like teaching nursery school, because I am helping the young children to get knowledgeable. Because I stayed for a time at home without employment, I can only thank God for giving me this job. While I am at school, the two younger children are here with my mother, but the oldest girl goes to school now.

If I were married, would I want my husband to give rũracio? No. That is one of those traditions of the past. When my mother was married, my father gave so many goats and cattle, but today a man is expected to give shillings if a girl has been to school. Sometimes the relatives ask for a lot of shillings if a girl has completed Form Six or gone to university. But I think it is a stupidity. It makes it seem like a girl is nothing but an object if a man must pay a cash price to marry her. I would not want a man to pay rũracio for me because then he would feel he has complete control over me and can do what he wants, even beating me if he feels like it! To me, that tradition is meaningless in today's world.

Nowadays a woman has to be self-sufficient, because you can't depend upon a husband. Whether a woman is married or not makes no difference, you are still responsible for your children. Of all my roles, I think the one of mother is most important. That's the one that changed me the most because now I began to think about how to get money to buy clothes for my children and, later, to take them to school.

Farming and housework are the next most important. Living with my parents, I have to help cultivate and pick tea, do the cooking, and other things. Next, I would say that my role as a teacher is important because I like children, and the job gives me the money I need to help my children. Being a member of the church group is less important, but I like going because I meet my friends and we do things together. There is one role missing—I am a member of the church choir, too, but that role is least important.

The thing I'm proudest of is being a mother to my three children—that I am able to feed and clothe them well. What do I think of family planning? It is a good idea if one has the number of children she wants. Some women my age are having too many children—like rabbits, one after the other. Also, some girls get pregnant while they are still in school and it may not be their fault. A teacher [male] can play dirty tricks with a girl and then she ends up pregnant. And there are the "sugar daddies"—those who come and seduce schoolgirls. They are the ones who offer to buy a girl things—like new shoes or a dress—if the girl will become their friend. Usually, a girl is too young to understand and then she gets pregnant. She is forced to leave school and go home to her parents. It is a problem.

About my future dreams? I would like to be a businesswoman. I want to have a shop and sell things. If I could save enough money from picking tea leaves, then I could get a shop. My strongest character is being obedient—like now I obey my parents, because I have to depend upon them. I can't think of my weakest character—I don't think I have one. Being a woman means having children and taking care of them and the home. I think of myself first as Mũgĩkũyu because I speak the language. I was born Mũgĩkũyu. I only became a Kenyan citizen when we got our independence in 1963.

How do I think schooling differs from how we learned at home? At school we had certain lessons that had to be learned and these were put on the blackboard and we learned them by copying the teacher. There are subjects we had to learn in order to pass the examinations, whether we might need them or not. But in learning things at home, like cultivating and picking tea, nobody made us learn. We just went out and learned those things on our own in the best way that suited us. The trouble with the things one learns in school is that one may not be able to use what is learned unless one is lucky enough to get a job. But going to school is important these days so one can learn how to read and write and do figures. If I did not go to school, I would not be able to teach others or think of beginning my own business. So each is important in its own way.

9

The Life Histories
in Retrospect

Seven women's lives caught like slivers of glass in the kaleidoscope of a constantly changing twentieth century. Historical incidents, alluding distance, cast shadows larger than reality and shape future options. Cultural responses, timeless, yet timely, mediate history creating new formations among old patterns. Individual experiences and personal talents mark each woman's life with bold brushstrokes, capturing her uniqueness, shaping her development.

In the process of creating and recreating her life, each woman uses a variety of skills learned through the process of daily living. Observation and imitation from earliest childhood provide the cultural scaffolding for future competence as adults. Listening to elders opens the way to a rich network of relationships extending back in time to Mumbi and Gikuyu. Stories become models for future behavior. Ritual events form arenas in which youth test their readiness for the next life stage and learn the secrets of their elders. Discovering new talents under adverse conditions as an adult leads to changed perceptions of self. Recalling old events, long forgotten, makes possible a perspective from which to view change and one's place in cultural history.

The Impact of Sociocultural Change

When asked in the second session to list all the major changes in their lives, the older informants named *mbuci* and *matū, Irua,* and *ūhiki* (marriage). It was only later that idiosyncratic events were acknowledged as having brought changes. Though some women had participated in *mambura ma twana* (the children's ceremony that removes a child from her mother's bed), it was not mentioned as an important rite, perhaps because it is least remembered. By the time a girl went through *mbuci* and *matū* at the age of eleven or twelve, she was old enough to understand that it marked the first stage of separation from childhood in the life of a Gikuyu girl. Moreover, ear-piercing was a prerequisite for *Irua*—that most important of all rites.

The narrative details of *mbuci* and *matū* vary from one woman to the next, depending upon personality and family circumstances. Thus, Wamutira went with a sister to have her ears pierced at her mother's urging, whereas Wanoi had to pierce her own ears in secret because her oldest brother opposed *matū*. In almost all cases, permission for *mbuci* and *matū* was secured from the uncle—the mother's oldest brother. Wamutira admits that *matū* was painful, and Watoro relates that *mbuci* became infected. Both piercings seem to be visual symbols of an historic past and are rarely seen in women below the age of thirty-five. In fact, a number of older women have had *matu* stitched up to prevent the holes from being caught on something.

It is *Irua*, however, that marked the real transition in social status from girl to woman. Godfrey Muriūki, the Gikuyu historian, has said of *Irua*:

> In the absence of any formal centre of instruction, initiation served as one of the main educational channels in Kikuyu society. This education was both practical and theoretical and covered such fields as tribal traditions, religion, folklore, modes of behaviour and the duties of adults, taboos and sex. Also, the initiates were invested with important roles, responsibilities and privileges in the social system [1974:119]

Although religion and folklore are mentioned by Muriūki, there is very little evidence of it in the life history accounts of *Irua*. My guess is that the reason lies in gender-specific spheres of knowledge—spiritual knowledge, in particular, was linked with males. Male, rather than female elders, acted as intermediaries with *Ngai* and offered prayers on behalf of the community. It is for this reason that one finds no female *mūndū mugo*—shamanism belonged to the realm of men.

What Gikuyu women learned from female relatives concerning expectations of adult behavior and sexuality during *Irua* prepared them for accompanying responsibilities. *Irua*, as a ritual transition, created a disequilibrium that Monika Vizedom (1976) compares to the transitions that occur between developmental stages of growth. For the Gikuyu, *Irua* was characterized by disequilibrium—a liminal state in which the norms of behavior were suspended in the act of transmitting a new set of adult, gender-specific norms that served to reorient a girl's status to that of a woman. For girls, as for boys, circumcision was part of the ritual process that enabled the initiate to assume a new sexual and a new social status. Victor Turner's (1969) observation that "powerful drives and emotions associated with human physiology, especially the physiology of reproduction, are divested in the ritual process of their antisocial quality and attached to components of the moral order" (1969:53) is applicable to *Irua*.

Older women describe the process by which gender role expectations were transmitted by women elders through ritualized dance and songs during the ceremony. At the same time, a girl's biological sex was dramatized, with its accompanying potential for reproduction. The physical act of removing *rong'otho* (the clitoris) freed a Gikuyu female from categorical ambiguity, while it signaled her readiness to assume sexual relations upon marriage.

Not only status and gender became crystallized, but relations between age-groups were delineated with membership in a particular *riika*. *Irua* had an integrative role in enabling a girl to gain access to an age-set that had both historical and social significance. Historically, the attachment of a *riika* name provided a means of keeping track of events, as each age-group was identified with an event that occurred concurrently with *Irua*. Socially, *riika* meant identification with a "sisterhood" that provided solidarity and mutual aid throughout the lifespan. Finally, *Irua* was an enabling process that allowed the mother and father of the initiate to assume new role-statuses as elders in the community. Formerly, such a transition included eligibility for the *kiama* (council of elders), as we learned from Wanjiku's narrative.

At the individual level, each woman describes how she felt personally transformed by the experience. States Wamutira, "After I had gone through *Irua*, I felt different. I felt like I was a grown up girl now, ready for dances. And everybody termed us as adults. . . . Nowadays, you wouldn't know who is mature and who isn't. "

Irua marked the transition to adulthood for older women, but the two women in their twenties did not go through the ritual. All of the older women were intensely interested in talking about the social changes that have occurred surrounding *Irua*, as the discussion between Wamutira and her co-wives illustrates. Though none of the women believe the operation itself is beneficial, most feel that the end of *Irua* in terms of its symbolic meaning for the age-grade system is detrimental to the Gikuyu way of life. Wangeci even goes so far as to suggest that young women today are *outside* the culture—"*Irua* has no meaning to Agĩkũyũ girls today because now they have become *people of a different culture* (emphasis mine). The only important thing to them is schooling—to pass or fail."

By the time Wanja and Nyambura were eligible for circumcision, independence had been won, female circumcision was no longer a symbol of nationalism for the Gikuyu, and the girls' parents had converted to Christianity. The Gikuyu, now in power, embraced "modernization." Though Wanja indicates that female circumcision was still prevalent when she was a girl in the 1960s, by the 1970s, educated Christian women were questioning the relevance of clitoridectomy.

Brought to the forefront of discussions at the UN Decade of Women Conference in Copenhagen in 1980, female circumcision became an issue between African and Euro-American women. Media coverage in Kenya of the medical dangers involved in clitoridectomizing young women under often unsterile conditions began to appear. International opinion condemning the operation added fuel to the fire. Urban educated women joined the debate. Under such pressure, a ban on female circumcision was initiated by President Moi in 1982.

All of the life history informants in their fifties and twenties are aware of the ban and supported its intent—at least to me. Though one woman in her fifties confidentially told me that her oldest daughter had been circumcised, neither of the other women with daughters desires to have her daughters go through the same kind of pain she experienced. What accounts for the change in attitudes over the twenty-year period?

First, although clitoridectomy was viewed as a symbol of cultural loyalty (and as a symbol of defiance against European colonialism) during the Mau Mau struggle, it no longer had the same significance once independence was gained. Second, the post-independence conversion of many Gikuyu women to Christianity, with its accompanying lessons—Wanoi cites the fact that the Biblical Mary was uncircumcised as a basis for her changed attitudes—made clitoridectomy less meaningful. Finally, the impact of formal schooling which acts as a "modernizing agent," including the transmission of western values, contributed to a social climate in which cultural tradition slowly gave way to health considerations and "progress." The rationale currently given by Gikuyu women for no longer practicing clitoridectomy is based not upon sexual rights or sexuality (except among educated urban feminists), but upon health dangers—cited by Wamutira—and cultural asynchronicity, illustrated by Wanja and Nyambura's comments that *Irua* no longer has meaning.

If *Irua*, in fact, is no longer practiced, how then do younger women know when they have made the transition to adult status? Nyambura has an answer: "When you are a girl and then give birth, you find that you are changed. Your body features change . . . and show that you are no longer a girl. And you change mentally, too, because you are always thinking about your children. So you have gone from girlhood to womanhood." Wanja concurs: "Before, *Irua* made the difference (between girls and women), but now that it is no longer practiced, the only division is when a girl becomes a mother."

Today's young women lack the ritually marked social transition from girlhood to womanhood that their mothers and grandmothers experienced. At the same time, there seems to be a felt need on their parts to validate their transition to adult female status. In place of a *socially recognized* event they seek a *biologically recognized* event to mark the transition. Motherhood, with or without marriage, has taken the place of *Irua* as the validating event.   Such a change in attitude, has, in part, led an increasing number of young women to have children outside of marriage—a phenomenon that concerns both young women like Nyambura and Wanja and older women like Wanjiku and Wangeci who often find themselves responsible for the child care of their daughters' children.

In addition to *Irua*, the five older women refer to *ũhiki* as being a significant change in their lives. Marriage is a transition not only in social status but in location. Even today, a girl leaves her father's homestead and travels with her husband to his homestead to live (as I discovered in attending several Christian weddings in which women escorted the bride to the husband's compound once the Christian ceremony was completed). All the older women expressed sadness at leaving their natal homes when they married, and some even resisted on the way as we learn from Wamutira: "I went slowly with Murage, sometimes sitting down because I did not want to go. Sometimes I wondered whether I could escape and go back home, but then I was threatened with a beating and I would start walking again."

When a woman marries, she becomes a part of her husband's extended family. Though she will see members of her own family and clan during ceremonies and visits, her affiliation is now with her husband's people and any children she bears will be members of his clan. For the older women, the first month was often spent isolated in the sleeping quarters of the husband's mother's house as a sign of respect for the older woman. The bride was being symbolically reborn as the daughter of her husband's mother, according to Wangeci: "She [sister-in-law] took me to Ngiricii's mother's house. Ngiricii's mother lit a fire but I went into the room where the bed was . . . to show that now I had become her child."

Fear and loneliness were not uncommon feelings at such a time, as Wamutira and Watoro testify. The young bride was, and still is, very much at the beck and call of her mother-in-law. The isolation period constituted a form of marital apprenticeship, when the new wife learned from the older woman the normative behavior expected of married women, as Wanjiku (the oldest woman) relates: "When I first came here, I stayed in Wamai's mother's house. . . . During the time when I was staying with the mother, I was observing how she was cooking food and taking care of her house. She also gave me *kirira*." *Kirira* consisted of the secret knowledge and moral codes that only older people knew and had the power to share with younger ones. Watoro relates that her husband's mother warned her not to wander, or stray, from the husband. Wangeci learned that she should not sleep with her husband if she was having her menstrual period.

If a newly married woman was a second or third wife, she had to adjust to co-wives and their personalities, as Watoro and Muthoni, Wamutira's younger co-wife, explain. Watoro, upon arriving at her husband's compound, suddenly realized that the eldest wife was angry with her husband for taking a second wife. "Wangui, the first wife, was there, and I could tell she was not happy to see me. That scared me. Right away she started screaming and abusing me. She had known me before, but now she had different feelings because she didn't want the husband to marry another wife. He insisted. . . . I learned that she had had no say in the marriage. So she and I stayed that way abusing one another." Being a young wife in the husband's compound was not always a pleasant experience—homesickness and feelings of inadequacy might plague a woman for the first time. LeVine and Pfeifer point out that among Gusii women in Western Kenya, a new wife relocated to her husband's home, tends to idealize her natal home—"from a distance her parents appear generous and wise, her siblings and grandparents are remembered as loving, and the family farm seems bountiful, in contrast to the ambivalence, coldness and depriving circumstances of her new home" (1982:66).

At the same time, a young woman knows that once *rūracio* has been exchanged, she has a commitment to make her marriage work. She must obey her husband now, as she obeyed her parents in the past. Wanjiku explains the advice she got prior to marriage:

"My mother warned me that if people (at the husband's place) discovered I had *ng'aa* and did not care for other people there, the *rūracio* might be taken back because it showed that I was one who could not be ruled. . . . "Now that you are going to your husband's place," she said, "you are no longer in my hands, but under your husband's care and rule. Respect him and do what he wants."

From the life histories, we learn that marriage was actually a sequentially arranged series of rituals among Gikuyu. First, came formal exchanges of tobacco and beer. Second, were the negotiations for *rūracio*, followed by *gūthokia*—the period during which a young woman shared beer or porridge with the young man's friends. The third event was *gūthinjiro* —a blood sacrifice was made that bound the two extended families together. Finally, the bride went to her husband's homestead, where she served as an apprenticeship in the house of her husband's mother that could last anywhere from a month to three years. The last ritual was *kumanda*, when a bride was officially welcomed by her parents-in-law into her own house and could start residing with her husband. The last ritual was a significant moment for the bride, because it symbolized her mother-in-law's willingness to allow her to cook for her son and to sleep with him. It also meant that the young wife had to do more things for herself, as Watoro explains: "When I moved there, I found a big change because now I was required to fetch my own firewood. . . . I was fetching my own water and washing my own utensils and keeping the house clean all by myself."

Today, most steps described by the older women have disappeared, with the exception of *rūracio*. Bridewealth is still an accepted practice, though it has become capitalized with the transfer of shillings as well as herd animals. The amount of shillings is dependent upon the bride's level of education, with university-educated women's families' receiving the highest amounts. It is for this reason that young women like Wanja (and my research assistant) reject the idea of *rūracio*. They feel that attaching a monetary value to bridewealth commoditizes the wife and gives too much power to the husband. However, not all young women agree. Nyambura, for example, views *rūracio* as a validating aspect of marriage—one that she supports as a sign of respect for the bride's parents.

Typically, a young woman moves into her future husband's home once she discovers she is pregnant by him. Sometime later, when the couple have saved enough money for a ceremony and feasting, they will legalize their marriage through a civil or church wedding with all the trimmings. Several middle-aged women who earlier had had customary weddings, prior to the enactment of post-independence marriage laws, were "renewing their vows" with church weddings during the year and a half I was in Mutira Location.

Marriage, for Gikuyu women, has always meant children. Formerly, it was not long after a woman began living with her husband in the same house that she discovered she was pregnant. If she did not become pregnant, she sought the advice of a *mūndū mugo*, as in Wamutira's case. Though most women were ill informed about pregnancy and relied on older women to guide them, the news that a woman was going to bear a child was greeted with joy, because motherhood validated a woman's marriage. It was not until the birth of a woman's first child that she achieved full status among the other women in her husband's compound (Mathu 1971). Motherhood affirmed a woman's position in her husband's home and brought security in the marital relationship. Given such circumstances, it is not hard to understand why Wamutira became so anxious when she did not become pregnant in the first year of her marriage. The transition to marriage implied a transition to motherhood, and the woman who did not bear children, for one reason or another, was in danger of being returned to her natal home. Marriage, then, resulted in intra-psychic tension—a tension that was not resolved until a woman proved her ability to bear children.

Whereas formerly women gave birth at home with the assistance of a midwife, increasingly women are now seeking hospital births. Both Wanja and Nyambura gave birth to their children in hospitals. This means that midwives like Wanoi are less often called upon to help with births in the community. However, *itega*—the custom of women taking offerings of food, firewood, and, now, baby items to the new mother and her baby—is still very much a part of Gikuyu culture. It gives women in rural areas a chance to get together and celebrate with singing, dancing, and feasting.

The birth of a first child was, and still is, a critical event in Gikuyu women's lives. Wanoi views it as the most significant change in her life—"Of all the changes I've told you about, the one that changed me the most was when I gave birth. That's because I knew then that I had become a woman, entitled to some duties and respect." Nyambura, twenty years younger, concurs. "When I became a mother—that was the biggest change for me." When women in Mutira were asked what constitutes womanhood for the Agĩkũyũ, the majority responded that next to agricultural production, motherhood is the most important aspect of being a woman. Nevertheless, a woman's functional role as a mother (reproducer) does not supercede her role as a cultivator or wage earner (producer), as I indicated in the first chapter.

From Nyambura and Wanja's accounts, we find that the relationship between marriage and motherhood is undergoing change. If a woman became a *mũkoma ndi* (unmarried pregnant woman) in Wangeci's time, she did not have the chance of becoming a man's first wife, and she felt shame. Today, threats of becoming a *mũkoma ndi* seem to have little effect. The younger women's narratives illustrate that childbirth may precede marriage—a phenomenon I observed to be increasing in the years between 1975 (when I first visited Kenya) and on subsequent visits up through 1983–1984, when I did my fieldwork. Male informants with whom I've discussed this changing pattern argue that having a child before marriage ensures a man that the woman he plans to marry is fertile before he begins bridewealth negotiations. Younger women hope that once they become pregnant, a man will feel compelled to marry them—a scenario that does not always work out, as we learn from Wanja's account.

Finally, the narratives of older women reveal that by the time they reached an age when their first child was circumcised, *nyumithio*, which formerly initiated a woman into elder status, was no longer practised. Wanjiku had become a Christian by the time her oldest son was circumcised in the 1950s and no longer adhered to the old ways. Women in their fifties relate that the custom had long since disappeared.

Of all the cultural changes that have occurred during the older women's lives, the slow dissolution of *mariika* seems to have the most significance. Older women hold school—an institution they can't imagine and have never experienced—to be responsible. Somehow in the process of being "educated," their children and grandchildren have come to accept a different set of social principles that structure their behavior. Social distance is giving way to cross-age groupings. Boys play and talk with girls in a way their elders find offensive. And young girls act and dress in ways that are provocative, according to Wangeci. In her view, the increased social intercourse between sexes leads to promiscuity. "Look at young men nowadays," she argues, "they are tiring easily and growing old fast because they think all the time they are enjoying sex, but they are not. The girls, too, are growing old very fast using up a lot of sexual energy for nothing."

For Wangeci, the answer is not preventive contraception, it is sexual abstinence. However, Wanoi supports the idea of contraception and as a midwife even learned how to insert IUDs at the training course in Nyeri. Of the two younger women, Nyambura resists family planning methods (contraception) whereas Wanja supports them. Their attitudes are indicative of the dichotomy that prevails among women of their generation. Women with more formal education tend to consider family planning as an alternative. Less well educated women tend to resist it for cultural or religious reasons or out of fear of reprisal from their husbands, who still take pride in large families.

Along with a change in social mores, according to older women, comes the problem of increased fecundity—"A young girl marries today and gets a child year after year, and after five or six years she looks older than her mother and dies early because she is wearing out." Wangeci argues that Gikuyu formerly had their own forms of family planning, which involved post-natal abstinence for up to four or five years while a mother nursed her child and regained her strength.

Although these were not part of my scheduled interviews, several women in their late thirties and forties who had had all the children they desired, initiated conversations with me about pregnancy prevention. They wanted to know how I managed to have only three children. During my stay in the field, I had a chance, on several occasions, to accompany a Gikuyu woman who is a family planning community educator, and a mother of seven, on her visits to local homesteads. During such visits I learned that an increasing number of women are seeking tubal ligations once they have had the number of children desired. However, such a procedure does require the written permission of a husband, and several women expressed concern that their husbands would never give consent. Nonetheless, a demographer with an international family planning agency in Nairobi confirmed that tubal ligation is currently the fastest growing form of pregnancy prevention in Kenya (Merritt 1984, personal communication).

Finally, how have women's cultural roles as agricultural producers changed over the seventy-year period? Wanjiku notes that women were alloted several plots of land in different ecological niches when she was growing up. As a woman in her husband's father's homestead, she was granted sufficient *migūnda* (gardens) to cultivate. Likewise, women had a variety of *migūnda* when the women in their fifties were children. The major change seems to have occurred during the 1950s, when all the women were relocated—either to Nairobi or to internment villages during Mau Mau. Wamutira relates that during her absence in Nairobi, the goats and cows were *gūtaho*—comandeered by British soldiers to feed the colonial army. It is likely that the fields were also plundered.[1] Wamutira describes how they began rebuilding the homestead once Gikuyu were allowed to return from the villages.

In our formal interviews, Wanoi did not describe the changes in her husband's homestead that took place during Mau Mau, but in the process of helping her pick beans and tomatoes one day, she explained that what I saw—four different plots of land interspersed between coffee fields amounting to less than an acre—was all she had. She also observed that her mother had had access to more *migūnda*. Before Mau Mau and independence, there had been no coffee, only food crops.

Wanoi is the major producer in her family. She produces most of the food they eat, selling harvested fruits such as avocados, mangos, and passion fruits in the market to buy commodities such as tea and sugar. She harvests the coffee berries largely with the help of her children. However, it is her husband who receives the proceeds, which he may or may not share with Wanoi. Her husband is employed intermittently in a town some distance from Mutira. Necessarily, Wanoi has learned to be self-sufficient: "Like the granary I'm adding here at the homestead, I will not ask my husband for a cent, even though he got his coffee harvest money just the other day. If I rely on him to give me money, the day he misses I will have a problem."

In a study of rural Gikuyu women's perceptions of themselves and their roles, sociologist Priscilla Kariŭki reports the observation of one woman that "most women do not rely on their husbands today. They try to get money for themselves selling vegetables, clothes, or making handicrafts and selling them. They have an obligation to make sure that children do not sleep hungry or go without clothes" (1985:224). Each woman speaks for an increasing number of Gikuyu women who find their husbands coming and going as wage earners, but whose husbands' physical and economic presence in terms of labor and income are unpredictable.

For Watoro, Wangeci, and Wanjiku, husbands are not an issue. They are single women, totally reliant upon their own resources, or in the case of Wanjiku, dependent upon sons and daughters-in-law. Watoro, as indicated earlier, lost her access to cropland when she left her husband and is dependent upon cultivating migŭnda that belonged to her recently deceased father, and coffee that belongs to her brother. During the drought in 1984, she was in desperate need of cash to buy unga (maize meal) for her children and grandchildren. Had she lived thirty years earlier, she might have had several migŭn-da in different ecological niches, but today she has only three gardens amounting to less than an acre located in the same area. She dreams of coming to the coffee shamba and finding abundant food crops growing or waking up to find herself holding a fistful of money. Like many other single women around the world, Wanoi is among the poorest of the poor (Clark 1984).

Wangeci's husband's land seems to have been little disturbed by the ravages of war in the 1950s, perhaps because it is at the higher elevation adjacent to the Mount Kenya Forest. Like Wanjiku, who lives at the same elevation, she returned after the end of the emergency eager to clear the land and plant tea. Similarly, Wanja's parents returned home from an internment village and began to cultivate tea. In each case, the land had previously belonged to a particular mbari, or land-holding patrilineage, prior to the 1950s. When land consolidation and registration were extended to this area in the mid-1960s, the land was subdivided between male members of the lineage under separate titles. Most women here have adequate numbers of migŭnda —both at the tops of ridges and near streams below. In addition, they cleared the steep ridges of brush in the 1960s and planted tea. Of the seven women, those living on the high, moisture-laden ridges were less affected by changes in land consolidation than those living at lower elevations.

Wanja represents a particular case because she has completed secondary school and has a wage occupation that brings her an income. Nevertheless, as a single woman she has no direct access to land except through the generosity of her father, who makes available to her several plots for food crops, which she cultivates together with her mother. She yearns for the security of owning her own land.

When I returned to the field in 1985, I discovered that those women who were cultivating tea at the higher elevations had significantly increased their incomes over the previous year because the price of tea leaves per kilo had increased considerably. Those benefiting from the sudden prosperity were spending the proceeds on improving their homesteads—particularly the construction of wells or more permanent houses and granaries. What most failed to realize was that the price of tea could just as easily drop in the next year. Women in Mutira have become dependent upon a world commodities market that structures their daily existence, but which they do not comprehend.

Changes in Women's Personal Lives

In contrast to historic and sociocultural changes, at times individuals experience events unique to their lives that may alter their behavior (Neugarten and Datan 1973; Riegel 1975; Gergen 1980). What kinds of events have had the most impact on the lives of the seven Gikuyu women? How does each woman go about explaining their significance? What kinds of changes do they imply for a woman's life span development? I will limit the discussion to events that suddenly altered a woman's social status or to life crises that precipitated changes in behavior patterns.

In the case of widowhood or separation, Gikuyu women experience a change in status that often has negative repercussions in a society in which the normative pattern for adult women is marriage. Wanjiku, as a young widow, finds herself in a quandary because she is left with a baby to raise alone. When the baby dies, she wants to return to her natal home. However, her husband's parents have grown fond of her and wish her to remain. The younger brother reveals his affection for her and assumes the position of her husband—a normative solution in many African societies. Wanjiku's period of feeling asynchronous lasts only a short time before her remarriage to Kamau. The scenario is different for Wangeci, who is left a widow in her late thirties.

Wangeci's adjustment to widowhood leads to a transformation in her pattern of living. After the shock of her husband's death wears off, Wangeci realizes that she no longer "fits" into the norm of her age group—she feels alone and cut off from her peers. "I just decided, there and then, to stand on my own. . . . The hardest change for me was to refrain from moving with women who had their husbands, and learning to stay alone with my work. . . . So I decided to keep to myself and be self-reliant." Wangeci has been advised by her husband not to count on outside advisers, and she takes his advice. She learns not to move with married women who might be jealous, but to stay home, learning to master the tasks that she formerly took for granted as her husband's responsibilities. Part of the change she experiences as a widow is the discovery that she can do things that before she assumed she could not—like trapping moles.

At the same time, Wangeci perceives her asynchronous status within a larger historical frame: "Nowadays, in our society widows do not get help. They say each has his mother. It means that even the father's [deceased man's] brothers can't help, as they are interested only in their children. . . . But long ago in Agĩkũyũ society, if there was a feast somewhere, a share of meat would be brought to the widow, and the father's [father of the widow's children] brother took over father's role."

Wangeci feels isolated: "Even in the community, people say that you, a widow, are rich with all the things left to you by your husband. So they never think to help someone like me." But Wangeci compensates for her isolation by working hard to gain the respect of the community. "So being a widow, one needs to do her work first, single-handed, slowly by slowly. . . . That way, one will win the respect of the people in her area." Hard work has become her therapy.

It is clear from Wangeci's account that her attitudes and her patterns of behavior have changed with widowhood. She *feels* isolated. She must now assume responsibilities that were formerly shared. Nor can she count on her husband's brothers or the community for help. Necessarily, she grows in her ability to be self-suffcient and gains in self-confidence as she learns new skills. Widowhood becomes a catalyst for change.

Although Watoro experiences a changed status when she decides to leave her husband and return to her father's home, it is a crisis—the death of her only daughter—that makes the greatest impact on her personally. The death teaches Watoro that she can never depend upon her husband, and his complete lack of understanding of her psychological needs amplifies other shortcomings. Watoro realizes that if she wants to make a life for herself and her remaining children, she will have to do it on her own. Whereas prior to the death, Watoro was able to cope with marital stress, now the factor of multiple stress as a result of the death causes a crisis in her life. Watoro weighs the consequences and decides to leave her husband. The separation combined with her daughter's death are perceived by Watoro to be the greatest changes in her life.

Wamutira also experiences the death of a nine-year-old daughter, Kanugu, which has a profound effect upon her life: "I changed very much after that child's death. I started fearing that I might never be given others. The ones I had later, after Kanugu's death, I took very much care of so they might not die—like making sure they were clean, had good food, and went for clinic. . . . There are none of my children that I take for granted. Kanugu's death taught me that lesson." In addition, Kanugu's death raises certain philosophical questions that Wamutira finds herself struggling with intellectually: "At times I would keep quiet and think, 'I have had very strong children who have died compared to ones I have now.' . . . When the two-year-old boy died, I prayed, asking, 'Why has God taken the bigger one and left this tiny one (Wamutira's newborn infant)?'"

The death of Wamutira's daughter accomplishes three changes in her life: (1) It alters her knowledge of death in relation to life; (2) it brings about a personal change in attitudes both toward herself as a mother and toward her children, who become more valuable; (3) such a change motivates Wamutira to take better care of her children. For Wamutira, the death becomes a learning experience.

Wanoi also experiences the death of a child. She relates that she felt very much changed by Wacera's death—and perhaps may even feel some guilt because she refused at first to take him to the hospital. Nonetheless, she does not name Wacera's death as one of the greatest changes in her life. Two other events are of greater significance and help shape her later development. The first is her experience with a woman giving birth in a sugarcane field that prompted her to become a midwife. The other is her conversion to Christianity.

Wanoi relates that when she first heard the pregnant woman calling to her for help, her impulse was to run away. "I started wondering what to do and was feeling a bit scared, but a voice deep within me told me to go back and help her." With that decision, Wanoi changes the pattern of her development. She learns, despite her initial fear, that she can deliver a baby. The knowledge is reinforced when she has to make another emergency delivery. She now perceives herself to be a midwife and begins to deliver other women's babies, discovering in the process that she is able to devise creative solutions when the need arises—as in the case of the stubborn afterbirth.

Wanoi's profession, in turn, leads her to other learning experiences—with an in-service training course for midwives and eventually to enroll in an adult education course. The "voice deep within"—her conscience—proves to be a turning point in her lifelong development.

The second event that alters Wanoi's life is her conversion to Christianity. One of the initial questions I had when I began collecting the life histories relates to the timing of conversion in women's lives. Wanoi fits the normative pattern of her age group—she joined the church after independence as an adult. Conversion is transformative because it changes her perceptions of herself in relationship to her family and community, as she testifies: "So there is a big change (since she became a Christian). I am able to humble myself now and follow Jesus's teaching that even when he was abused, mocked, and saliva thrown at him, he only humbled himself . . . if I have abused Kamani (husband) the night before, I go and apologize and so make good our relationship." Wangeci describes a similar change in behavior with her conversion. "Becoming a Christian changed my life—even my soul—because in the days before I became a Christian I used to cook and drink liquor. . . . But after becoming a Christian, I stopped. . . . Before, I would abuse anyone who tried to abuse me. . . . But now, even if somebody comes and abuses me or tries to fight with me, I will not fight back." Christianity modifies patterns of behavior because it places the responsibility for actions on the individual rather than on external forces, for example, witchcraft or evil omens.

Like Wanoi and Wangeci, the oldest informant, Wanjiku, feels that becoming 'saved' as a Christian had a profound impact on her life. The circumstances of her being saved are related to the wound on her face—even the *mũndũ mugo* cannot heal her and that shakes her faith in indigenous healing practices. Wanjiku believes that it was her faith in God's healing powers that cured her wound. When the wound heals of its own accord, Wanjiku becomes a committed Christian who gives up "abusing others," "drinking beer," and "taking snuff." She views herself to be transformed.

Neither of the youngest informants remembers an idiosyncratic event that transformed their attitudes or behavior. Nonetheless, Nyambura's relocation to her aunt's home to become a "maid" certainly included learning new skills and attitudes that she applied to her later life. In addition, the abuse and lack of commitment she received from her husband taught her that she must be self-sufficient if she is to survive as a young mother. Wanja's boarding school experience broadened her perceptions and led her to believe she was capable of becoming a wage earner—a goal she eventually achieved. Yet, when asked what the greatest change in their lives had been, each stated unequivocally that becoming a mother was the greatest change so far. If asked twenty years from now, each might have a different story to tell.

Idiosyncratic changes affect women's lives differently. What constitutes change is totally dependent upon the way an individual perceives a particular event in her life: It is the *significance of meaning* that the individual attaches to the change in a subjective retrospective account that is of importance (Cohler 1982). Similar occurrences—for instance, the death of a child—may affect women differently. In addition, each approaches change differently; some rationalize an unavoidable change, whereas others resist it or use it for personal growth.

How do Gikuyu women mediate such changes in their lives to give them meaning? Watoro justifies the change from married to single status by viewing the latter as problem-free at first. Later, she realizes that raising her children without a husband is financially difficult. Wamutira sees her husband's absence from home as an opportunity to seek a co-wife, and later justifies the addition of a third wife by acknowledging that Murage is the one who "pushes the pedals." She views the death of her daughter as an opportunity to learn new skills. Wanoi perceives herself as a midwife once she's proved to herself that she can deliver a baby. Wangeci views becoming a widow as an opportunity to become self-sufficient. Nyambura perceives her move to her aunt's home as an opportunity to gain new skills, rather than as the end of schooling.

Apart from unavoidable changes, some women actively seek change in their lives, for example, by joining a church, a women's group, or an adult education class. Wanoi embraces changes in the way she practices her profession, joining the in-service training course for midwives in Nyeri and attending an adult education class to learn the skills she needs for recordkeeping as a midwife. She joins the women's self-help group and learns a new form of basketry. Wanoi uses change creatively, as does Wangeci. Watoro acknowledges changes in her personal life that were necessary for her own personal survival, but her poverty confines her from having the kinds of choice available to Wangeci. Wanja equates the completion of her education with a chance to make a change in her socioeconomic position by seeking wage work. At first she is frustrated by lack of jobs, but rather than opting to relocate to Nairobi or another urban area, she decides to stay at home and eventually lands a position as a teacher. She has made a clear choice to stay in rural Mutira rather than join the urban throng.

The life histories illustrate that Gikuyu women view themselves either as a part of their culture or as separate individuals in varying degrees. Social variations and personal life experience influence each woman's ability to see herself as a distinct individual mediating change as well as being shaped by it. Thus, the life histories demonstrate a range of possibilities among Gikuyu women in an age of rapid change.

Significance of the Life Histories for the Global Study of Women

Having discovered the possibilities, what significance do these individual accounts of change have for women in other parts of Africa? For women in so-called developing countries? Or for women in developed countries?

Collectively, the narratives illustrate ways in which women, as distinct from men, mediate changes encroaching on their lives. Because women have priorities that often, though not always, include bearing, nursing, and caring for children during most of their child-bearing years, their needs often relate directly to these priorities. Needs include better health care for themselves and their children, more permanent housing, closer sources of water, and formal education for their children, regardless of the cost to themselves. Equally important, Gikuyu women, like other rural African women, view themselves as primary economic providers for their children (Obbo 1982; Kariũki 1985). This section is primarily concerned with changes in agriculture, family planning, and education. I also include a brief discussion of idiosyncratic changes viewed in cross-cultural perspective.

Changes in Agricultural Production

Of vital importance to Gikuyu women, as the life histories vividly illustrate, is their commitment to production either through agricultural labor on their family's farm or through off-farm wage labor. Such a priority is often overlooked by Western-educated policy planners who assume that male "heads of household" are the critical factor in economic development. Agricultural extension programs and capital for agricultural expansion, for example, are designed and targeted for male landowners, with little consideration for female producers of either food or cash crops (Staudt 1982; Spring 1985; El-Hassan and Holding 1985). Agricultural inputs that would increase women's production, such as access to improved seed, fertilizer, or plows, are beyond the reach of most rural women. Furthermore, credit is not available to the majority of female farmers in rural areas because they do not have the necessary collateral in land (Staudt 1982; Obbo 1982).

Since World War I, Gikuyu women have seen a dramatic change in the kinds of crops planted, in the way they are cultivated, and in their distribution. Similar to other African women, they once controlled the majority of subsistence crops, including processing and distribution (Kaberry 1952; Bryson 1979; Okali 1983; Guyer 1984; Nasimiyu 1985). The infiltration of cash crops, either for national or international distribution, and intensification of land use have jointly undermined women's primary control of agricultural production (Boserup 1970). The life histories demonstrate that although Gikuyu women may participate in cash crop production, they do not fully understand the implications of being tied to a world market system that dictates the price these women will receive for their coffee or tea harvests.

Since the 1950s, Gikuyu women's customary guaranteed access to land through kinship and family ties has been preempted, first, by colonial land policies and, later, by national policies requiring consolidation of scattered holdings and registration in the name of one individual—typically male. A major concern of these women today is that there will be enough land for all of their children—a concern expressed by other women in Kenya (see Pala 1978).

Although most rural development programs designed to increase production are addressed to male heads of households, among the small sample of life history subjects, four out of the seven women are, in fact, single female heads of households. One other—Wanoi—is a de facto head of household. Female-headed households in Mutira, similar to women-headed households globally, are an underenumerated and often ignored segment of the population (Clark 1984; Buvinic 1983; Schmink 1984). Nonetheless, examining the individual lives of the four single women in the life history sample reveals that two—Wanjiku and Wanja—have access to economic support from family members, whereas the other two—Watoro and Wangeci—are totally dependent upon their own resources. Such an investigation at the individual level indicates the need for disaggregating data collected for female-headed households in Africa (and elsewhere) to learn more about causes, existing circumstances, and future opportunities, both perceived and real.

Changes in Health and Family Planning

Related to women's priorities concerning children is the question of family planning, particularly in a country where the population growth rate is one of the highest in the world. Examining the lives of several Gikuyu women reveals that their attitudes toward reproduction reflect a culture that values wealth in people—particularly children, who theoretically provide security in old age. Further, cultural beliefs and practices legitimize the existence of large numbers of children, as indicated in the first chapter of this book.

Formerly, plentiful land and indigenous practices of family planning that allowed for spacing between children worked in tandem to ensure that children would have future access to land as adults. Today, improved health and sanitation measures guarantee that increased numbers of children will be born and survive to adulthood. At the same time, cultural constraints that historically limited reproduction, such as taboos on premarital sexual relations and postnatal abstinence, have been superceded by Western concepts of morality that place the burden of responsibility on individual choice rather than on group consensus. A rapidly increasing population on a limited arable land base (17 percent of Kenya's total land) means that population density per square mile will continue to increase.

Although sociocultural mores prevented unmarried girls from becoming pregnant thirty years ago, such constraints no longer exist. The consequence in Kenya, as elsewhere (for example, Mbilinyi 1985, on Tanzania), is increased numbers of unmarried school-age mothers. Because Kenya has no social welfare program to aid single parent families, the burden of support falls on the extended family, including mothers and grandmothers.

An array of internationally sponsored family planning programs largely advocating Western contraceptive methods exists in Kenya. There is little attempt to incorporate indigenous methods in such efforts. The life narratives (and my own observations) suggest that although there is some concern over population growth, little consensus exists among women—even young women—about the benefits of family planning. Men still count their wealth in children, and cultural ideals prevail in many areas. The only family planning method that has made any headway seems to be tubal ligation for women who have had all the children they desire. Educational and economic constraints—such as paying for children's schooling and landlessness—will be the determining factors in bringing about changes in the present pattern of growth. Western advocates of population planning may suggest changes, but until the actors at the local level feel directly the consequences of increased population, the family planning message will be largely ignored.

Changes in Education

The life histories indicate that Gikuyu women, as mothers, desire the best future for their children they can envision; such a vision includes schooling and wage occupations (also see Kariũki 1985). At the same time, older Gikuyu women view school as the institution that breaks down normative social structures such as *mariika* and causes lack of respect for elders among children and grandchildren. New kinds of knowledge imbue young people with power. Nonliterate women, in particular, feel defenseless in the face of such power. The result is not so different from the "generation gap" that exists between immigrants and their children, who have access to schooling in a new country.

If the future of family planning depends on education, education equally depends upon family. The narratives verify that learning, as a lifelong process, begins in the home, with mothers as the primary socializing agents. Learning continues in the community regardless of whether a person becomes literate or not. Indigenous modes of learning emphasize observation and demonstration; school learning emphasizes listening and recitation. Formal schooling not only explicitly encourages different modes of learning skills, such as reading and mathematics, but implicit is the learning of new social patterns that challenge old cultural norms. Although Gikuyu children usually adjust to school learning, their mothers and grandmothers learn best when learning is synchronous with indigenous modes of education and relates directly to their basic needs. Consequently, education that maximizes women's participation and addresses significant family and community issues, such as the Freirean approach (Freire 1973), better meets the needs of rural women than a model dependent upon schooling.

The life histories illuminate the preference of some women—for example, Wanoi and Wangeci—to learn on their own through discovery or inspiration. Discovery arises out of need—an immediate need to solve a problem associated with a particular situation. In the context of Wanoi's profession, the problem was how to remove the afterbirth in a difficult delivery. Inspiration, or what we might term "creative thinking," solved the problem. Creativity, as one aspect of learning, merits careful cross-cultural investigation.

Idiosyncratic Changes

Women (and men), regardless of where they live, respond to idiosyncratic changes in similar ways; some rationalize the significance of particular events whereas others use them as a learning experience to enhance their own personal development. Among the life history informants, several women experienced life crises—the death of a spouse or child, marital separation. The range of the women's responses, as illuminated in their narratives, including shock, disbelief, anger, rationalization, and, for some, acceptance—resembles that of crisis responses of women and men in European and North American cultures. The parallels suggest that human beings in crisis respond similarly regardless of cultural differences. Cross-cultural comparisons of human responses to life crises might contribute to our knowledge of the role that culture plays in shaping such responses.

Women's Voices

I began this study of women's lives by asking how Gikuyu women in one location in Kenya are mediating change and to what extent their experiences may be compared with women in other parts of the globe. In examining their life histories, we have learned that Mutira women are "like all other women, like some other women, and yet are like no other women." Similarities and contrasting differences make up the fabric of their lives. With one voice and with separate voices, the women of Mutira have spoken. Their sonorous accounts, like their bare footprints firmly embedded in the dusty path to Kirinyaga, link the past with the future. And their voices echo those of other rural women throughout the world who struggle for a daily existence and fall into bed exhausted every night. They are born, they give birth, and they often live to see one or two of their children die. They outlabor and outlive their husbands but never attain commensurate economic power. All in all, life's ironies amuse them and they laugh; its injustices anger them and they shout to be heard. It is time for us to listen.

Note

1. See Appendix B.

Appendix A

TABLE 1
Sample Population By Age Group

Age Group	Number of Women	% of Total Sample
20–29	16	15.8 [b]
30–39	20	19.8
40–49	18	17.8
50–55[a]	18	17.8
56–69	14	13.8
70–79	15	14.8
Totals:	101	99.8%

[a] Target sample for four life-history informants in their early fifties.

[b] Rounded to nearest tenth.

TABLE 2

Marital Status by Age Group

Age Group	Total per Group	Monog-amous	Polyg-ynous	Sepa-rated	Widowed	Single
20-29	16	13	0	0	0	3
30-39	20	15	5	0	0	0
40-49	18	8	9	0	1	0
50-55[a]	18	6	5	2	4	1
56-69	14	6	4	1	3	0
70-79	15	4	4	0	7	0
Totals:	101	52	27	3	15	4

[a] Target sample for four life-history informants in their early fifties.

TABLE 3

Child Mortality Among Mutira Women

Age Group	Total per Group	No. Who Had Lost Children	No. Who Had Lost None	Never Had Children
20-29	16	1	15	0
30-39	20	5	15	0
40-49	18	9	9	0
50-55[a]	18	11	6	1
56-69	14	11	3	0
70-79	15	9	5	1
Totals:	101	46	53	2

[a] Represents target sample of women in their early fifties.

TABLE 4

Religion

Age Group	No. per Group	Anglican	Catholic	Full Gospel	African Holy Ghost	Christian	Non-Christian
20-29	16	5	8	1	0	1	0
30-39	20	10	8	1	1	0	0
40-49	18	11	5	0	1	1	1
50-55[a]	18	8	10	0	0	0	0
56-69	14	7	4	2	0	1	0
70-79	15	6	7	0	0	1	1
Totals :	101	47	42	4	2	4	2

[a] Represents target sample of women in their early fifties.

TABLE 5

Participation in Formal Education

Age Group	Total per Group	Ever attended school			Ever attended adult ed. classes	
		No.	percent	Mean no. years	No.	percent
20-29	16	14	87.5	6.4	3	18.8
30-39	20	9	45	4.7	6	30
40-49	18	7	38.8	5.8	7	38.8
50-59	20	5	25	3.6	5	25
60-69	12	3	25	1.0	2	16.6
70-79	15	4	26.7	0.6	6	40
Totals:	101	41	40.5	3.7	29	28.7

TABLE 6

Women's Participation in Women's Groups

Age Group	No. per Group	No. in Self-Help Groups	No. in Church Groups	Total % in Both Types
20–29	16	5	1	37.5%
30–39	20	8	5	65.0
40–49	18	7	4	61.0
50–55[a]	18	6	5	61.0
56–69	14	5	6	78.6
70–79	15	5	4	60.0
Totals:	101	36	27	62.4%

[a]Represents target sample of women in their early fifties.

Appendix B

The Emergency Regulation for the Control of Crops, Food, and Dwellings.

(Enacted by the Emergency War Council, 1953)

The Provincial Commissioner where is is necessary or expedient in the interests of public order to do so, may by order:

a.   prohibit the planting of crops or of any specified crop.

b.   require the removal and disposal, or the destruction, of crops or any specified crop.

c.   require any person to deliver his or their crop or crops to such person or persons as the Provincial Commissioner may specify.

Source: Kenya National Archives, Government Notice No. 796 of the Emergency Regulations, 1953:n.p.

Glossary

Note: In Kikuyu ũ is pronounced as a soft`o´and ĩ as soft`a.´

Agĩkũyũ (Mũgĩkũyũ, s.)	Gikuyu
andũ akũrũ	old people
athoni (mũthoni, s.)	in-laws
aririri	trill of women when child is born
baraza (Kiswahili)	outdoor public meeting
ciũthi	children's game similar to jacks
cuka	piece of material worn around waist to cover lower half of body
gakenge	newborn child
gikabu	large, woven basket used for hauling tea leaves
gũtara matũ	piercing of earlobes
gũthinjiro	blood sacrifice to seal betrothal
gũthokia	giving of beer during betrothal
gwothoka	process of binding together plant fibers into string for weaving baskets

haiya	expression of exclamation somewhere between "wow" and "brother"
ĩi (pronounced "aye")	yes
irio	general term for food
Irua	initiation-circumcision ceremony
itega	custom of bringing gifts to new mother
ithangu (mathangu, pl.)	leaf
ithitu (githitu, s.)	containers for medicine
itumbi (matumbi, pl.)	literally means egg, but used to refer to egg-shaped items such as gourds
jembe (Kiswahili)	hoe
kaana	infant
kahĩĩ	small uncircumcised boy
kanini	small one
karathiro	blessing preceding a ceremony
karigũ	small girl
kiama	council of elders
kibanga (Kiswahili is panga)	machete
kienji	broad-bladed knife used in circumcision ceremonies
kiondu	woven basket
kirigũ (irigũ, pl.)	a big, uncircumcised girl

kirira	secret knowledge
kiumbi	handsome, talkative
kithuni	bachelor's hut
kubibo	blood sucking ritual
kumanda	when bride brings vegetables from her shamba to cook for her mother-in-law
mabati (Kiswahili)	corregated iron roofing
mambura	ceremony (also menstruation)
mambura ma twana	ceremony of the children
mariika (riika, s.)	age-sets (those circumcised at the same time)
mathaga	women's dress
matũ	earlobe that is pierced
mathakwa (ithakwa, s.)	velvet-like leaves used during Irua
mathangu (ithangu, s.)	leaves
mbari	landholding patrilineage
mbuci	upper rim of the ear that is pierced
mbũgũ	objects such as bones, stones used in the mũndũ mugo's healing ceremony
migio	native plant with suitable fibers for for weaving
mikwa	large ear plugs
miti dawa	tree medicine
mũcii (micii, pl.)	compound with several dwellings

mũgũnda (migũnda, pl.)	garden
mũhiki	bride with young child
muiko	long handled wooden spoon, flattened on one side and used for mashing food
mũirĩtu	adult "circumcised" girl
mũkoma ndi	"loose," unmarried woman
mũkwa	sisal or leather tumpline
mũndũ mugo	medicine man
muongia	old woman past menopause
muratina	beanpod from native tree used as a fermenting agent (also refers to the brew made with muratina beanpod)
muthaiga	white medicinal powder
mũthuri (athuri, pl.)	man
mũthuru	skirt with slits
mũtũmia (atũmia, pl.)	woman with several children
mwanake (anake, pl.)	young, circumcised man
mwanake kiumbi	handsome, talkative young man
mwengu	goatskin skirt with flaps for girls
mweretho	dance for young people in which young men would toss their female partners high in the air while the girls shook their bodies
ndebe	type of earplug, also a storage tin

ndigi	string
ndoma	arrowroots
nduka	shop
ng'aa	false talk, empty feelings
Ngai	Creator, God
ngatha	industrious, self-reliant, stays at home
ngoni	type of earplug
ngunga	type of herb used to cause an abortion
ngutwii	stinging nettle
ngwatio	women's work group
nja	pounded earth yard in a compound
njohi	homemade sugarcane beer
nyumithio	ceremony to advance to elderhood
oma	short-handled garden fork
retho	pieces of cloth tied around shoulders
rigi	wooden movable walls (screens)
riiko	central fireplace for cooking
rŭkoro	strip of goat skin worn around wrist
rŭracio	bridewealth
shamba (Kiswahili; mashamba, pl.)	tilled field

skuma-wiki (Kiswahili)	kale
tatha	insides of intestines of a goat or sheep used to smear the body during ritual
thegi	place where goats are kept indoors
thira	reed and bead skirt worn during Irua
thiri	secret
twana (mwana, s.)	children
ũgo	healing ceremony of the mũndũ mugo
ũhiki	marriage
wamũng'ii	woman with several children, one of whom is circumcised

References

Abbott, Susan. 1974. "Full Time Farmers And Weekend Wives: Change And
Stress Among Rural Kikuyu Women. " Ph. D. dissertation, University of
North Carolina.

Andreski, Iris. 1970. *Old Wives Tales: Life Stories From Ibibioland*. New York:
Schocken Books.

Barnes, Carolyn. 1983. "Differentiation by Sex Among Small Scale Farming
Households in Kenya. " *Rural Africana*, 15/16: 41–63.

Barrett, Donald, and Karigo Muchai. 1973. *The Hardcore*. Richmond, B. C. :
LMB Press.

Barrett, Donald, and Karani Njama. 1966. *Mau Mau From Within: An Analysis
of Kenya's Peasant Revolt*. New York: Modern Reader Paperbacks.

Bay, Edna, ed. 1982. *Women and Work in Africa*. Boulder, Colo. : Westview
Press.

Bledsoe, Caroline H. 1980. *Women And Marriage In Kpelle Society*. Stanford:
Stanford University Press.

Bogden, Robert, and Steven J. Taylor. 1975. *Introduction to Qualitative Research
Methods: A Phenomenological Approach to the Social Sciences*. New York: John
Wiley.

Boserup, Ester. 1970. *Woman's Role in Economic Development*. New York: St.
Martin's Press.

Bryson, Judy. 1979. *Women And Economic Development in Cameroon*.
Washington D. C. : Women in Development Program, USAID.

Buvinic, Mayra. 1983. "Women's Issues in Third World Poverty: A Policy
Analysis. " In *Women And Poverty in the Third World*, edited by M. Buvinic,
and M. Lycette, & W. McGreevy. Baltimore: John Hopkins University
Press.

Caplan, Anne P. 1975. *Choice And Constraint in a Swahili Community*. Oxford:
Oxford University Press.

Castro, Alfonso P. 1983. "Tree Planting and Fuel Use in Kirinyaga District. "
In *Fuelwood Use in Rural Kenya: Impacts of Deforestration*, edited by D.
Brokensha, B. Riley, and A. Castro. New York: Institute For Development
Anthropology.

Chodorow, Nancy. 1978. *The Reproduction of Mothering: Psychoanalysis and the
Sociology of Gender*. Berkeley: University of California Press.

Clark, Carolyn. 1971. *Conflict in Kikuyu Kinship*. Nairobi: Institute of African
Studies.

Clark, Mari. 1984. "Women-headed Households and Poverty," *Signs*,

10:19–26.

Cohler, B. J. 1982. "Personal Narrative and Life Course. " In *Life-span Development and Behavior*, vol. 4, edited by P. B. Baltes and O. G. Brim, Jr. New YorK: Academic Press.

Crapanzano, Vincent. 1980. *Tuhami: Portrait of a Moroccan*. Chicago: Chicago University Press.

Davison, Jean. 1985. "Achievements and Constraints Among Rural Kenyan Women: A Case Study. " In *Women and Development in Africa*, edited by G. S. Were Nairobi: Gideon Were Press.

———. 1988. "Land and Women's Agricultural Production: The Context." In *Agriculture, Women and Land: The African Experience*, edited by J. Davison Boulder, Colo. : Westview Press.

Due, Jean. 1985. Women Made Visible: *Their Contributions to Farming System And Household Incomes in Zambia and Tanzania*. University of Illinois, Department of Agricultural Economy.

El-Hassam, Salim, and Christine Holding. 1985. "Food Production: A Suggested Change in Emphasis in Women's Training. " Paper presented at the Workshop on the Role of Women in Development and Population Activities, Khartoum, 1984 (mimeo).

Fisher, Jeanne. n. d. *The Anatomy of Kikuyu Domesticity and Husbandry*. Nairobi: Ministry of Agriculture, Department of Technical Cooperation.

Freire, Paulo. 1973. *Education for Critical Consciousness*. New York: Seabury.

Georges, Robert, and Michael Jones. 1980. *People Studying People: The Human Element in Fieldwork*. Berkeley: University of California Press.

Gergen, Kenneth. 1980. "The Emerging Crisis in Life-Span Developmental Theory. " In *Life Span Development and Behavior*, edited by Paul Baltes and O. G. Brim. New York: Academic Press.

Giele, Janet Z. , and Audrey C. Smock. 1977. *Women: Roles and Status in Eight Countries*. New York: John Wiley.

Gollock, Georgina A. 1928. *Lives of Eminent Africans*. New York: Longmans.

Guyer, Jane. 1984. *Family and Farm in Southern Cameroon*. Boston: Boston University Press.

Herzog, A. 1971. *Fertility and Cultural Values: Kikuyu Naming Customs and the Preference for Four or More Children*. Nairobi: Bureau of Educational Research, Kenyatta University.

Hobley, Charles W. 1910. "Kikuyu Customs and Beliefs. " *Journal of the Royal Anthropological Institute*, 40:428–445.

———. 1938. *Bantu Beliefs and Magic*. London: H. F. & G. Witherby.

Hoorweg, Jan and Rudo Niemeyer. 1980. "Preliminary Studies on Some Aspects of Kikuyu Food Habits. " *Ecology of Food and Nutrition*, 9:139–150.

Kaberry, Priscilla. 1952. *Women of the Grassfields: A Study of the Economic Position of Women in Bamenda, British Cameroons*. London: Her Majesty's Stationary Office.

Kariuki, Priscilla. 1985. "Women's Aspirations and Self-perceptions of Their Own Situation in Society. " In *Women and Development in Africa*, edited by G. S. Were. Nairobi: Gideon Were Press.

Karoki, Flora. 1977. Interview. Gatwe, August 23.

Kenya, Central Bureau of Statistics. 1984. *Agricultural Census of Large Farms,*

1981–1982. Nairobi: Government Printers.

Kenya, National Archives. 1927a. *"Resolution of Ft. Hall Local Native Council"* (9/27).

———. 1927b. *"Report of Nyeri Native Council"* (9/3/27) DC/PC 9/3/27.

———. 1930. *"Correspondence from D. C. , Ft. Hall To P. C. , Nyeri"* (4/3/30) DC/PC, Central Province.

———. 1934. *"Provincial Commissioner's Report, Central Province"* (PC/DC 9/9/4).

———. 1954. *"Handing over Report: Embu District"* (R. A. Wilkinson, D. C.) DC/PC, Embu District.

Kenyatta, Jomo. 1968 (1938), *Facing Mt. Kenya*. London: Secker & Warburg.

Kershaw, Greet. 1975/76. "The Changing Roles of Men and Women in the Kikuyu Family by Socioeconomic Strata. " *Rural Afriana* 29:173–194.

Kirinyaga District. 1982. *Annual Report*. Kerugoya, Kenya: Government Printers.

Kluckhohn, Clyde. 1945. "Personal Document in Anthropological Science. " In *The Use of Personal Document in History, Anthropology, and Sociology,* edited by L. Gottschalk, C. Kluckhohn, and R. Angell. New York: Social Science Research Council, Bulletin No. 53.

Kluckhohn, Clyde, and H. A. Murray 1953. "Personality Formation: The Determinants. " In *Personality in Nature, Society and Culture,* edited by C. Kluckhohn, H. Murray, and D. Schneider. New York: Knopf.

Kuper, Hilda. 1978. *Sobhuza II, Ngwenyama and King of Swaziland: The Story of an Hereditary Ruler and His Country*. New York: Africana Publishing.

Lambert, H. E. 1956. *Kikuyu Social and Political Institutions*. London: Oxford University Press.

Langness, L. L. and Geyla Frank. 1981. *Lives: An Anthropological Approach to Biography*. Novato, Calif.: Chandler and Sharp Publishers.

Laurentin, Anne. 1963. "Nzakara Women (Central African Republic)." In *Women in Tropical Africa,* edited by Denise Paulme. London: Routledge and Kegan Paul.

Leakey, L. S. B. 1977. *The Southern Kikuyu Before 1903*. London And New York: Academic Press.

Leo, Christopher. 1984. *Land and Class in Kenya*. Toronto: University of Toronto Press.

LeVine, Sarah. 1979. *Mothers and Wives: Gusii Women of East Africa*. Chicago: Chicago University Press.

LeVine, Sarah, and Gary Pfeifer. 1982. "Separation and Individuation in an African Society: The Developmental Tasks of the Gusii Married Woman. " *Psychiatry* 45:61–75.

Leys, Colin. 1975. *Underdevelopment in Kenya*. London: Heinemann.

Mathu, George 1971. *Gikuyu Marriage: Beliefs and Practises*. Nairobi: Institute of African Studies.

Mbilinyi, Marjorie. 1985. "Struggles Concerning Sexuality Among Female Youth. " In *Women and Development in Africa,* edited by G. S. Were. Nairobi: Gideon Were Press.

Merritt, Gary. 1984. Interview. Nairobi, October 8.

Middleton, John. 1953. *The Central Tribes of the North-Eastern Bantu*. London:

International African Institute.

Mullings, Leith. 1976. "Women and Economic Change in Africa. " In *Women in Africa*, edited by Nancy Hafkin and Edna Bay. Stanford: Stanford University Press.

Muriuki, Godfrey. 1974. *A History of the Kikuyu: 1500-1900*. Nairobi: Oxford University Press.

Nasimiyu, Ruth. 1985. "Women in the Colonial Economy of Bungoma: Role of Women in Agriculture: 1902–1960. " In *Women and Developmnet in Africa*, edited by G. S. Were. Nairobi: Gideon Were Press.

Neugarten, Beatrice L., and Nancy Datan. 1973. "Sociological Perspectives on the Life Cycle. " In *Life-Span Developmental Psychology*, edited by Paul Baltes and K. Warner Schaie. New York: Academic Press.

Obbo, Christine. 1980. *African Women: Their Struggle for Economic Independence*. London: Zed Press.

———. 1982. "The Effects of Land Tenure Change upon Women in East African Smallholder Agriculture." Paper presented at the Colloquium on Issues in African Land Tenure, Land Tenure Center, University of Wisconsin, Madison.

Oboler, Regina S. 1985. *Women, Power and Economic Change: The Nandi of Kenya*. Stanford: Stanford University Press.

Okali, Christine. 1983. *Cocoa and Kinship in Ghana: The Matrilineal Akan of Ghana*. London and Boston: Kegan Paul International.

Pala, Achola. 1976. *African Women in Rural Development: Research Trends and Priorities*. Washington, D. C. : Overseas Liason Committee, Paper no. 12, American Council on Education.

———. 1978. *Women's Access to Land and Their Role in Agriculture And Decision-making on the Farm: Experiences of the Joluo Of Kenya*. Nairobi: Institute for Development Studies, University of Nairobi.

Perham, Marjorie, ed. 1936. *Ten Africans*. London: Faber & Faber.

Plummer, Ken. 1983. *Documents of Life*. London: George Allen & Unwin.

Riegel, Klaus F. 1975. "Adult Life Crises: A Dialectic Interpretation of Development. " In *Life Span Developmental Psychology: Normative Life Crises*, edited by Nancy Datan and Leon Ginsberg. New York: Academic Press.

Robertson, Claire. 1976. "Ga Women and Socioeconomic Change in Accra, Ghana. " In *Women in Africa*, edited by Nancy Hafkin and Edna Bay. Stanford: Stanford University Press.

Romero, Patricia W. , ed. 1988. *Life Histories of African Women*. London: The Ashfield Press.

Rosaldo, Renato 1976. "The Story of Tukbaw:'They Listen as He Orates. '" In *The Biographical Process*, edited by F. Reynolds and D. Crapps. The Hague: Mouton & Company.

Routledge, William S. and Katherine Routledge. 1910. *With A Prehistoric People: The Agikuyu Of East Africa*. London: Edward Arnold.

Sachs, Wulf. 1937. *Black Hamlet: The Mind of an African Negro Revealed by Psychoanalysis*. London: Geoffrey Books.

Safilios-Rothchild, Constantina. 1982. *Persistence of Women's Invisibility in Agriculture: Theoretical and Policy Lessons from Lesotho and Sierra Leone*. New

York: Population Council, Center for Policy Studies.

Sandgren, David P. 1982. "Twentieth Century Religious and Political Division: Among the Kikuyu of Kenya. " *African Studies Review*, 25, no. 2/3:195–207.

Schmink, Marianne. 1984 "Household Economic Strategies: Review and Research Agenda. " *Latin American Research Review*, 8:87–101.

Shostak, Marjorie 1981. *Nisa: The Live and Words of a !Kung Woman.* Cambridge, Mass.: Harvard University Press.

Smith, Mary F. 1954. *Baba of Karo.* London: Faber & Faber.

Spring, Anita. 1985. "Profiles of Men and Women Smallholder Farmers In Malawi." Paper presented at the African Studies Association meeting, New Orleans, October-November.

Staudt, Kathleen. 1982. "Women Farmers and Inequities in Agricultural Services. " In *Women and Work in Africa*, edited by Edna Bay. Boulder, Colo.: Westview Press.

Tinker, Irene, and Michele Bramsen. 1976. *Women and World Development.* Washington, D. C. : Overseas Development Council.

Turner, Victor. 1969. *The Ritual Process.* Ithaca: Cornell University Press.

Van Gennep, Arnold. 1960 (1908). *Rites of Passage.* New York: Vintage Press.

Vizedom, Monika 1976. *Rites and Relationships: Rites of Passage and Contemporary Anthropology.* Beverly Hills, Calif.: Sage Publications.

Wacuima, Charity. 1969. *Daughter of Mumbi.* Nairobi: East Africa Publishing.

Wa Thiong'o, Ngugi. 1967. A Grain of Wheat. London: Heinemann.

———. 1977. *Petals of Blood.* London: Heinemann.

Winter, Edward H. 1965. *Boyond the Mountains of the Moon: The Lives of Four Africans* Urbana: University of Illinois Press.

Worthman, Carol M. 1985. "Social Management of Developmental Differences: Kikuyu Adolescents." Paper presented at the American Anthropological Association meeting, Washington, D. C., December 5, 1985.